MUTINIES

DEDICATION

For Yvonne, Jackson and Truman—the best family a guy ever had. 'Drink up me hearties, YO-HO!'

TRUE CRIME & PUNISHMENT

MUTINIES

SHOCKING REAL-LIFE STORIES OF SUBVERSION AT SEA

BARRY STONE

PIER 9

CONTENTS

INTRODUCTION

In the vast, empty oceans of the eighteenth and nineteenth centuries a ship of sea was a nation unto itself, an imperfect representation of the country under whose flag it flew, carrying the ideals, the laws and the values of its government to the farthest corners of the world. All that stood between life and death for its officers and crew was the respect the crew had for its captain, and the ability of that captain to lead and inspire his men.

The notion of a ship as a sovereign entity wasn't lost on the mutineer Richard Parker in 1797, when he called the rebel ships of Britain's North Sea Fleet that fell under his command in the River Thames his 'Floating Republic'. Mutiny was an act heavy in symbolism, and a ship that was without its officers and under the control of mutineers was a rogue state—a law unto itself. The significance of the term was not lost on the British Government either. Such acts were unacceptable to governments whose power and continued longevity were often dependent upon control of the military and the maintenance of discipline and a proper chain of command. Stung into action by Parker's bold declaration, the authorities brutally put down the mutiny and promptly hanged Parker and twenty-nine of his accomplices from the yardarm of HMS *Sandwich.*

To refuse an order from a superior officer at sea, which is mutiny's broad and grossly inadequate definition, carries far greater significance than simply disobeying an order. Whether it is a refusal to go into battle or just to swab a deck, refusing an order is a direct challenge to the legitimacy of the government, a revolution in miniature. For a sailor or group of sailors to have their privileges withdrawn, or grievances ignored, to the point that they see even a 'technical' act of mutiny as the only recourse left to them is an almost unheard-of event, and still retains the capacity to send shockwaves through a nation's navy and its government.

In the days of sail the cramped, squalid living quarters in the bow that were home to a ship's enlisted men were a stark contrast to the spacious officers' cabins aft, emphasising the sense of separateness that magnified discontent and providing troublemakers with all the privacy they needed for the hatching of treasonous schemes. A ship can be a haven for disturbed minds and violent personalities, as was the case with *Wager* (1741), and small ships provide few places to hide from a mutineer's bayonet, cutlass or pistol. With many vessels out of sight of land for months at a time, with their myriad hidden spaces and darkened corners ideally suited for facilitating the fermenting of grievances and the formulating of desperate acts of redress and retribution, it should come as no surprise that mutinies occur most easily at sea.

Of course, if a mutiny can occur at sea it can also happen in port, on land and in the streets, and governments have always been acutely conscious of the symbolic power even a failed mutiny can wield. A mutiny at sea involving a single ship is bad enough, but mutinies in home ports have a habit of spreading and encompassing entire fleets, particularly when vessels are moored in close proximity to one another and crews can coordinate their actions. In 1797 at Spithead, an anchorage in the waters off Portsmouth, a coordinated strike erupted in the Channel Fleet, Britain's first line of defence against the navies of France, Spain and the Netherlands. The action began on the deck of HMS *Royal Sovereign*, was cheered on by the crew of HMS *Queen Charlotte* anchored nearby, and in no time the entire fleet was in open revolt. In Germany in 1918, what began as a mutiny among the sailors of the German Fleet moored in Wilhelmshaven and Kiel spread to shore and resulted, just days later, in the abdication of the Emperor Kaiser Wilhelm II and the end of a monarchy that had been in place since 1871.

Despite the pervasive familiarity of the events involving William Bligh and HMAV *Bounty*, mutinies cannot be categorised or reduced to a convenient formula. The reasons that provoke them and the circumstances in which they occur are as varied as the crews that sail the oceans. A mutiny can be the result of the universal human desire for freedom and liberty, as it was with the Spanish-owned slave ship *La Amistad* in 1839, or a lightning rod for the igniting of a revolution, as with the Russian battleship *Potemkin* in 1905. Of course a mutiny can also be a bloody affair, as witnessed on the decks of HMS *Hermione* in 1797 when nine Royal Navy officers and *Hermione*'s commander Captain Hugh Pigot, were slaughtered by a frenzied crew pushed to breaking point by their tyrannical captain.

But a mutiny can be almost endearing in its aims and motivations, like the day in 1954 when seven crewmembers of a Polish fishing trawler called *Puszczyk* beat up their captain, locked him in the lavatory, and sailed their boat into the English North Sea port of Whitby to ask for asylum and a new life free of communism. With the overwhelming support of more than 200,000 British Poles, the seven fishermen fought for their freedom in Britain's High Court against a Polish Government determined to get them back, and won. *Puszczyk*'s was an honorable mutiny.

Thirteen of the twenty-three mutinies studied in this book occurred after the Age of Sail; they include events aboard a merchant ship, battleships, minesweepers and destroyers. Even so, mutinies are increasingly a thing of the past. Two or three people cannot take over a modern warship. Unlike the days of sail, when all that was needed to commandeer a ship was the support of an experienced boatswain and navigator, to successfully wrest control of a modern ship from its officers requires the participation of enough sailors to maintain a sophisticated engine room, bridge and communications centre—which makes Valery Sablin's methodical and audacious commandeering of the Russian guided-missile frigate *Storozhevoy* in 1975 all the more remarkable.

Sailors have historically been moved to mutiny not because of a desire to gain some new right or privilege, or to grasp by using the tools of force and intimidation something that was never theirs, but as a last resort to regain something they once had that had been taken from them. Mutinies are rarely a question of loyalty to the flag the ship is flying—they are born of requests for decent food, better pay, more humane living conditions. Even in the midst of mutiny, mutineers have for the most part remained loyal to their navy and to the flag it flies. Mostly, what some might view as mutinous activity is nothing more than the acquatic equivalent of a factory-floor strike or an industrial dispute involving little more than the presentation of a list of grievances. They are lock-ins. Sit-downs. For a period in the 1940s the Royal Canadian Navy almost owned the phrase: 'Sir, the men won't come out.' It is rarely a question of sedition.

Mutinous behaviour is more common than naval records indicate, hardly surprising considering a mutiny is seen as both a stain on a navy's reputation and an embarrassing admission of poor treatment of its servicemen and women. In the twentieth century, particularly as navies around the world have become more sophisticated, naval bureaucracies have gone to extraordinary lengths to avoid the stain of mutiny being placed upon them.

In 1919, crewmembers of the freighter USS *Robert M. Thompson* were protesting the ship's abysmal living conditions and disobeyed the direct orders of their ensign to retire below decks. The refusal met all the textbook definitions of mutiny and was so called by the ship's officers in their report to Naval Headquarters in Washington, but when it came to trial all references to a mutiny had been removed and the men were tried for disobedience. An incident in 1949 on the Canadian destroyer *Athabaskan* saw the ship's commander, Captain Medland, casually place his cap over a list of demands presented to him by dozens of his crew so he could later claim not to have noticed them, to—in effect—cover up their massed declaration of grievances, one of the prerequisites of a mutiny.

In 1972, the commander of the 61,000-tonne (60,000 ton) aircraft carrier USS *Constellation* insisted before a Congressional hearing that recent events below decks involving 110 conscripted African-American sailors and approximately a dozen whites protesting discrimination constituted mutiny, plain and simple. The incident was even referred to by the *New York Times* as 'the first mass mutiny in the history of the US Navy. But there would be no reprisals, no embarrassing trials. Those involved were either reassigned to other vessels or quietly discharged, and the Navy plumbed the dictionary for euphemisms in its determination to use any word in the English language but 'mutiny' to describe what had occurred.

There have been countless mutinies throughout history, the vast majority benign affairs not worthy of the emotive power of the word.

Occasionally, however, mutinies do go beyond the realm of protest, and it is for the most part these mutinies: the bloodthirsty, the audacious, the historic and the tragic, that are revisited in the pages ahead.

‘I WOULD RATHER BE HANGED AT HOME THAN STARVED ABROAD.’

Henry Greene, mutineer, *Discovery*

1611

THE HENRY HUDSON MUTINY

John Maler Collier (1850–1934) was an English author, humanist and a leading painter in the Pre-Raphaelite style, specialising in vibrant portraits of everyone from George V, future king of England, to Rudyard Kipling and Charles Darwin, and was without peer when it came to depicting a seated subject on canvas. In 1881, at London's Royal Academy he unveiled a pivotal work that proved he was also a master at depicting moments in human history that no one could possibly have witnessed.

The painting shows two men and a male child adrift in an open boat, encircled by icebergs, utterly isolated. Their plight appears hopeless. Their boat has no sail and they seem to be bereft of provisions. The child is looking up into the eyes of his father, who is steering a doomed path through the fridgid, deadly waters with a look of complete resignation. The other man slumps beneath a fur rug, staring blankly into the inhospitable wilderness. No one is speaking. They are resigned to their fate.

The man steering the boat is the famed English navigator and explorer Henry Hudson, cast adrift by a mutinous group from his ship *Discovery*. Collier's painting captures the horrifying moment when the three confront the fact they will soon perish. *The Last Voyage of Henry Hudson* has come to be the accepted image of Hudson's final ordeal in the same way that da Vinci's *Last Supper* is seen as the quintessential image of Christ's last meal.

THE SEARCH FOR AN ICE-FREE ROUTE

Little is known of Hudson's early life. Born in or around 1570; he enters the historical record in 1607 with his reputation as a navigator already well established. In the late sixteenth and early seventeenth centuries the Dutch and English were in a race to discover a northerly passage to the Pacific Ocean and the riches of Asia. In 1607 Hudson was engaged by the Muscovy Company of England to find a northerly passage above North America to Asia, aboard his 81-tonne (80-ton) coaster *Hopewell*. Though unsuccessful, he set a new record in sailing beyond the Arctic Circle, reaching a point north of the island of Svalbard, a mere 577 nautical miles from the North Pole. His observations of whale numbers saw him partly responsible for the creation of the Spitzbergen whaling industry. In 1608, again in command of *Hopewell*, he attempted a northeast route through the arctic waters north of Russia, but got only as far as the archipelago of Novaya Zemlya.

In 1609 the Dutch East India Company approached him with a similar request, and provided him with *Halve Maen* (*Half Moon*), a fast *vlieboat* known to the British as a flyboat, but he was not able to progress beyond Norway's North Cape due to the presence of polar ice and an obstinate crew who refused to take the ship any further. In a direct contravention of his commission Hudson then decided to turn westward and sail towards the warmer waters of the New World. Following the coastline south until he reached what is now known as the mouth of New York's aptly-named Hudson River, he took *Half Moon* up it as far as present-day Albany before the river's increasingly shallow waters ended any hope that this was the route he had been looking for, and Hudson was forced to turn back.

Then in 1610 Sir Thomas Smythe of the Virginia Company, named in honour of the late 'Virgin Queen' Elizabeth I, and two other influential members of the court of James I, John Wolstenholme and Sir Dudley Digges, asked Hudson to search again for the imagined ice-free route to the riches of the Orient. In assembling his crew for this new voyage Hudson again chose to include Robert Juet, the mariner who had accompanied him as first mate on his second and third voyages aboard *Hopewell* and *Half Moon*. He also invited along an acquaintance, Henry Greene, a man he had only recently met and helped through a difficult period after being disowned by his own family—a decision that would prove fatal.

A DISCONSOLATE CREW

Hudson's new ship, *Discovery*, was another flyboat, stout-hulled and slightly larger than his previous vessels with a complement of thirty-five. It sailed from the port of Gravesend on the banks of the River Thames on 17 April 1610. On exiting the Thames Hudson turned north along the English east coast towards the Orkney Islands before setting a course for Iceland. Discontent began to grow early in the voyage with many of the crew resenting the close relationship between Greene and Hudson. The resentment grew after Greene got into a physical altercation with the ship's twenty-two-year-old surgeon, Edward Wilson, while *Discovery* was at anchor in Iceland, and was made worse when Hudson blamed Wilson for starting the quarrel. Juet added fuel to the mutterings of favouritism when he began spreading a rumour that Greene had been asked by Hudson to secretly report to him on the mood of the crew.

Hudson sighted the southern tip of Greenland on 4 June and three weeks later sailed through the Hudson Strait between Baffin Island and Labrador. Hudson wasn't the first European to sail the waters that would one day bear his name. The English navigator John Davis entered the passage in 1585 and Captain George Weymouth sailed almost 500 kilometres (310 miles) into it in 1602 before being forced to turn back by his crew.

It was in the waters of the Hudson Strait near Akpatok Island that Robert Juet led an initial attempt at mutiny, one that was easily put down. Hudson was so furious with Juet that he threatened to maroon him at the next landfall. Six weeks later, after successfully charting the manifold dangers of the strait that saw *Discovery* covering as little as 16 kilometres (10 miles) a day in often impenetrable fogs, they passed Digges Island and

Cape Wolstenholme in present-day Quebec. They must have thought the expedition's goal of seeking a northwest passage was an unqualified success when they reached the end of the narrows and saw for the first time the Pacific-like vastness of what proved to be Hudson Bay.

Before entering the bay Hudson sent his boatswain Robert Bylot, navigator Abacuk Pricket and Henry Greene ashore on Digges Island. They returned with reports of verdant pastures filled with wildfowl and the suggestion that it would be wise to allow a day or two to replenish their supplies. But Hudson believed that he had just emulated the feat of the great explorer Ferdinand Magellan, the first European to sail into the Pacific after navigating his ship *Victoria* through the Straits of Magellan in 1520. The empty stomachs of his crew could wait. History was calling.

Still basking in his newly acquired prestige, Hudson chose to use the moment to punish Juet for his earlier attempt at mutiny by charging him with the lesser crime of 'incitement to disobedience' and demoting him to the rank of common seaman. Juet was replaced by Robert Bylot, who would one day rise to captain his own ship in the British Royal Navy.

SUB-ZERO CONDITIONS

By October, *Discovery* had made its way south along the Hudson Bay coastline into the maze of islands that was James Bay, described by Hudson as 'a labyrinth without end'. Instead of heeding the crew's wishes and turning back, Hudson persisted in searching for a non-existent southern escape route. Encroaching ice propelled by uncommonly fast tides repeatedly caused icebergs to smash into *Discovery*'s hull, and with winter fast approaching the ship eventually found itself hemmed in by sea ice, giving Hudson no choice but to moor *Discovery* in the bay's sub-zero waters for the duration near the mouth of either the Rupert or Nottaway rivers.

Tragedy soon struck when John Williams, *Discovery*'s gunner, wandered into the forest and was later found frozen to death. After a seaman's death it was customary to gather together his belongings and auction them off. One of the items most coveted by the crew was Williams' overcoat. But before a single bid, Hudson decided to sell the coat to his friend Henry Greene. Hudson's favouritism increased the crew's resentment towards him.

A month earlier the ship's carpenter, Philip Staffe, had urged Hudson to allow him to build some shelters on shore for the crew, but Hudson had refused. Now he changed his mind, but Staffe claimed the weather had deteriorated so much that the shelters could not be built. Hudson berated Staffe in front of the entire crew, yelling abuse and at one point even threatening to hang him. When Henry Greene turned against his benefactor and voiced his support of Staffe, Hudson took back the overcoat and told him he would sequester his wages if he took his disrespect any further. The shelters were duly built.

Before November's freezing weather Hudson had contemplated returning home, but he was increasingly aware of his place in history and insisted to his crew that enduring the winter and pressing on anew in the spring would yield success. Before leaving England, however, Hudson was conscious that he could be spending much of his time sailing in shallow coastal waters and had therefore taken on fewer provisions—so *Discovery* would sit high in the water. The lack of provisions has caused some historians to suggest this was a secret mission, known only to Hudson, to survey and map the region for possible exploitation of its minerals by his wealthy backers. This theory only gains credence when one considers the fact that Hudson carried no letters of introduction to those rulers who lived beyond the Northwest Passage, and no goods with which to trade should he have met them. It also appears odd that Hudson failed to conclude that the shallow, river-fed waters of James Bay were unlikely to be hiding a deep passage to the northwest.

In any case the lack of provisions was now becoming an issue as the first signs of scurvy began to sweep through the crew, and with temperatures dropping it was becoming increasingly difficult to find fresh game on shore. With eight months of virtual idleness ahead of them waiting for the newly formed ice sheet to thaw, conditions soon became ripe for a disgruntled and hungry crew to begin the first mutterings of mutiny.

On 12 June 1611, Hudson at last realised the patience of the crew was at an end and made the decision to sail for England. The remaining provisions were portioned out and the crew was assured that *Discovery* would stop at Digges Island to gather further provisions. It was an attempt by Hudson to placate his crew, but it had come too late. According to the personal journal of the landsman and agent of the voyage's backers, Abacuk Pricket, Hudson was then caught hoarding food, and when this was made known it led to further resentment. Hudson's authority was eroding faster than he could repair it.

Arguments began to break out with Hudson accusing certain crewmembers of hoarding food and the crew in turn accusing Hudson of doing the same.

On the evening of 23 June, Juet, Greene and William Wilson, the *Discovery*'s boatswain, told Pricket of their intention to put Hudson, his son, and several of the sickest crewmen overboard and divide their food between those left. Pricket said he would not intervene if they promised they would treat those to be marooned 'humanely', though he failed to explain in his journal how putting men overboard in a small boat with meagre provisions and few prospects of survival could in any way be termed humane.

The following day the mutinous group led, ironically, by Henry Greene, grabbed Hudson as he emerged from his cabin, as well as his son, the ship's mathematician Thomas Wydowse, the carpenter Philip Staffe and five others, manhandled them into the open shallop and tethered it to *Discovery*'s stern. For several hours Hudson and his companions were towed north through the waters of James Bay before finally the tow rope was cut and they were set adrift, never to be seen again. For a while Hudson and the others rowed after the ship in the hope the mutineers would relent, but the mutineers raised sail and left the castaways in *Discovery*'s wake.

Henry Greene, once a homeless vagabond and now in charge of his own vessel, needed an experienced navigator and turned to Robert Bylot, who had earlier been stripped of his rank by Hudson for reasons unknown, but generally thought to be linked to his sympathy towards the mutineers. Bylot guided *Discovery* back to Digges Island where Greene took an unarmed party ashore in the hope of securing provisions from local Inuit for the voyage home. Unfortunately Greene possessed little in the way of diplomatic savvy and the encounter quickly degenerated into a pitched battle. As the landing party scrambled back into the ship's boat Greene was struck and killed by an arrow. William Wilson and two others were fatally wounded. The survivors managed to row to another part of the island, where they gathered some wildfowl before returning to *Discovery*.

Discovery continued on to England under the command of Robert Bylot. A shortage of food continued to bedevil the crew, who at one point were forced to eat seagulls that came to rest in the rigging. In August Robert Juet died of starvation and his body was committed to the deep.

Of the nine crewmembers who returned to England alive, only one was asked by the British Admiralty to produce a deposition, and it would be six long years before just four of the crew were committed to trial for murder. All were acquitted after it was felt that it could not be termed murder to set men adrift near a shoreline that had food sources and fresh water. As for being tried on charges of mutiny, it was agreed that most if not all the principal mutineers had died on the voyage home, so who was there left to prosecute? It was also felt that those who returned possessed unique perspectives on the New World and were too valuable to be put to death.

HUDSON'S ULTIMATE FATE

Despite the remnants of what could have been a shelter having been located on nearby Danby Island in 1631 by Captain Thomas James, and other signs of human habitation located in the same area by Captain Zachariah Gillian during his expedition of 1668–70, it is impossible to say who their original inhabitants might have been. Though it is tempting to suggest Hudson may have sheltered there, the fact is no evidence of Henry Hudson or any of those who were set adrift with him has ever been found.

Robert Bylot's skill as a navigator in returning the ship and its crew to England earned him a pardon. The following year he returned to Hudson Bay with Sir Thomas Button in yet another unsuccessful attempt to locate a northwest passage. Then in 1615, in a demonstration of historic irony, Bylot went on to prove conclusively that Hudson Bay possessed no outlet to the west and was not in fact the sought-after shortcut to the Orient that Hudson and the majority of maritime England believed it to be.

Legends persist about the fate of Hudson. One story insists Hudson and some of his crew were taken by boat down the Ottawa River by local Inuit. Another claims a band of Inuit found a boat filled with the bodies of Europeans and took the only survivor, a small boy, back to their camp. The local Cree Indians have an oral tradition that says Hudson lived among them until he was an old man. They even have a word—*wamstuksheesh* (little white man)—for a series of traplines designed to snare small animals said to have been named in Hudson's honour. There were also numerous stories of so-called 'ape-men', perhaps bearded Europeans, seen sailing between James Bay's numerous offshore islands. And in 1920 the *Baltimore Sun* claimed that the last will and testament of Hudson had been found by a trapper.

‘NO MAN WILL BE A SAILOR WHO HAS CONTRIVANCE ENOUGH TO GET HIMSELF INTO A GAOL, FOR BEING IN A SHIP IS BEING IN A GAOL WITH A CHANCE OF BEING DROWNED.’

Samuel Johnson, eighteenth century English author

‘WHENEVER I SEE A FELLOW LOOK AS IF HE WERE THINKING, I SAY THAT IS MUTINY.’

Captain Thomas Troubridge, HMS *Culloden*

1628
THE *BATAVIA* MUTINY

In 1963, in the waters surrounding the Houtman Abrolhos archipelago off the coast of Western Australia, a local fisherman escorted two divers to what remained of the wreckage of a seventeenth century trading ship. Seven years later the remains of *Batavia*, the pride of the Dutch Fleet, began to be raised from the shallow seabed surrounding the reef on which it came to grief 341 years earlier.

Expectations for salvage were high from the team at the Department of Maritime Archaeology at the Western Australian Museum, and over time some 8000 artifacts, scattered across an area of almost a square kilometre (about one-third of a square mile) of ocean floor, were recovered. They included rare salt-glazed ceramics, surgeon's tools, the remains of a sandstone arch, German and Dutch coins dating to as early as 1542, and a bronze astrolabe, a navigational device used to plot the position of the sun, moon and stars.

The recovery of these artifacts and the window they provide on seventeenth century life, however, do not even begin to tell the story of the events surrounding this famous shipwreck and, worse still, the grisly fate of its human cargo. They don't even come close.

The Dutch East India Company vessel *Batavia* sank on 4 June 1629, and would enjoy the status of Australia's oldest shipwreck if it weren't for the loss of the English East India Company ship *Trial* off the northwest coast of Australia in 1622. Of the original complement of 322 men, women and children aboard *Batavia*, more than 160 would perish. Forty people died as the ship broke up, but the deaths of the other 110 or so would not be as a result of the smashing of *Batavia*'s hull on the reef that surrounded the islands, nor from drowning, nor from injuries sustained in the struggle to swim to shore. The horrific truth is that more than a third of the 322 souls aboard *Batavia* would die at the hands of a small group of mutineers long after the splintered remains of the ship descended to the seabed—killed in a murderous rampage that took the lives even of women and children in what became one of the darkest and bloodiest pages in Australian maritime history.

THE *TITANIC* OF ITS DAY

Batavia was no ordinary ship. In fact, in many ways it was the *Titanic* of its time. The newest ship in the Dutch East India Company (VOC) fleet, *Batavia* was, like all VOC vessels, built for long, gruelling voyages. The strong double hull of 3-inch (7.5-centimetre) thick oak, with the layers separated by a waterproof lining of tarred horsehair, had an outer sheathing of pine as a barrier against infestation by teredos (marine worms). Over this again were tacked several hundred cowhides, which would rot and drop off in the course of the vessel's maiden voyage. *Batavia* was also one of the most heavily armed merchant ships of its time, with twenty-four cast-iron cannon, and was considered, like *Titanic*, to be virtually unsinkable. Also like *Titanic*, *Batavia* was destined to perish on its maiden voyage.

When the *Batavia* left the Dutch port of Texel for the Indonesian city of Batavia (now Jakarta) and the headquarters of the Dutch East India Company on 28 October 1628, it did so in company with seven other VOC ships, among them the storeship *Assendelft*, the small yacht *Kleine David* and the warship *Buren*. *Batavia* was under the command of Captain Francisco Pelsaert, a company-appointed *opperkoopman* (uppermerchant), and the ship's regular skipper, Ariaen Jacobsz, and was carrying a fortune in silver, gold and precious gems that required an armed escort of seventy soldiers. *Batavia* was built for the spice trade, specifically for the transport of items such as nutmeg, cloves and pepper, and at times cargoes of china ware and cotton garments, that were transferred to larger merchant vessels for the voyage back to Amsterdam, then the commercial capital of Europe.

Pelsaert and Jacobsz had very different personalities. They clashed early in the voyage over the affections of a woman, to the point where mutiny was discussed between Jacobsz and the man whose murderous excesses would soon be known to all, the *onderkoopman* (undermerchant) Jeronimus Cornelisz. Cornelisz suggested to Jacobsz that they could overwhelm the other ship's officers, throw Pelsaert overboard, seize control of the ship and the treasure it was carrying, and live a life of piracy among the islands and hidden coves of the Indonesian archipelago, masquerading as a Dutch East India Company ship under the VOC flag and raiding other Company vessels. As the voyage wore on and a few other malcontents were brought into the plot, it was agreed that Jacobsz would initiate the mutiny during the course of a disciplinary hearing that was shortly to take place over the mistreatment of one of the wealthy passengers by a member of the crew.

By the time *Batavia* was approaching the treacherous waters of the Houtman Abrolhos, the ship had been at sea for eight months, and living standards had become nothing short of abysmal. Drinking water was in short supply and the ship's stores had become stale. The crew knew they would never benefit from the treasure *Batavia* was transporting and the spices it would soon be amassing for a prosperous European aristocracy. There is little doubt that conditions were ripe for mutiny, but before the small group of mutineers could put their plan into effect, fate intervened.

Like *Titanic*, *Batavia* came to grief while travelling at high speed in calm seas under a night sky, following a route that had been pioneered by the VOC in 1611 that took its ships a considerable distance south from the Cape of Good Hope, then east, finally turning north to Batavia. The route was much faster and healthier than the old route across the Indian Ocean, but passed close to the mythical *Terra Australis Incognita*. The great southern land was sighted for the first time by a Dutch trader in 1606 and in 1616 by the Dutch explorer Dirk Hartog. Propelled through the water by more than 1170 square metres (12,570 square feet) of sail, *Batavia* ran aground 65 kilometres (40 miles) off the west coast of Australia in the midst of a collection of coral reefs and low-lying atolls surrounding the Houtman Abrolhos. The impact was such that Pelsaert was knocked from his bunk. To make matters worse, the grounding occurred at high tide, making it all but impossible to repair and refloat the ship, although several attempts were made.

A TREACHEROUS RESCUE MISSION

The passengers and crew had no choice but to row ashore on Beacon Island in the ship's two longboats, taking with them most of the remaining supplies of food and water. Four days later, on 8 June, Pelsaert, Jacobsz, and a chosen group of senior officers, crew and passengers set sail in the longboats for Batavia to arrange rescue, a voyage that would take thirty-three days and go down in history as one of the great feats of open boat navigation. This decision was not altogether popular, for many of those left behind would have preferred to take their chances in the longboats rather than be abandoned on a group of low-lying coral islands that had, on initial inspection, no natural sources of fresh water, no sources of food save what might be caught in the surrounding ocean, and no shelter. Such was the degree of resentment that they named one of the islands Traitor's Island, a designation it retains to this day.

Reaching the headquarters of the Dutch East India Company in Batavia at the end of the historic thirty-three-day open-water voyage, Pelsaert immediately had *Batavia*'s high boatswain, Jan Evertsz, and Jacobsz arrested for negligence for running the ship aground. He then recounted their ordeal to the Governor General, Jan Coen, who immediately gave him command of a small inter-island merchant ship, *Sardam*, originally part of the very flotilla that departed Texel with *Batavia* the previous October, and ordered him and his remaining officers to return to the site of the wreck and rescue the survivors. Pelsaert had not the slightest suspicion, however, that during the time it took to reach Batavia, and the two months that it would take to return to the Houtman Abrolhos, a murderous struggle for survival would arise among those who were left behind on the island that would come to be known as Batavia's Graveyard.

BATAVIA'S GRAVEYARD

One of those who had been left behind on the Houtman Abrolhos was Jeronimus Cornelisz, the undermerchant, the man responsible for the ship's stores who had earlier suggested mutiny to skipper Ariaen Jacobsz. Cornelisz was a recent employee of the Dutch East India Company. Little is known of him other than that he was a personal bankrupt and a member of the heretical Anabaptist sect, fleeing the Netherlands to escape persecution for his beliefs. When Pelsaert and Jacobsz sailed towards the horizon on their ambitious rescue mission, it was Cornelisz who was left behind as the company's senior representative. He took no time in revealing himself not only as a psychotic and domineering killer, but also a master manipulator, taking advantage of the panic that set in almost immediately upon the realisation the islands had, apparently, no reserves of fresh water.

Cornelisz had hatched a plan to commandeer the rescue vessel that he was certain would soon return, kill the crew, and load it with the 250,000 guilders of treasure that had been salvaged from the wreck. He decided those who opposed his plan had to be disposed of, and split the survivors into two groups, at low tide walking a group of men to a neighbouring atoll on the pretext of searching for water. He left them there, unarmed, in the hope they would perish—or, if they returned, would be so weakened that they could be disposed of easily. Unwittingly, Cornelisz had left the men, who included the twenty-one-year-old VOC soldier Wiebbe Hayes and a number of other soldiers, on West Wallabi, an island which had plentiful supplies of water and sufficient sources of food, including resident populations of wallabies and mutton birds, to sustain life. About three weeks later a smoke signal from West Wallabi revealed to the mutineers that at least some members of the abandoned group had found water and survived.

In the meantime, having divined Cornelisz's fell intent, Hayes's group constructed a series of rudimentary defences and, from the wreckage that was continually washing ashore, improvised weapons such as truncheons and wooden lances. They even retrieved some of the long, hand-forged nails used in *Batavia*'s construction, driving them through wooden planks to create crude but very effective weapons. By these means they were able to withstand a number of assaults by Cornelisz and his followers and survive until the return of *Sardam*.

After abandoning the group on West Wallabi, Cornelisz split the remaining survivors into small groups, ordering their dispersal over the nearby islands. He then gathered around him a small and loyal core of followers, composed mostly of junior ship's officers and soldiers, and convinced them of the necessity of killing an unspecified number of survivors in order to maximise the supplies of food and water available, not to mention that the fewer individuals still alive on the return of a rescue vessel meant the greater quantity of *Batavia*'s treasures each would receive. It wasn't long before a frenzy of killing—there were at least 110 deaths—saw even women and children strangled, knifed and drowned.

Pelsaert's journal cited one survivor's horrific recounting of the descent into madness under the reign of Jeronimus Cornelisz:

> *Jan Hendrycks confesses that one day he had been called by Jeronimus into his tent and that he gave him to know that at night time he must help him with the murder of the Predikant's [minister's] family. At night, Zeevonk has called outside Wiebrecht Clausen, a young girl, whom Jan Hendrycks stabbed with a dagger, and inside all people—the mother with her six children—had their heads battered in with axes ...*

Meanwhile the group under Wiebbe Hayes had slowly been gaining in number as refugees from the neighbouring islands fled on simple rafts to West Wallabi for sanctuary. Soon Hayes had forty-five people sheltering with him, compared to the thirty-six men loyal to Cornelisz.

The smoke signal from West Wallabi had not only revealed the presence of water on the island, but had also alerted the mutineers to the fact that Hayes was in a position to warn any rescue party of the dangers that awaited them. A series of skirmishes between the two groups began with an assault on West Wallabi by Cornelisz on 27 July after an unsuccessful attempt to tempt some of the soldiers with Hayes to join the mutineers. Along with constructing weaponry, Hayes and his men had built a small rock fort around a fresh-water source, as well as a variety of stone shelters, the remnants of which can still be seen. They remain Australia's oldest extant examples of European construction.

In August a second attack saw Cornelisz's men brandishing two salvaged muskets, neither of which could be fired, and they were again repulsed. Unable to break through Hayes's makeshift yet effective defences and eliminate the witnesses to the murderous rampages that had seen at least 110 survivors killed, Cornelisz began to show signs of desperation. In early September he unsuccessfully attempted to bribe the defenders out with offers of wine and blankets. A struggle ensued, Cornelisz himself was captured, and five of his most trusted confidants were killed. Even after his capture, however, senior figures from within his murderous group continued the bloodletting unabated.

TRIAL AND PUNISHMENT

On 16 September the crew of *Sardam* finally sighted the outer reefs of the Houtman Abrolhos and began to slowly navigate a path through the treacherous atolls and reefs. The following day saw the final assault by the mutineers on the defiant inhabitants of West Wallabi. During the course of the attack, Hayes and a small number of men rowed a makeshift raft out to meet the *Sardam* and warn Pelsaert and his crew of the mutineers' intent to capture the vessel. The mutineers were rounded up and confined, and Pelsaert immediately initiated an extensive and thorough investigation of events, which he went on to document in his personal journal.

Confessions were for the most part easily extracted and it didn't take long for a full picture of the horrors of the previous two months to emerge. A trial ensued and Jeronimus Cornelisz had both hands severed before being hanged on nearby Seal Island on 2 October. One of *Batavia*'s young cadets, Lenert Michielsz, was found guilty of complicity in the murder of twelve people, had one hand severed, and was hanged on the same day. Saloman Deschamps, a junior undermerchant, was keelhauled three times and whipped for strangling a young child whom Cornelisz had earlier poisoned. Mattys Beer, a twenty-one-year-old soldier, pleaded guilty to killing or contributing to the deaths of eighteen people and was also hanged, as was Allert Jansz, a twenty-four-year-old musketeer, for the murder of a cabin boy. The list goes on and on. It would appear, with such a collection of men all of whom had proved capable of the worst kind of atrocities imaginable, that if *Batavia* had not come to grief on the Houtman

Abrolhos the original mutiny proposed in hushed conversations between Ariaen Jacobsz and Jeronimus Cornelisz would almost certainly have been a savage and bloody success.

In addition to those summarily hanged, and the remainder who returned to Batavia aboard *Sardam* to face justice, there were two mutineers who suffered a very different fate. A cabin boy named Jan Pelgrom de Bye and the soldier Wouter Looes were marooned by Pelsaert on the central coast of Western Australia, near the mouth of the Murchison River. De Bye was found guilty of the murder of a small boy and complicit in several other murders. He had pleaded with Cornelisz to be allowed to decapitate one Coen Aldertsz, and became uncontrollable when the gruesome task was given to someone else. Wouter Looes had become the leader of the mutineers after Cornelisz was captured by Hayes, and was convicted of involvement in the murder of the Predikant's family. Despite never being heard from again, the two men nevertheless achieved a degree of notoriety by going into the history books as Australia's first European settlers, and could have been responsible for a number of lighter-skinned Aborigines with fair hair and blue eyes that are said to have been seen in the region in the decades to come. Add to this the mysterious painting on Western Australia's monolithic Walga Rock, 350 kilometres (220 miles) inland, showing a lone seventeenth century sailing ship among a plethora of traditional Aboriginal art. Where did it come from? Is it possible de Bye and Looes survived and together made their way into the interior? But why go there? Or is it perhaps a 'contact painting', composed by Indigenous Australians who witnessed one of the many Dutch trading vessels sailing off the Western Australian coast in the seventeenth and eighteenth centuries?

Wiebbe Hayes was rewarded for his heroism and promoted to the rank of sergeant with an annual salary of 216 guilders, twice his former pay, and was later made a lieutenant. When news of his resistance to Cornelisz eventually reached the Netherlands, he was elevated to the status of national hero. Eventual blame for the loss of *Batavia* was laid at Pelsaert's feet. He was accused at the subsequent board of inquiry to have lacked authority and exercised poor judgment. All his holdings and moneys were seized, and within a year of his return to the Indonesian island of Java he died a broken, disillusioned man.

The loss of *Batavia* was a major blow to the interests and prestige of the Dutch East India Company, and news of its loss came as a great shock to the people of the Netherlands. The first written account of the disaster was published in 1647: *The Disastrous Voyage of the Vessel Batavia,* by the Dutch historian Isaac Commelin. Two hundred fifty years later the first English translation of his story appeared in an edition of the *Western Mail,* a Perth-based weekly newspaper.

RESTORING THE *BATAVIA*

The coordinates of the original wreck site are 28° 30′S, and 113° 47′E on Batavia's Graveyard, today known as Beacon Island. *Batavia* is Australia's second-oldest shipwreck and a reconstructed portion of the vessel, as well as hundreds of artifacts including 137 sandstone blocks that were to be assembled as a triumphal portico at VOC headquarters in Batavia, can be seen today at the Western Australian maritime museums in Fremantle and Geraldton. After being restored over a period of years in the museum's Conservation Laboratory, the centrepiece of the display today is without doubt *Batavia*'s imposing port-side stern section, which includes a generous portion of the lower-level gun deck as well as the sternpost and transom.

In 1985, master boatbuilder Willem Vos of the Netherlands began to construct a replica of the *Batavia* using seventeenth century materials and methods. The project took ten years to complete. In September 1999, the new *Batavia* was transported to Australia by barge, and moored at the National Maritime Museum in Sydney. The vessel was the flagship for the Dutch Olympic Team during the 2000 Sydney Olympic Games. In 2001 it returned to its permanent home in the Dutch port of Lelystad, where it continues its life as a museum ship.

‘BOLD WERE THE MEN WHO
ON THE OCEAN FIRST

SPREAD THE NEW SAILS,
WHEN SHIPWRECK WAS
THE WORST:

MORE DANGERS NOW FROM
MAN ALONE WE FIND

THAN FROM THE ROCKS,
THE BILLOWS, AND THE WIND.’

Edmund Waller, seventeenth century English poet

‘I AM STARVING NOW,
ALMOST STARVED TO DEATH!
THEREFORE, FOR GOD’S SAKE,
GIVE ME MY SILVER CUP TO
GET ME SOME VICTUALS ...’

Twelve-year-old Thomas Capell, *Speedwell*

1741

THE *WAGER* MUTINY

Fear and superstition can play a large part in the life of a sailor. Some captains won't allow plants in the wheelhouse because they think they seek out dry land in the night. Some don't like to leave port on a Friday. You never kill an albatross because it might be carrying the spirit of a lost sailor in its bosom, and you never, ever, step off a boat with your left foot first.

One can only imagine, therefore, the impact the words that came softly from the lips of HMS *Wager*'s dying captain Dandy Kidd must have had upon the officers at his death-bed. As the fleet of which it was a part made its way through the South Atlantic, Kidd's body was being ravaged by scurvy. His gums were bleeding and his hair had begun to grow in an odd corkscrew shape, evidence of haemorrhaging within the hair follicles. His joints were so painful he could barely lift himself out of bed. As sick as he was however, Kidd felt compelled to share the vision he had just seen. Yes, there would indeed be riches ahead for those ships that could round the treacherous Cape Horn and go on to plunder the Spanish outposts along the Chilean coast, but for the officers and crew of *Wager* there was only poverty, disease, famine and death. Soon after uttering his chilling revelation, Dandy Kidd passed away and was buried at sea. Lieutenant David Cheap was promoted to fill the position of captain.

It's hard to imagine assuming command of a vessel in more challenging circumstances. *Wager* was approaching Cape Horn, one of the most demanding stretches of ocean in the world. Its captain had just died and its dispirited crew was left to ponder the implications of his apocalyptic vision. Cheap had never commanded a ship before and suddenly found he was captain of a cursed one. It was to be his first, and only, command.

THE WAR OF JENKINS' EAR

Anti-Spanish sentiments among the British people were more or less a constant in the early decades of the eighteenth century. First there was the War of the Quadruple Alliance (1718–20), then the Blockade of Porto Bello Harbour by the British (1726) and the Anglo–Spanish War that followed (1726–29), which included a failed Spanish attempt to capture the British-controlled Mediterranean island of Gibraltar. It perhaps should have come as no surprise, then, that the two nations were again destined to go to war over little more than a severed ear.

In 1731 Robert Jenkins, a British mariner, was in command of the brig *Rebecca* and engaging in piracy along the Spanish coast when his ship was boarded by the crew of a Spanish vessel. The Spanish captain, Julio Fandino, sliced off Jenkins' ear and handed it to him, telling him to take it back to his King with the warning that he would suffer the same indignity should he ever sail uninvited into Spanish waters. Seven years passed before Jenkins produced the severed ear in a vivid retelling of the incident to a packed House of Commons. This dramatic gesture proved to be a catalyst for war, though in reality the sending of English troops to the Spanish-held rock of Gibraltar, followed by the English resolutely refusing to provide Spain with compensation for its occupation, had more to do with igniting tensions. Nevertheless, the following year Great Britain named the conflict (1739–48), the War of Jenkins' Ear.

In September 1740, HMS *Wager*, a former trader converted to a 607-tonne (599-ton) man-of-war, sailed from England bound for the

Chilean coast with a squadron of seven other ships under the command of Commodore George Anson. Their mission was to sink Spanish shipping in the Pacific and to harass and capture whatever Spanish possessions they could find. Purchased from the Dutch East India Company in 1739, *Wager* was the least formidable ship in the group. Named after the commissioner who organised its purchase, the vessel was sluggish, unwieldy and outdated, but nevertheless considered good enough to be the fleet's storeship, carrying the bulk of the small armada's supplies of powder and small arms for the intended shore-raiding parties.

It is questionable just how effective the raiding parties would have been had they actually been required to fight. The fleet's so-called 'marines' were largely made up of almost 500 elderly conscripts from the Royal Hospital Chelsea, founded by King Charles II in 1682 and intended for the 'succour and relief of veterans broken by age and war', *Wager* carried the largest number of the infirm at 142, outnumbering its crew of 102. These recruits were effectively press-ganged into service and surely would have deserted if they'd been able-bodied enough to do so; their inclusion in the expedition was nothing short of a travesty.

Wager was also stocked to the hatches with merchandise designed to ingratiate the local populations the fleet would encounter. The tiny ship was carrying more than 406 tonnes (400 tons) of provisions, a massive cargo for a ship of its size, and a weight that it could ill-afford to maintain.

A HORRIBLE VOYAGE

It had been a horrible passage. The fleet was late leaving England and had been fighting persistent westerly winds for most of the voyage. This had it placed to round Cape Horn at the worst possible time of the year, when the easterly currents were at their peak. The majority of the crewmen had been on other missions prior to joining the fleet, and hadn't had enough time on land to replenish with a proper diet to guard against the outbreak of scurvy. The result was that the 'plague of the sea', caused by an acute deficiency of vitamin C, was soon ravaging every ship in the fleet.

The eight vessels of the fleet: the flagship *Centurion* and the warships *Gloucester*, *Severn*, *Pearl*, *Tryal* and *Wager*, with the two additional supply ships *Anna* and *Industry*, approached the Straits of Staten Island to the east of Cape Horn on 7 March 1741. Atrocious seas accompanied by a series of unusually strong and unremitting storms hampered the fleet's progress around the Cape. Sails froze in the icy winds and snow and sleet continually lashed the decks. Sailors, their numbers depleted by scurvy, suffered frostbitten fingers and were too exhausted even to throw the bodies of their dead comrades overboard. On one particular night Anson even sent his men up into the rigging to act as sails after *Centurion*'s mainsail had been stripped by the wind. Men were routinely swept overboard, and water flooded the lower decks so that there wasn't a dry place to be had. What began as a typical mission to 'annoy and distress' Spanish interests had become a fight for their very survival, and it was on one such night that *Wager*, its mizzenmast smashed, rigging damaged almost beyond repair and laden with supplies that made it sluggish in the water, lost contact with the rest of Anson's fleet.

GULF OF DISTRESS

In the weeks that followed the presumed loss of *Wager* the rest of the fleet didn't fare much better. Of the remaining five warships, *Pearl* and *Severn* were lost to heavy seas, and *Gloucester* was scuttled. In company with *Centurion*, the eight-gun sloop *Tryal* managed to round the Cape, but its hull had become so compromised it could go no further.

Wager meanwhile had also rounded the Cape and was limping northwards along Patagonia's wild western coast when on 13 May the ship's carpenter, John Cummins, and gunner John Bulkeley sighted land off the port side where there should only have been ocean. The crew soon realised they had strayed unwittingly into the waters of the appropriately named Golfo de Peñas (Gulf of Distress) and that what they were seeing was the peaks of Chile's Peninsula Tres Montes to the north. At 4.30 am Cheap ordered the ship turn south, only to strike a series of submerged rocks, off what is now known as Wager Island, with such force that the tiller was smashed, rendering the rudder inoperable. The sudden impact also loosed a spare anchor belonging to *Centurion*, which crashed straight through the hull into the ocean below. Forty-five men perished, either as a direct result of the collision or simply from being too ill to raise themselves from their hammocks and crawl up ladders to the upper deck.

Wager was stuck fast between two rock ledges, which at least kept it on the surface and allowed its stores to be taken ashore. Its refusal to sink resulted in some of the crew refusing to go ashore, with several dying after breaking into the stores of alcohol, becoming drunk and falling either into the sea or into one of the many flooded compartments. The 100 sailors who survived were ferried ashore on *Wager*'s yawl, cutter, barge and longboat. The officers, already conscious of the prospect of mutiny, disarmed any crewman who came ashore in possession of a weapon.

Over the following days the majority of the stores were brought ashore and distributed equally. On Saturday, 18 May a cask of beef was retrieved. The following day shirts, caps and supplies of cloth were salvaged. The following Wednesday some of the men began to build a shelter when it appeared they might be marooned there longer than at first thought. On 23 May more beef and pork was brought ashore, as well as some candles. Natives appeared and began to bring the crew food, including rock crabs, which were accepted with gratitude.

But with *Wager* also transporting the entire supply of alcohol for the fleet, it wasn't long before the chain of command began to be challenged. One crewman, who had been marooned once already in his employ with the British Navy, took it upon himself to remind the others that under the current law a sailor's wages ceased the moment he was shipwrecked. He then argued persuasively that if a sailor's wages ceased, then he was no longer in the employ of the navy and that therefore its entire disciplinary structure ceased to be of relevance, meaning an end to the following of orders and, if one so chooses, of the respect afforded a ship's captain.

HEADING IN OPPOSITE DIRECTIONS

Thanks to the skill of the ship's carpenter, who had reshaped and lengthened the longboat, named *Speedwell*, the survivors soon had a total of four boats to transport them through the labyrinth of islands that filled the Golfo de Peñas. The only decision to be made was in which direction they should travel. Cheap and his officers preferred to head north in the hope of making contact with Anson's fleet off Valparaiso. The majority, however, preferred a southerly route that would take them into the Portuguese-held region of southern Brazil. Weight of numbers saw Cheap remain on the island with the ship's yawl while seventy-nine of the crew, including First Lieutenant Baynes, Bulkeley and Cummins, headed south in *Speedwell* and the cutter towards the Strait of Magellan. Technically, Baynes, Bulkeley and Cummins had abandoned the captain of their ship and set off, if not in contravention of Cheap's direct orders, then at least against his better judgment. But is that all it was? Did Cheap order the men to stay? Had orders been openly defied? Had a mutiny, in fact, occurred at all? Or was the departure of Baynes and those who went with him simply the result of a mutual understanding?

A diary kept by midshipman Alexander Campbell, who determined to stay by his captain's side, seems to leave little doubt that force was brought to bear upon Captain Cheap to either join the majority in their southward journey to Brazil or relinquish his command over them:

> *all the men declared they would not go to the northward, and that in case the Captain should persist in his refusal to sign the paper [a document permitting them to go on their journey] he ought to have his command taken from him ... [and] therefore they determined to imprison him, which they did in a violent manner, tying his hands behind him with a rope, and leading him out of his tent in a shirt, they confined him in another tent, in which he remained until the boat went off.*

After an equitable split of provisions, the longboat and the cutter containing Lieutenant Baynes, Bulkeley, Cummins and the 'Magellans,' as they had come to be called, departed on 12 October. The Patagonian coast along which they were sailing was a vast archipelago of deeply incised fjords and inlets and affords those who know how to find it, a safe, calm, inside passage to the Strait that would have certainly saved lives and dramatically shortened the length of their journey. But Bulkeley, whose experience in seamanship and navigation, combined with a natural ability to lead and inspire others, which soon saw him emerge as the group's leader, had no knowledge of this route and so they continued on their tortuous way down the coast, not long afterward encountering their first misfortune. The cutter and a seaman were lost during a storm, and with *Speedwell* too large to be taken onto land they no longer had a craft capable of getting them to shore. Three of the crew volunteered and were granted permission to leave *Speedwell* in the hope of either finding the lost cutter or building a canoe and continuing on alone, but despite being left adequate provisions were never seen again.

Speedwell's journey through the Strait of Magellan was nothing short of appalling. By mid-November supplies had become so scarce that some of the men were screaming for food, and those with money purchased food that should have gone to others. Men began to die of starvation, at the rate of almost one a day. The smell of wet and putrid clothing filled the air. Then there was the trauma of sailing through sleet while trying to navigate a passage through the maze of channels and inlets that populate the Strait. The Magellans finally entered the Atlantic on 11 December and put into Port Desire (now Puerto Deseado) in southern Argentina to recuperate and slaughter as many of its resident penguins and sea lions as they could cram onto their boat.

On 28 January, three months after splitting with Captain Cheap, and with forty-nine of the original complement of seventy-nine lost to starvation, drowning or being stranded along the way, the *Speedwell* arrived in Rio Grande. The men had travelled over 5000 kilometres (3000 miles) in a cobbled-together open boat through sleet, hail and mountainous seas in one of the greatest feats of endurance and seamanship ever recorded. The Portuguese Governor of Rio Grande could scarcely believe his ears when told the tale and gave the sailors the freedom of the city. With their privations behind them, the thirty survivors of the *Speedwell* now steeled themselves for the journey home to England, to explain their seemingly mutinous actions to an unsympathetic British court.

The survivors departed Brazil on a variety of vessels. The first to arrive back in England was Lieutenant Baynes, who lost no time in denouncing Bulkeley and Cummins. Baynes, weak-willed and easily influenced, remembered all too well how he had been coerced and cajoled into taking command of the mutineers. With Cheap's condemnation still ringing in his ears and warning him that he would one day be held to account for his treachery, he was keen to distance himself from the mutiny. His condemnation of Bulkeley and Cummins resulted in the two men being detained for a fortnight on suspicion of mutiny after their arrival back at Spithead. Nothing came of it, however, and they were soon released and allowed to go home. It would be another three years before Captain Cheap arrived in England.

THE LONG JOURNEY HOME

As *Speedwell* and its cutter sailed south on that October day, Captain Cheap and almost twenty others, including the seventeen-year-old midshipman John Byron and Alexander Campbell, stayed on their windswept island, remaining there as the bitter Patagonian winter set in. In November the winds blew so ferociously and the temperatures were so cold they were prevented from foraging for shellfish, their only source of nutrition apart from the occasional seafowl and a rapidly dwindling store of flour. If it hadn't been for three casks of beef found by Campbell aboard *Wager*'s decaying remains in the first few days of December they may well have starved to death. But impatience to get off the island was growing, and on 15 December they boarded the barge and yawl, and set sail to the north.

What followed was eight weeks of privation that saw the loss of the yawl and four men before Captain Cheap decided to return to the island and abandon any hope of escape. It was then that a band of Indians agreed to guide them to the Spanish settlement of Castro, a journey that took four months and claimed the lives of a further ten men. On 6 January 1743, Captain Cheap, Campbell, Byron and Lieutenant Hamilton were sent to the Spanish-controlled port city of Valparaiso and kept under limited supervision. But their ordeal was over, and as Campbell was to record in his diary: 'Now we thought ourselves once more in the land of the living.' While in Valparaiso Campbell converted to Roman Catholicism and remained there, in the employ of the Spanish authorities.

In January 1745, after living in Chile for two years Cheap, Byron, and Hamilton were taken to the Argentine capital Buenos Aires and from there to Montevideo where on 13 October they boarded a Spanish ship for the voyage home to Europe. They made their way to France where they were collected in a cutter belonging to the English frigate *Squirrel* and taken to Dover. Byron, who was later to write a classic tale of their adventures, *The Narrative of the Honorable John Byron* (1768), was especially keen to return to his house in London but when he got there found it had been boarded up. No one expected him to return, and in his absence, life had gone on. Byron's sister had married and moved to the district of Soho. When he found her home the doorman failed to recognise him and refused him admittance until his sister, whom he hadn't seen in over five years, appeared, and they threw their arms around one another in rapturous joy.

GETTING OFF LIGHTLY

In Bulkeley's account of the *Wager*'s misadventures, *Voyages to the South Seas* (1743), he maintains that both he and Cummins avoided hanging on a technicality that echoed the argument made by the disgruntled sailor in the days after the *Wager* came to grief in the Golfo de Peñas, namely, that as they were no longer receiving wages they were deemed not to be in the service of the navy and so could not be held accountable for their defiance.

What is clear is that by the time Captain Cheap returned to London on 24 March 1746, the planned court martial had been watered down to nothing more than an inquiry into how the *Wager* had come to be wrecked in the first place, rather than representing any real attempt to determine whether any subsequent acts might be regarded as mutinous. There was also a groundswell of interest in the case because the miraculous nature of the journey had captured the public's imagination. In the eyes of the man on the street, the crew of the *Speedwell* were heroes, not villains.

In fact the only participant to receive any form of dressing-down was Lieutenant Baynes, who was given a 'severe reprimand', Despite the *Wager*'s rudder being disabled upon hitting the rocks he was nonetheless found guilty of failing to 'put the wheel over soon enough' after the impact, an action that would have been impossible given the circumstances. All other participants, including Cummins and Bulkeley, were simply acquitted.

Not long after his return to London, Cheap was given command of the Royal Navy frigate *Lark*; he engaged a Spanish galleon off the coast of Madeira before returning to London and promptly disappearing from history.

The loss of *Wager* led to the decision that in future the wages of a seaman would continue even if he were unfortunate enough to be shipwrecked. A corps of marines was also established, separate to the navy, which meant an end to the forced conscription of prisoners and the infirm.

For John Byron (1723–86), the ship's loss represented one unfortunate incident in an otherwise stellar career. In July 1760 he commanded a squadron that decimated the French naval forces at the Battle of Restigouche in New France, and in May 1766 completed the first circumnavigation of the world to take less than two years. He was appointed Governor of Newfoundland in 1769 and in 1778 became Vice-Admiral of the British Fleet. He died in the same year that his grandson George Gordon Byron, better known as the famous poet Lord Byron, was born.

'THE MEN ARE READY
FOR ANYTHING.'

Midshipman George Stewart to Fletcher Christian, the day before the mutiny, 27 April 1789

'SIR, YOUR OFFICERS ARE
NOW IN THE BOAT, AND
YOU MUST GO WITH THEM.'

Fletcher Christian to Lieutenant William Bligh, 28 April 1789

1789

MUTINY ON THE *BOUNTY*

The late 1700s was the Golden Age of Botany. By the 1780s 'botanising' had grown into global big business as the seafaring nations of the era amassed encyclopaedic collections of seeds and plants from around the world for propagation and study. In England the great explorer and botanist Joseph Banks, who had accompanied Captain James Cook on his voyages through the South Pacific in the 1770s, was put in charge of the new botanical garden in Kew, often used by King George III as a retreat from the intrigues of London's Royal Court. Banks set himself the personal challenge of gathering together the most extensive collection of exotic plant species in Europe. His longstanding connections with London's Royal Society, and the fascination of royalty in particular with the gathering of endemic species from around the world, enabled him to establish Kew as Britain's centre for botanic research and streamline the financing and organising of expeditions.

Banks was particularly keen to experiment with the transplantation of a primary food source from one part of the world to another. He found a perfect candidate in the exotic breadfruit tree, an attractive, fast-growing tree that can grow to over 23.5 metres (80 feet) in height with large, pear-shaped fruit that have a soft, fibrous interior not unlike bread. The tree is endemic to the Malay Peninsula and the western islands of the South Pacific but was first recorded growing by Europeans in the islands of French Polynesia in 1606.

BLIGH AND THE *BOUNTY*

In the early 1780s a number of destructive hurricanes alternated with a pernicious, ongoing drought that decimated the food supply on the British-held Caribbean island of Jamaica. Jamaican planters, concerned that an ongoing food shortage would drastically reduce the output of the island's slaves, petitioned King George III to mount an expedition to find a tree that was said to provide 'year-round bread', and in 1787, after consultation with Banks, it was decided to mount an expedition to Otaheite, as Tahiti was then known, and transport the breadfruit tree to Jamaica. The commander of the expedition would be Lieutenant William Bligh, a thirty-three-year-old seaman who had sailed with Captain Cook as a sailing master on his historic third and final journey in the *Resolution* in 1776–79. Bligh received much praise from Cook for the accuracy of his chart surveys and it was Bligh who safely navigated the *Resolution* safely back to England after the death of Cook at Kealakekua Bay, Hawaii in 1779.

Although Britain had a 600-strong navy in the late 1780s, none of its ships had been designed with a view to one day hauling hundreds of pots of breadfruit cuttings halfway around the world. To locate a suitable vessel the navy turned its attention to the country's fleet of merchant ships, and after considering six, settled on *Bethia*, a small, three-masted 224-tonne (220-ton) vessel originally built to haul coal. The navy purchased the collier for £1950 on 23 May 1787 and it was sent to the navy yards at Deptford for what proved to be an expensive and extensive refit. Copper plates were attached to the underside of its hull to prevent infestation by teredos (marine worms), and the captain's cabin aft was modified and lengthened in order to store the planned 1000 potted saplings on their long voyage home. Lead containers to store water for the plants were installed on the deck, and for armament the ship was provided with four 4-pounder guns and ten swivel guns. Even the sail area had to be reduced to better withstand the gale-force winds expected in the harsh southern latitudes around Cape Horn. When complete the cost of the refit came to almost £4500, more than double the ship's original purchase price. *Bethia* was then given a new name, becoming His Majesty's Armed Vessel (HMAV) *Bounty*, and commissioned into the Royal Navy on 8 June 1787.

Bounty sailed from Spithead on 23 December 1787 with a forty-five-strong, all-volunteer crew, a rarity in an age where the majority of crews were press-ganged into service. Volunteer crews were usually easier to handle and came on board with few of the grievances associated with men being forcibly sent to sea. It was a good omen. Several men who had sailed with Bligh beforehand had asked to join him, including the sailmaker Lawrence LeBouge and botanist David Nelson. *Bounty* had been transformed from a coastal collier to a cutter, not much more than half the size of a sloop-of-war, which was the Admiralty's preferred ship type for such a mission. It was so small, in fact, that it wasn't deemed large enough to warrant a detachment of marines to help maintain order, nor was Bligh provided with any commissioned officers. He would also be given a very young and impressionable crew, fourteen of whom, according to *Bounty*'s Muster Book, signed on as deserters. But he did have an experienced sailing master's mate, John Fryer, appointed by the Admiralty, and a senior master's mate, Fletcher Christian.

FLETCHER CHRISTIAN

Fletcher Christian was born on 25 September 1764 on a farm at Mooreland Close near Cumbria's Lake District, into an aristocratic lineage that stretched back twenty-five generations. No pictures of him exist but accounts describe him as having a commanding presence and 'a pleasant countenance'. He went to sea at the age of eighteen on HMS *Cambridge*, which coincidentally also carried a young 6th lieutenant, William Bligh. Christian was appointed master's mate on a voyage to India on HMS *Eurydice*, and then came two further voyages to Jamaica with Bligh before joining *Bounty* at Bligh's request for the voyage to Tahiti.

Bligh's orders stated he was to sail to Tahiti via the treacherous waters of Cape Horn, which would have proved a much simpler task had *Bounty* been able to depart England as scheduled in late November. With poor weather conditions in the English Channel forcing a delay until late December, this meant *Bounty* would be approaching the southern latitudes of Tierra del Fuego in late March, a treacherous time of year characterised by fierce storms that meant ships of its size could spend weeks or even months fighting the oncoming winds. In the end, on 22 April, after twenty-nine fruitless days that did nothing but sap the strength and endurance of his crew, Bligh was forced to abandon rounding the Cape Horn and set a new course for the Cape of Good Hope, which he reached on 24 May. By the time *Bounty* reached Matavai Bay in Tahiti on 26 October 1788, the crew had been at sea for more than ten months, and had covered more than 43,000 kilometres (27,000 miles).

Despite the arduous voyage there had been relatively few examples of the sort of brutality and short-temperedness that Bligh was known for. In over ten months there had only been two instances of flogging, one for behaviour akin to mutiny and one for neglect of duty, far less than the Royal Navy average, which led Bligh to record in his log: 'I had hoped I could have performed this voyage without punishment to anyone.' Bligh demoted John Fryer from his position as sailing master and promoted Fletcher Christian to acting lieutenant on 2 March, but there appeared to be little lasting enmity as a result. Instead of a crew driven to breaking point by a difficult voyage, *Bounty* arrived in Tahiti with a healthy and relatively content crew who were looking forward to a period of shore leave and becoming familiar with the local people and their traditional hospitality. When it was realised that their very late arrival meant they had missed the transplanting season for breadfruit and would have to remain anchored in Matavai Bay for the next five months, the mood of the crew bordered on euphoric.

To the casual observer it must have seemed that of all the 600 crews presently serving around the world in Royal Navy ships, none was less likely to mutiny than this one, serving their King in paradise aboard HMAV *Bounty*.

A TASTE PARADISE

Bligh permitted his crew to live ashore. It was a practical decision that allowed them to properly care for and tend to the breadfruit plants they were amassing, but it also allowed his crew to socialise with the local

Tahitians, whose women Bligh somewhat coyly referred to in his diary as 'handsome and delicate'. It also resulted in the first real test of Bligh's leadership when John Millward, Charles Churchill and William Muspratt, stole one of the ship's lifeboats and some muskets and deserted. Bligh set off in pursuit after putting midshipman Thomas Hayward, the officer of the watch at the time, in chains for being asleep. It took three weeks, but Bligh found them and gave them each a flogging on *Bounty*'s return to Tahiti, a more humane punishment than hanging, the navy's usual response to desertion, and yet another example of the leniency that has caused historians in recent times to re-evaluate Bligh's caricatured image as a tyrant.

Several accounts exist of the relationships that were formed between many of the crewmen and the local women, and it is beyond any doubt that the severance of these relationships was a catalyst to the mutiny that was to come. One of the better documented instances is that of Maimiti, the daughter of a Tahitian chieftain, who took an instant liking to Fletcher Christian, *Bounty*'s handsome twenty-three-year-old acting lieutenant. Bligh seemed unaware of the level of emotional discontent and resentment swirling through the crew when *Bounty* eventually departed Tahiti on 4 April 1789, forcing the break-up of several relationships. At the same time, his famously intemperate bad language began to re-emerge.

THE GULF BETWEEN BLIGH AND FLETCHER

On 23 April *Bounty* anchored at Nomuka in the Friendly (Tongan) Islands and Bligh sent Christian and a small party of men ashore to search for water, ordering them to leave their weapons in their landing boat. When the group encountered a number of Tongan warriors who chased them, brandishing spears and clubs, they had no choice but to head back to the boat and return to *Bounty*. Bligh was furious and called Christian a coward in front of the crew. There was no more-derogatory word one man could use against another at a time when a man's most cherished possession was his honour. If they'd been in England the incident would certainly have ended in a duel. Then on 27 April, a violent argument erupted between Bligh and Christian over the theft of some coconuts from a stash kept between two of *Bounty*'s deck guns that included coconuts from Bligh's personal store. Bligh accused Christian of theft in front of the entire crew: '... dam'd Hound ... you must have stolen them from me ... God damn you, you scoundrels, you are all thieves alike!'

If Bligh could be accused of contributing anything to the ensuing mutiny it was his complete lack of understanding of the impact his insults and rages had upon other people. Though bad language was hardly uncommon in the British Navy, Bligh seemed to be alone in his ability to deliver an assemblage of particularly humiliating phrases that would strip men of their dignity. In 1805 he was court-martialled (although he escaped with a reprimand) for oppressive and abusive language, a rare charge indeed for a Royal Navy captain to face.

An awkward, unspoken gulf had emerged between Bligh and his acting lieutenant, and added to that was the problem of an increasingly belligerent crew who were having a difficult time adjusting to the discipline and routine of life aboard ship after five months of shore leave in a place where the people, it was said, 'knew no other god but love'. Bligh himself seemed more short-tempered than ever, ranting and threatening his crew at every turn. But although Bligh had a quick temper he was also quick to calm down, and would often ask Christian to dine with him just hours after castigating him for some minor indiscretion. Nevertheless, twenty-four days after leaving Tahiti and his beloved Maimiti, Fletcher Christian couldn't bear the separation and Bligh's humiliating treatment any longer.

'THE MEN ARE READY FOR ANYTHING'

Much has been speculated regarding Fletcher Christian's mental state. He had fallen in love with Maimiti, and their relationship, unlike most others formed between the Tahitians and members of the crew, was strictly monogamous and genuine. Three weeks into the voyage home, Christian had suffered several outbursts from Bligh and was planning to desert the ship; he had even begun to make a small raft, although he was talked out of the idea by midshipman Edward Young—who reminded him of the prevalence of sharks. Midshipman George Stewart also did his best to dissuade Christian from leaving the ship, uttering a phrase that very well may have given the world its most famous mutiny. Leaning over towards Christian, Stewart said: 'The men are ready for anything.' Though historians differ over whether or not his statement was intended to suggest mutiny, it nevertheless stands out as a pivotal moment, a line in the sand for what was to come.

Before sunrise on 28 April 1789, some 1130 nautical miles west of Tahiti, William Bligh was asleep in his cabin when Fletcher Christian, ship's corporal Charles Churchill, and others armed with muskets entered his cabin, tied his hands behind his back with a heavy cord, and led him on deck dressed in little more than his nightshirt. Bligh screamed at his officers to assist him, but armed guards had been placed at their doors and they were unable to intervene. As he was dragged away Bligh saw John Fryer standing in his cabin, which was across from his own, holding what appeared to be two loaded pistols. Bligh later recorded that 'a firm resolution might have made good use of them'. When he confronted Fryer over the incident, Fryer replied that he was so 'flurried' by what he was witnessing that he couldn't recollect having the guns in his hands.

On deck Christian restrained Bligh at the point of a bayonet as Thomas Burkitt and Alexander Smith stood behind him with loaded muskets at his back. It was decided that Bligh and those who wished to go with him would be set adrift, and *Bounty*'s jollyboat, a small lifeboat, was prepared. It was found, however, to be riddled with worm and unseaworthy, as was a second boat. This left the launch as the only option, although it was designed to carry a maximum of fifteen on very short trips with few provisions. Then it was decided who would be made to follow their captain into the launch and who would remain behind. Eighteen men who became known as the 'Bligh Loyalists' went with Bligh into the launch, though it was more likely a love of country and a chance, however slight, of returning home that prompted their inclusion rather than any personal loyalty to Bligh. Once these eighteen men were seated Bligh's hands were untied and he was led at gunpoint into the boat. His request for firearms was denied, but he was given four cutlasses.

The men who shared Bligh's fate were John Fryer, acting lieutenant; William Elphinstone, master's mate; William Cole, boatswain; William Peckover, gunner; William Purcell, carpenter; Thomas Ledward, surgeon's mate; Thomas Hayward, midshipman; John Hallet, midshipman; Peter

Linkletter, quartermaster; John Norton, quartermaster; George Simpson, quartermaster's mate; Thomas Hall, cook; Robert Lamb, butcher; David Nelson, botanist; Lawrence LeBouge, sailmaker; John Samuel, clerk/steward; John Smith, servant/cook; and Robert Tinkler, able seaman.

Twenty-five men remained behind. Nine men made up the inner ring of hardcore mutineers, and sixteen chose to stay even though they had not committed themselves to the mutiny. This was hardly surprising considering that those in the launch were given only enough food and water for five days. As if the prospects for those in the launch weren't already bleak enough, it only measured a pitiful 7 metres (23 feet) in length, had a beam of just over 1.8 metres (6 feet), was crammed with nineteen men, and was constantly in danger of foundering, lying so low in the water that even the smallest wave splashed over the gunwale. They were given sixteen pieces of meat, around 135 litres (30 gallons) of water, 70 kilograms (150 pounds) of bread, a generous supply of rum and a medicine bag. A tool chest had also been smuggled aboard by William Purcell, the ship's carpenter. The launch was equipped with two four-cornered lugsails, a few additional yards of canvas and some coils of rope and six oars. They had no charts and no compass, their only navigational tools being a sextant to calculate latitude and a pocket watch. The personal books of drawings, observations and remarks that Bligh had spent fifteen years compiling were denied him, as were his collection of rare books, his maps and many of his instruments.

Those who remained aboard *Bounty*, even those for whom circumstances had left them with little choice, were fully aware that no matter what followed they would be regarded under the Articles of War as mutineers, and would be tried and punished as though each one of them had personally held the bayonet at Bligh's throat. It wasn't much of a choice: either be set adrift in a small boat to await eventual starvation or drowning, or stay with Fletcher Christian to one day swing from a hangman's noose after being hunted down by a relentless and unsympathetic Royal Navy.

The mutiny on board HMAV *Bounty* has been studied for more than 200 years in an effort to come to an understanding of the events and motivations that led to Fletcher Christian and his accomplices taking the actions they did. There was no obvious moment where insurrection was sparked, no act of physical abuse on a crewmember by the ship's captain. In the end no observations are any more valid in explaining why it occurred than Bligh's own insights. Almost every Royal Navy ship, he was to write, that had anchored in the waters of the Society Islands had experienced a measure of desertion. The contrast of living a life on board ship as opposed to one of these islands is obvious. In *Bounty*'s case this contrast was magnified by the length of its stay, which had resulted not only in a number of physical relationships but other enticements as well: the chieftains had become so fond of many of the crew that they promised them land if they stayed.

A VOYAGE OF THE MOST EXTRAORDINARY NATURE

What followed for Bligh and his loyal comrades would become one of the greatest tales of survival at sea ever told. Having been set adrift just 30 nautical miles from the island of Tofua in the Friendly Islands, Bligh decided to make the island his first landfall in the hope of gathering provisions for the long voyage ahead. They set down in a small cove Bligh ironically named Murderer's Cove, as the mutiny itself had been quite bloodless. As if to live up to the cove's new name, the local population proved less than friendly. It was here that quartermaster John Norton lost his life on the beach, trying to hold off a group of unarmed islanders who had chased the landing party almost to the launch itself. The other men rowed the boat into deeper water and watched helplessly as in front of them Norton was mercilessly beaten about the head with rocks.

Upon leaving the shores of Tofua an inventory was taken of their provisions. Despite the aggressiveness of the locals, the island had provided them with some yams, some breadfruit and about thirty coconuts, all of which were consumed over the coming days. But they had also come within seconds of death. The South Seas were suddenly hostile, on land as well as on the sea, and Bligh realised their only hope of rescue lay not in finding refuge on a Pacific island but in reaching the colonised islands of the Dutch East Indies, from whose ports they would be able to take passage for England. Bligh estimated the voyage would take fifty days and divided the provisions accordingly. Each man was given 28 grams (1 ounce) of bread and 125 millilitres (4 fluid ounces) of water per day.

Over the next forty-seven days the tiny boat limped its way across the Pacific, through heavy seas that saw its occupants almost constantly bailing out water. Along the way Bligh became the first European to chart the 'Bligh Islands' (Fiji Islands) with observations so accurate they could still be used today. He navigated the little boat through Australia's Great Barrier Reef to Restoration Island and from there to the Timorese port town of Coupang (Kupang, modern capital of Timor), an odyssey of 3618 nautical miles. Its significance was not lost on Bligh, who later recorded in his journal that it had been 'a voyage of the most extraordinary nature that ever happened in the world'. When they arrived their bodies were covered in all manner of sores, Bligh describing their appearance as amounting to little more than 'skin and bones'. Timor's governor, William Adrian van Este, offered Bligh and his men every courtesy and gave Bligh the only unoccupied house in Coupang in which to recuperate.

'WE SHALL NEVER LEAVE YOU, MR CHRISTIAN'

Meanwhile, back in the waters of the South Pacific, Fletcher Christian had been sailing an impressive voyage of his own. From the day of the mutiny to the day he sighted Pitcairn Island, Fletcher Christian sailed *Bounty* across more than 6749 nautical miles of ocean. On abandoning Bligh, he headed first to Tubuai, 297 nautical miles to the south of Tahiti in the hope of establishing a colony there, but was confronted by a hostile armada of fifty canoes filled with armed natives. He turned back to Tahiti, where he collected 312 pigs as well as goats and chickens to take to Tubuai, which he had found was devoid of animals. He again set sail for Tubuai, taking with him six Tahitian men and eleven women, but on *Bounty*'s arrival made the fatal mistake of releasing all the pigs on the island. The ever-opportunistic animals began to destroy the gardens of the house-proud Tubuaians, and the already tenuous relationship with the islanders quickly deteriorated.

At this point Christian made a famous speech, promising to take *Bounty*'s crewmen anywhere they asked. At the conclusion of the speech Edward Young leaped to his feet and yelled: 'We shall never leave you, Mr Christian, go where you will!' After barely three months on Tubuai, Christian left for the last time and returned to Tahiti, where the sixteen men who had refused to commit themselves to the mutiny were put ashore. Christian married Maimiti in a traditional Tahitian wedding on 16 June and gave her the name Isabella before leaving Tahiti to search for a place he had read about five months earlier in Bligh's copy of *Voyages*, by the explorer John Hawkesworth. He had been intrigued by the description of a small island in the southern Pacific Ocean with mountains so high it could be seen from a distance of 70 kilometres (15 leagues), first spotted in 1767 by a young lookout with the surname of Pitcairn.

It was to be another four months, however, before Christian, his eight fellow mutineers, and the seventeen Tahitians, sighted Pitcairn. In the meantime they became the first Europeans to sight Raratonga in the Cook Islands, before sailing on to the Lau Islands in the Fijian archipelago. From there they sailed to Tongatabu, the main island of the Tongan group, before eventually arriving in the waters off Pitcairn Island on 15 January 1790. It was a 6.5 kilometres (2½ square mile) outcrop of volcanic rock, thick with vegetation, isolated, and was incorrectly, and thus conveniently, referenced on charts as 190 nautical miles west of its true position, which of course would make it awkward to find for any pursuing Royal Navy ships. It seemed the perfect place to settle. On 23 January, after determining the uninhabited island was large enough and diverse enough to provide for their survival, the mutineers set *Bounty* alight and scuttled it. The new occupants built homes, fenced off vegetable plots and dug pits to trap wild hogs, and for a time all seemed well. But life on Pitcairn would soon prove to be anything but idyllic.

'MASSACRE DAY'

In October 1790 Fletcher Christian and Maimiti had a son whom they named Thursday October Christian, and in 1792 a son named Charles Christian. In 1793 their daughter Mary Ann Christian was born. Despite this, Fletcher Christian did not adapt well to life on Pitcairn, becoming increasingly isolated from the others and spending much of his time living away from the group. Edward Young filled the vacuum and became the de facto leader, but arguments began to break out over everything from the sharing of provisions to land rights and work duties and, most particularly, over the women. The ratio of women to men was already poor, and the accidental deaths of two of the women did nothing to alleviate the problem. Then in late 1793, on what has become known as 'Massacre Day', four of the Tahitian men attacked and murdered William Brown, John Mills, John Williams, Isaac Martin and Fletcher Christian. Four Tahitians were also killed in a frenzy that saw almost half the island's population slaughtered.

William McCoy, a violent man who often mistreated the Polynesians, and on Massacre Day only narrowly escaped being killed himself, learned how to distil a potent alcoholic drink from the roots of the local Ti plant, and committed suicide during a fit of drunken rage in 1798. In 1799 Matthew Quintal, the first on the original voyage to be flogged and who, along with Christian and Churchill, had been most ardently in favour of mutiny, was murdered by Young and Adams after he threatened to kill everyone on the island. On Christmas Day 1800 Edward Young died from an asthma attack. In 1808, Captain Mayhew Folger in the seal-hunter *Topaz* became the first person to visit Pitcairn Island since *Bounty*'s arrival; he found John Adams, the last surviving mutineer, living with a number of Polynesian women and their children, the offspring of the mutineers.

'PANDORA'S BOX'

Just ten days after Bligh returned to England, King George III ordered a ship be dispatched to bring the *Bounty* mutineers to justice. Eight months later, on 7 November 1790, the twenty-four-gun, 521-tonne (513-ton) frigate HMS *Pandora*, with a crew of 134 under the command of Captain Edward Edwards, sailed from Portsmouth and reached Tahiti on 23 March 1791. Edwards wasted no time rounding up the men Fletcher Christian had left behind and had them placed in irons inside a special cage he ordered built on *Pandora*'s deck, which came to be known as 'Pandora's Box'. It measured just 5.4 x 3.3 metres (18 x 11 feet) and the hammocks the fourteen men were given to sleep in were riddled with lice and vermin. Edwards spent four months scouring the Pacific looking for the remaining mutineers, to no avail. On 28 August 1791, at 7.20 pm, with the sun low in the west, making it difficult for the lookouts to see ahead, and pushed along by a strong tidal current, HMS *Pandora* struck the outer Great Barrier Reef in the Torres Strait and sank with the loss of four mutineers and thirty-one crew. Ninety-nine of its original complement of 134 survived, and arrived in Timor in four open boats on 16 September.

Ten mutineers survived the ordeal to face trial in England aboard HMS *Duke* in Portsmouth Harbour on 12 August 1792. Those charged with mutiny and desertion were Joseph Coleman, Charles Norman, Thomas McIntosh, Peter Heywood, James Morrison, John Millward, William Muspratt, Thomas Burkitt, Thomas Ellison and Michael Byrne. Of the six found guilty only Ellison, Burkitt and Millward were later hanged on board HMS *Brunswick* in Portsmouth Harbour on 29 October. Heywood and Morrison received royal pardons. William Muspratt, the *Bounty*'s assistant cook and the only able-bodied seaman in the group able to pay for the services of an attorney, was also found guilty but was subsequently freed on appeal.

The American explorer and diver Luis Marden spotted *Bounty*'s rudder on display in the Fiji Museum in Suva, and discovered the remains of the ship itself in Pitcairn Island's Bounty Bay in January 1957. The wreck of HMS *Pandora*, after lying hidden for 186 years beneath the waters of the Torres Strait, was discovered in November 1977 on what is now called Pandora Reef. Less than 30 per cent of the hull remains intact and it is unlikely it will ever be raised.

The *Bounty* was not just the world's most famous mutiny—it was also the least bloody. In fact, the only injury that occurred on the day Bligh and his 'loyalists' were set adrift was the pain caused to Bligh's wrists from the rope that bound them as he was marched from his cabin to the deck. It is also ironic that the character of the two chief protagonists, Bligh and Christian, both appear to be in need of revision. Stereotypical images of Bligh as a tyrant do not seem to be supported by the facts, and any romantic or heroic aspects attached to Christian should perhaps be re-evaluated in light of what was an ill-conceived and spontaneous act of mutiny spurred on by a lovesick heart and a confused mind, rather than a high-minded pursuit of anything that was noble, and compounded by the sobering image of a weak and indecisive leader on Pitcairn, as demonstrated by the virtual abandonment of his role as leader and retreat into seclusion.

‘I CANNOT COMMAND THE FLEET AS ALL AUTHORITY IS TAKEN FROM ME ... MY MIND IS TOO DEEPLY WOUNDED ... I AM SO UNWELL THAT I CAN SCARCELY HOLD MY PEN TO WRITE THESE SENTIMENTS OF DISTRESS.’

Admiral Lord Bridport in a letter to Earl Spencer, First Lord of the Admiralty

1797 THE MUTINIES OF THE BRITISH FLEET AT SPITHEAD AND THE NORE

Between 1774 and 1790 more than a quarter of the men in Britain's Royal Navy deserted their ships. Half of all deaths in the navy were caused by disease, and of the other half, forty out of fifty were the result of accident or misadventure. Just five of every 100 deaths were caused by action against the enemy. Surgery was crude and ships' surgeons had to provide their own medicines and equipment. Four thousand sailors a year developed hernias as a result of heavy lifting and had to be supplied with trusses.

At the close of the eighteenth century the life of many a British sailor was little more than a form of enslavement in a floating prison. They existed on a diet of substandard food, suffering brutal working conditions, and were subject to the daily whims of exacting commanders. Sailors lived and slept in the section of the bow known as the fo'c'sle (forecastle), a narrow, cramped environment deemed unsuitable for the storage of cargo but good enough for enlisted men—it was the part of the ship that took the full force of the waves that broke over the gunwales above, spilling down through deck hatches and making life a damp, dank misery.

Despite these difficulties, however, sailors who were determined to make something of themselves could have a good life. The professional sailor was a resourceful and highly skilled individual who could, at least in theory, rise to become an officer regardless of their social class. Britain had by far the most highly skilled and trained seamen of any of the world's navies. They set their sails more quickly, fired their cannon faster and kept their ships cleaner than any other nation's navy, which was supported at home by a vast network of dockyards and an industry geared to provide them with every necessity required to maintain Britain's dominance at sea. But the eighteenth century was also an era of gross inequities in sailors' pay, and some were beginning to think it was about time the worth of an ordinary and able seaman was properly reflected in what His Majesty's Government was prepared to pay him.

POOR PAY AND CONDITIONS

By the 1790s the level of discontent over pay and living conditions was reaching breaking point. England was at war with France and the fight was not going well, though it would certainly have gone far worse if English losses on the ground in Europe hadn't been offset by the Royal Navy's dominance over the navy of the French Republic. The Royal Navy needed thousands more men during times of war than it did during times of peace and, because sufficient volunteers were not forthcoming, impressment (compelling eligible men between the ages of eighteen and forty-five years to serve in the navy by force and without notice) was used to raise crews for the nation's vast armada. The numerous 'landsmen' (those with non-sailing backgrounds) also picked up by this system did not always mix well with established crews. At the same time, advances in technology were resulting in longer and more demanding voyages. The coppering of a ship's hull below the water line to prevent the wooden hull from rotting meant a ship could now spend much longer periods at sea, testing the endurance and patience of crews and their officers. The demands upon Royal Navy crews were increasing year by year. Time spent at sea was increasing. Engagements with enemy ships were increasing. Everything was going up; everything, that is, except the crewmen's pay.

Sailors' rates of pay were first set in 1653 and hadn't altered since, which might at first glance seem reason enough for an uprising. But for over a hundred years prices in Britain had remained remarkably stable, and the purchasing power of a sailor's wage in the mid-1700s was much the same as it had been in 1653. In the latter decades of the eighteenth century, however, persistently high inflation began to severely erode the purchasing power of a Royal Navy sailor. In the 1790s a string of poor harvests saw the price of food more than double. A sailor's wage no longer bought what it used to.

In 1797, 114,000 men were serving in the Royal Navy. The government was spending £30 million a year on its impregnable 'wooden wall' of warships, all that stood between a free Britain and the might of Napoleon's armies encamped on the other side of the English Channel, and it was the ordinary and able seamen who provided the manpower that allowed this 'wooden wall' to function. Yet for much of the previous 100 years an ordinary seaman with between one and two years' experience received just £11 and 10 shillings a year. Able-bodied seamen with over two years' experience were paid £14 a year. Even petty officers had cause for complaint, receiving anywhere between £20 and £27 a year depending on their grade. Ships' surgeons were paid a respectable £60, lieutenants £100, and if you were a first rate captain you received £336 a year, thirty times the pay of an ordinary seaman—and these officers had just lodged another claim for an increase. Those on the lowest rate of pay were the 'landsmen', the unfortunate citizens grabbed off the street and press-ganged into service. Landsmen earned just £10 a year, but in their growing numbers they were beginning to alter the mix and expectations of Britain's sailors. Coming from increasingly educated backgrounds, their presence resulted in crews becoming more politically and ideologically savvy, adept at organising themselves into groups and initiating protests.

SHARING THE SPOILS

Even when Royal Navy ships captured a Spanish sloop or successfully laid siege to a Spanish or French seaport, the formula for dividing up the spoils of war did little to engender morale among the enlisted men. The Battle of Havana in 1762, for instance, saw the British Fleet's commanders divide almost a quarter of a million pounds' worth of treasure between them, while the ordinary seamen under their command received on average just £4 each. How the treasure of a captured enemy ship was divided among a Royal Navy crew was determined by the *Cruisers and Convoys Act* of 1708. The captain would receive three-eighths of the total, the captain of the marines, master and ship's surgeon would divide one-eighth between them, the ship's lieutenants, warrant officers, chaplain and all master's mates would share another eighth, and the midshipmen, the lesser warrant officers and marine sergeants shared another eighth. The final two-eighths of the prize would then be divided among the rest of the crew, which often numbered over a hundred men. An enlisted man in the Royal Navy was never going to make his fortune from plunder.

All a Royal Navy sailor had to do to be reminded of how little he was valued was to look across the bow at sailors in the merchant fleet. Merchant sailors enjoyed far shorter times at sea, earned four times the wages of an ordinary seaman, and didn't have their wages deliberately held back for up to six months to prevent desertion. To make matters worse, two years earlier soldiers in Britain's land army received a pay rise while the sailors were forgotten. By 1797, crews on some of the ships moored at the Nore, an offshore anchorage in the Thames Estuary, hadn't been paid for more than ten years, and in other cases fifteen years. The Royal Navy had a deserved reputation for being poor payers, but enough was enough. A good mutiny was long overdue, and the sailors duly obliged with two, the first at Spithead, the second at the Nore.

THE MUTINY AT SPITHEAD

Spithead was the traditional Royal Navy anchorage in the Solent, the stretch of water separating the coastal city of Portsmouth in the southern British county of Hampshire from the Isle of Wight and the English Channel. Since 1400 the Solent had been the site of Britain's Fleet Review, a demonstration in which the Royal Navy would occasionally, in times of war or pending war, sail in massive flotillas before its reigning monarch with intimidating displays of firepower designed to make its European rivals think twice before considering an invasion.

Spithead was no stranger to drama. In 1782, HMS *Royal George*, a first-rate 100-gun ship of the line and the largest warship in the world at its launching in 1756, sank while undergoing repairs at Spithead with the loss of almost 900 lives, and remains to this day the greatest single loss of life in the Royal Navy's history. In March the next year, crews at Spithead advised the Admiralty that they would run every ship aground and set them alight if a long-running dispute over unpaid wages was not resolved, and it was at Spithead in 1792 that the mutineers of HMAV *Bounty* were hanged above the decks of HMS *Brunswick*. Now a new chapter was about to be written in Spithead's history, one which saw the red flag of mutiny raised above its ships and a crisis emerge that had the Lords of the Admiralty referring to it as potentially the greatest challenge maritime England had ever faced.

The 1790s was a time of increased awareness among the general population of what should constitute a human being's basic rights. *The Rights of Man* (1791–92), by Thomas Paine, had sold an unheard of 200,000 copies in Britain, one copy for every fifty citizens. Paine argued that a government's sole reason for existing was to safeguard the rights of its people, and if this was not done then revolution was an acceptable response. Among the Channel Fleet crews, secret committees were formed to organise lists of grievances and the writing of petitions, actions in themselves that could be interpreted as acts of mutiny, which were sent to a blinkered and unsympathetic Earl Spencer, First Lord of the Admiralty, whose personal view was that a pay rise for the navy's enlisted men was out of the question.

In February 1797, eleven petitions were sent to the seventy-one-year-old retired Admiral Lord Howe, who was believed to be sympathetic to the woes of the enlisted men. At first Howe believed the petitions to have been fabricated, although by the end of the month and with fresh petitions arriving almost daily, he finally took them to Earl Spencer. Some weeks later, however, at an Admiralty meeting on 22 March, Spencer thought a course of inaction was best taken with regard to the growing calls for a review. He was more concerned at the prospect of a backlash from Britain's taxpayers, who would be asked to pay for any increase, than he was from his navy.

Perhaps the polite phrasing of the petitions caused the Admiralty to think that they were nothing more than requests and could be ignored without the risk of violent repercussions. An extract from a petition of 28 February read in part:

> *Your petitioners relying on your goodness and benevolence humbly implores that my Lords Commissioners of the Admiralty will comply with the prayers of this petition, and grant such addition will be made in their pay as their Lordship's wisdom they shall think meet. And your petitioners will in duty bound ever pray.*

They were hardly fighting words.

In the Admiralty's view there was nothing untoward brewing at Spithead; in fact, the Lords were so little concerned that Howe's successor, Admiral Alexander Bridport, was permitted in the last week of March to go on annual leave until 10 April. For the moment, the sailors at Spithead waited patiently for their concerns to be addressed.

On 13 April, after it became apparent that no reply would be forthcoming, Sir Peter Parker, Port Admiral at Portsmouth, was handed another petition from delegates representing the sixteen ships of Britain's Channel Fleet. This petition said that the Fleet's sailors were preparing to refuse their orders and would not allow their ships to leave their moorings. The significance of this was obvious to all. With the Channel Fleet tied up at anchor, the entire southern coastline of England was vulnerable to an attack by the French Navy. Portsmouth's Transport Officer was immediately ordered to send a message via a chain of shutter telegraph stations to the Admiralty in London: 'Mutiny brewing at Spithead.'

Returning from leave on 10 April, Admiral Bridport, who had not been privy to the petitions, sensed a disagreeable mood within the Fleet. He took his concerns to Spencer, who informed Bridport of the petitions and ventured the opinion that they amounted to nothing. Bridport was incensed that he had not been notified and privately thought Spencer a fool for disregarding them. Then on 16 April, Easter Sunday, the Admiralty gave the order that Bridport knew would uncover the extent of discontent. The squadron, under the command of Admiral Gardiner in HMS *Royal Sovereign*, was ordered to sail to St Helens anchorage, just three miles from Spithead. Bridport, in *Royal George*, passed on the order, but *Royal Sovereign*'s crew refused to weigh anchor; what followed was a lot of gesticulating and ordering on the part of its officers and very little evidence of a compliant crew.

The crew of HMS *Queen Charlotte*, anchored nearby, saw the confusion erupting on the deck of *Royal Sovereign* and, realising that their own timetable for rebellion had been usurped, began to climb into the rigging and cheer their shipmates on. The mutiny at Spithead had begun.

Within minutes of the crew of *Royal Sovereign* refusing their orders, boats from *Queen Charlotte* set out to every ship in the fleet requesting each ship's delegates to meet on board *Queen Charlotte* that evening to discuss the way ahead. The delegates from the rebel ships were mostly petty officers and midshipmen who realised early on that they stood a better chance of having their demands met if they didn't make them too unreasonable and at the same time continued to demonstrate a willingness to maintain discipline. This was not a politically inspired mutiny led by revolutionaries with an ideological agenda. The Spithead mutineers were professional sailors with a devotion to duty who continued to obey the captains of their ships at every turn short of putting out to sea. In fact the only deviation from the daily routine associated with being at anchor was seen every morning at 8 am and every evening at sunset in the days to come, when the crews ascended into the rigging to cheer and fill the air surrounding the defiantly still-furled sails with song.

DEMANDS OF THE SEAMEN

Meanwhile the mutineers set themselves up in the Admiral's cabin aboard HMS *Queen Charlotte* and gave the Admiralty forty-eight hours to agree to their requests, which were:

- an increase in pay
- the abolition of the so-called 'purser's pound,' the tradition that for every pound of food, that is, 460 grams (16 ounces), that a ship's manifest said was to go to the sailors, the ship's purser

would pass on only 400 grams (14 ounces) and keep 60 grams (2 ounces) for himself
- the provision of vegetables when at anchor in a British port
- greater attendance given to crewmembers who fall ill
- lengthier periods of shore leave, although acknowledging a boundary should be set lest a sailor stray too far
- if a sailor is wounded in action his pay will continue until he either recovers and returns to duty or is discharged.

On 18 April Earl Spencer arrived and offered the sailors what amounted to a 15 per cent increase in pay—but failed to address any of their other concerns. The mutineers rejected the offer. A subsequent Admiralty request to Bridport to arrest the ringleaders only served to highlight the Admiralty's failure to grasp the extent of the mutiny, for Bridport was forced to reply that to arrest those responsible was impossible—because the entire fleet had mutinied. Events then began to spiral out of control. Admiral Gardiner called all the ships' delegates together and told them they would be forgiven if they returned to duty, and would hang if they didn't. At this point the call of 'Remember the *Culloden*!' went out among the delegates, a reminder that the mutineers aboard HMS *Culloden* at Spithead in 1793 were also told they'd be forgiven if they ended their mutiny, which was little more than a refusal to put to sea in what they considered to be a leaky and unseaworthy vessel. They ended their mutiny as requested, and five mutineers were promptly hanged.

Negotiations with Bridport and Gardiner, predictably, collapsed. The red flag of mutiny was raised across the fleet. Spencer sent a small army to Portsmouth and ordered coastal gun emplacements to prepare for action.

To their credit the mutineers not only kept their nerve, they asked for a royal pardon and again reiterated their demands. Spencer was the first to blink. On 22 April he secured the mutineers their royal pardon; on the following day a promise to address their grievances was received from Parliament and read to the assembled crews. A relatively incident-free two weeks ensued, until on 5 May newspapers began to run stories saying the Seamen's Bill was expected to be voted down by Parliament. The fragile truce that had been built up over the previous two weeks was shattered. When an order came to send four ships from St Helens anchorage to assess the whereabouts of a French squadron, their crews, who had relinquished control of their ships in an act of good faith, again took command in what amounted to a second mutiny and refused to set sail.

On the evening of 6 May, unpopular officers were removed from the fleet, with courtesy if possible but unceremoniously if not, and delegates went from ship to ship ordering their crews to sail to St Helen's anchorage, where they would be out of range of the army assembling along the Portsmouth shoreline. Only the officers of HMS *London* put up any resistance. The *London*'s commander, Admiral Colpoy, who had helped negotiate an end to the *Culloden* mutiny, ordered its lower gunports closed and its trailing boats brought in to prevent the mutineers' delegates from boarding. The mutineers climbed aboard anyway, and the *London*'s First Lieutenant Peter Bover shot and killed a sailor standing on the ship's forecastle. A gunfight ensued which left nine people dead, among them three sailors, a midshipman and an officer, and an incensed crew wanting to hang Bover there and then. This may well have happened were it not for the intervention of the delegates, who urged the crew not to undermine all they had so far managed to achieve.

The Seamen's Bill was passed in Parliament and given royal assent on 10 May. In an effort to regain the trust of the mutineers Lord Howe, still a heroic figure despite his disregard of the petitions, was appointed as the Crown's representative over the hated Earl Spencer. On 11 May, Howe visited the *Duke*, *Queen Charlotte* and *Royal George* to argue the merits of the bill. The crews of *Duke* and *Mars* felt inclined to press for more, but when the rest of the fleet felt obliged to accept it the renegade crews fell into line. What continued to be argued over, however, was the fate of the more than 100 officers the mutineers had put ashore. The Admiralty could not be seen to allow this as it would give the impression that the crews of the Channel Fleet, alone among the navies of the world, had the luxury of choosing who would command them, an intolerable situation with obvious disciplinary repercussions. In the end fifty-nine officers were reassigned to other vessels, and the negotiations were over.

On 15 May there was a day of celebration and pageantry. Bands played 'God Save the King' in the streets of Portsmouth and barges full of revellers sailed through the fleet. The Channel Fleet's beloved Lord Howe was taken by barge from ship to ship where he read the royal pardon to cheering crews. At the end of a long day Lord Howe, exhausted and looking frail, was hoisted upon the shoulders of the fleet delegates and carried to the Portsmouth home of the British Prime Minister, William Pitt. On 17 May, Bridport finally gave the order to sail out and search for the suspect French Fleet, which, in the end, had not put to sea.

The crew of the Channel Fleet at Spithead had won a great victory, but it was only for them. The sailors at the Nore wouldn't be so lucky.

THE MUTINY AT THE NORE

Not quite forty years before the Spithead mutiny, HMS *Sandwich* had been a proud warship. Launched in 1759 as a ninty-gun ship of the line, it was the flagship of Admiral Sir George Rodney in the famous Battle of Cape St Vincent (1780) that saw the capture of six Spanish ships of the line. The *Sandwich*, however, had endured more than its fair share of storms. It lost its main topmast twice and had to dock in Spithead for repairs, and in the late 1770s was almost wrecked off the French coast. In 1780, ageing, worn out and beyond repair, it was converted to a floating gun battery, and in 1790 became a depot and receiving ship for the Port Admiral at the Nore, an offshore anchorage in the Thames Estuary some 40 kilometres (25 miles) downstream from London. Built for a complement of 750 when at sea, *Sandwich* now was packed from bow to stern with almost 1600 men waiting to be posted to various ships, living in cramped and unsanitary conditions that routinely saw the ship's surgeon, John Snipe, pleading to no avail with its commander, Captain Mosse, to ease the congestion.

Sandwich was attached to Britain's North Sea Fleet. Unlike the Channel Fleet, however, whose large ships of the line spent a lot of time in port, relying on smaller, more manoeuvrable frigates to shadow the French fleet and report back with their movements, the North Sea Fleet spent much of its time at sea, split between three strategic locations: the Nore, which was not a fleet station like Spithead but rather an assembly point, Great Yarmouth 145 kilometres (90 miles) to the north on the coast of Norfolk, and on patrol near the island of Texel in the Wadden Sea, within sight of the Dutch coast to the northeast. The commander of the fleet, Admiral Adam Duncan, spent much of his time aboard his flagship HMS *Venerable*, sailing between the three locations, which made it difficult for him to keep a close watch on the mood of his men.

THE NORE GRIEVANCES

On 19 May the Nore mutineers came into possession of Lord Howe's documents detailing the agreement reached at Spithead, which they believed put them in a strong position to formulate some very specific demands of their own. On 20 May Admiral Buckner boarded HMS *Sandwich* and was handed the following list of grievances:

- ARTICLE #1: Every indulgence that was granted to the mutineers at Spithead was to be given to them.
- ARTICLE #2: Every man when in port shall be given sufficient shore leave to visit their families and friends. (This demand was not granted to the Spithead mutineers.)
- ARTICLE #3: The navy would scrupulously adhere to its own laws and guidelines and pay every sailor all moneys owed prior to any voyage.
- ARTICLE #4: No officer that has been dismissed from a Royal Navy ship shall be appointed to that ship again without consent from the crew.
- ARTICLE #5: Pressed men to receive two months' pay in advance of a voyage to prevent pursers' on-board 'credit shops' extorting higher prices.
- ARTICLE #6: That an indemnification be offered to anyone deemed to be a deserter from a ship in mutiny.
- ARTICLE #7: A more equitable distribution of money and treasures from captured enemy ships.
- ARTICLE #8: Alterations to be made to various Articles of War (non-specific).

On 22 May the Admiralty's response to the Nore mutineers' grievances was to dispatch two armed regiments to nearby Sheerness. Many in the top echelons of the navy remained unhappy with the concessions made at Spithead; they were determined to hold the line at the Nore and prevent the desire for change from spreading throughout the entire British Fleet.

Meanwhile the rebellious ships had been formed into two crescent-shaped defensive lines strengthened by eight gunboats from the garrison town of Sheerness, brazenly captured by the mutineers in open boats and placed along the flanks of what had already become known as the 'Floating Republic'. This intimidating assemblage of firepower was moored almost within striking distance of the Houses of Parliament in London. Some in the Admiralty favoured ordering Duncan to bring the ships from Great Yarmouth and end the mutiny with a show of force, but could the crews at Great Yarmouth be trusted?

On 26 May the Lord Chancellor issued a statement saying the agreement at Spithead did not apply to the Nore mutineers, who immediately threatened to blockade the Thames. On 27 May Duncan, in command of HMS *Venerable*, received orders to put to sea after unconfirmed reports were received that the Dutch Fleet was preparing to sail from Texel. *Adamant*, *Repulse* and *Agamemnon* followed *Venerable* to sea. The crew of *Nassau* refused to weigh anchor, as did the crew of *Montagu*, due to their ships' unseaworthy condition. Two days later, however, on 29 May *Adamant* and *Repulse* turned back to port to join the mutiny, as did the sixty-four-gun *Agamemnon*, known throughout Britain as Lord Nelson's favourite ship. When the ships at Great Yarmouth joined the mutiny on 31 May, Duncan's North Sea Fleet had all but disintegrated.

But the British Government had learned its lessons at Spithead. On 1 June Prime Minister William Pitt introduced a Bill to 'prevent and punish' any attempts to woo sailors away from their oath of allegiance and to encourage them towards disobedience. A subsequent Bill established guidelines that enabled the Admiralty to declare a ship to be mutinous and to label mutineers and those sympathetic to them as 'pirates,' a charge punishable by death. The noose was tightening.

On 7 June the Admiralty issued a statement saying the Nore mutineers were nothing more than rebels, which meant that if they were captured they would certainly be hanged. Talk began to spread of escaping to France, but in anticipation of a mass exodus the Admiralty ordered the destruction of all the markers that provided vessels with safe passage through the Thames sandbanks and out to the open sea. Most sailors could not swim, and thus to be trapped on a sandbank meant almost certain death. On 9 June the rebel ships defied an order from President of the Delegates Richard Parker to sail, and on 13 June Parker chaired a meeting on *Sandwich* where it was agreed to end the mutiny.

On 14 June Parker was arrested and charged with disobeying orders, of being contemptuous of the authority of an officer, and with various acts of mutiny. He represented himself at his trial aboard HMS *Neptune*, and despite receiving some kind words of understanding from officers who were sympathetic to his aim of bettering conditions for his fellow sailors, was nonetheless found guilty and sentenced to death. In total 412 men were court-martialled, fifty-nine of whom were sentenced to death; of those, twenty-nine were executed. Richard Parker was hanged from the yardarm of *Sandwich* on 30 June. His body was swung from *Neptune*'s yardarm as a warning to others.

In the final analysis, what contributed to the Admiralty seeing the Nore mutineers as revolutionaries and treating their mutiny accordingly, as opposed to the gentlemanly dialogue with the 'honest sailors' at Spithead, was Richard Parker bestowing upon the ships assembled at the Nore the title of 'Floating Republic'. To a government already nervous over increased unionisation at home and left-wing revolutions abroad, the establishment of a so-called republic on the very outskirts of London, albeit self-proclaimed and transient, fuelled fears of the importation of a French Jacobin-style revolution, thus ensuring the mutiny was destined to be ruthlessly and mercilessly dealt with.

'YOU'VE SHOWN NO MERCY YOURSELF AND THEREFORE DESERVE NONE.'

Mutineer to Captain Hugh Pigot, HMS *Hermione*

'I STABBED THE CAPTAIN IN THE GUTS.'

John Phillips, sailmaker, HMS *Hermione*

'LET ME HAVE A CUT AT HIM.'

James Allen, servant of Second Lieutenant Archibald Douglas, upon seeing his master being dragged topside

1797

MUTINY ON HMS *HERMIONE*

In September of 1797 HMS *Hermione*, a thirty-two-gun Royal Navy frigate based at the Jamaica station, in company with HMS *Diligence*, was in the Mona Passage, between Puerto Rico and the Dominican Republic, halfway through a seven-week patrol in search of Spanish privateers, when the ships became engulfed by a violent wind squall.

Hermione's commanding officer, Captain Hugh Pigot, who had taken up his posting only seven months earlier, ordered his topmen into the rigging to reef the sails. This was to prevent the sails being torn from the masts or, worse, the wind-filled sails heeling the ship over to founder in the heavy seas. Clambering up wet rigging, unsecured, as a ship pitched and yawed in high winds was, for an experienced topman more or less routine, and not considered overly dangerous, though even the best topman was never more than one ill-timed step away from falling to his death below.

Hugh Pigot, however, was one of the Royal Navy's most brutal and sadistic captains. He flogged sailors for failing to make haste when given orders, for pausing while climbing the rigging, frequently for being the last man down. Reefing the sails required concentration and precision.

The last thing a topman needed was the distraction of a flogging awaiting him should he be the last to descend.

On this particular night, 20 September 1797, Pigot screamed out through his speaking trumpet that he would flog the last man down. Desperate to avoid this fate, three mizzentopmen, each attempting to clamber over the others in their efforts to get to the quarterdeck first, fell to their deaths. The youngest was aged just sixteen. Pigot, ignoring navy protocol and any semblance of human decency, dispensed with the 'fuss' of a Christian burial, and standing over their broken bodies gave the order: 'Throw the lubbers overboard.' When some of the deceased men's fellow topmen complained that the threat of a flogging had been unnecessary and had contributed to their deaths, Pigot ordered them to be flogged on the spot, and again the following morning.

ONE FLOGGING TOO MANY

During all this a Spanish privateer, which *Hermione* and *Diligence* had been shadowing through the night, managed to slip away. Pigot signalled to the *Diligence* to set a new tack, and the two ships sailed away from each other for the last time.

Pigot's unseemly disposal of the bodies of the three mizzentopmen was by no means the only disgraceful action that the crew had witnessed. A week earlier David O'Brien Casey, a young Irishman who was one of the ship's most capable midshipmen, was on his way down from setting a sail when he saw an improperly tied reef-point and paused in the rigging until a yardsman moved across to re-tie it. When he reached the deck an enraged Pigot insulted Casey in front of the entire crew and demanded he fall to his knees and apologise for pausing in the rigging. When Casey refused, Pigot ordered that he be stripped of his shirt and that boatswain William Martin administer twelve lashes, the maximum allowed under naval regulations. Although floggings were a common occurrence under Pigot's command, there was something different this time. Casey was a respected midshipman, held in high regard not only by the crew but also by many of the officers. The flogging, and the humiliating and degrading manner in which Pigot had attempted to force an apology from him, left a particularly sour taste in the mouths of the crew.

These incidents drove the crew to breaking point. They had, at last, seen enough. The next day, aided by the sort of courage that a barrel of rum provides, an orgy of savagery and vengeance turned the decks of HMS *Hermione* into the stage for the most bloodthirsty act of mutiny in the history of the British Navy.

AN OVER-INDULGED PIGOT

Hugh Pigot was born in Staffordshire, England in 1769 and grew up in a world of authority, power and influence. His father was a Royal Navy Admiral and a personal friend of Prime Minister Augustus Fitzroy, and an uncle held the rank of lieutenant general in the British Army. With his father often away from home, Pigot was sent to Ireland to be raised under the stewardship of his uncle—at a time when the English ruthlessly ruled over Ireland and treated the Irish with utter contempt. His life until he joined the navy at the age of twelve was one of a complete lack of accountability and absolute indulgence. Even then, his family connections permitted him to avoid the usual training and with it the instilling of proper naval discipline and values. Hugh Pigot must have felt that he could do as he pleased in life, even before he assumed the role of captain, which bestowed with it autocracy enough.

In 1782 he sailed to the West Indies as an admiral's servant on HMS *Jupiter*, observing firsthand the wielding of discipline on a Royal Navy ship. He was given his first command, the sloop HMS *Swan*, in 1794 and later that year was in command when *Swan* rammed a merchant ship in the English Channel. Pigot laid the blame for the collision squarely on the shoulders of the master of the merchant ship and soon afterward, perhaps as the result of some parental string-pulling, was given command of the 32-gun frigate HMS *Success*. During his twenty-seven months as captain of this ship Pigot began to build an unequalled reputation for barbarity.

Pigot had become a true believer in flogging as the primary tool in the maintenance of discipline at sea, and wasted no time in demonstrating his philosophy to his hapless crew. In his first fourteen months as captain of HMS *Success* he ordered more than a hundred floggings, one for every two men under his command. Despite their mistreatment, however, the men of *Success* never took it upon themselves to mutiny. By the time Pigot received his new commission on HMS *Hermione* he would surely have felt his authority as a captain was akin to that of a despot, an absolute monarch who could not be touched.

DISPOSAL OF PIGOT

There was one aspect of *Hermione*'s crew, however, that presaged a degree of unpredictability that Pigot would have done well to consider. When the ship set out on the seven-week patrol of the Mona Passage almost the entire complement of 170 men had been on board for three full years and most had not enjoyed so much as a single day of shore leave. *Hermione* had become, for those who were pressed into service and for those who had volunteered, a floating wooden prison, a humid, scurvy-ridden hellhole.

All that was needed was a spark. The treatment of Midshipman Casey, the deaths of the three young mizzentopmen, and the flogging of those who had complained, provided spark enough.

The following evening, a few minutes after the 11 pm time check, a group of eighteen men, having imbibed courage from a barrel of rum stolen from the fo'c'sle, armed themselves with tomahawks and cutlasses and moved towards the door of Captain Hugh Pigot's cabin, overpowering a marine guard. As the angry mob smashed their way in, Pigot grabbed for his sailor's dirk, a shortened sword used as a ceremonial sidearm by Royal Navy officers, and attempted to fight them off. The men slashed at him repeatedly, but no one managed to land a fatal blow. Pigot, his nightshirt drenched with blood, fought back valiantly until a bayonet pierced his defences and was driven into his side. Still alive, Pigot was forced to the cabin window and thrown out into the dark, still waters of the Caribbean. It was later claimed that his fading cries for help could be heard as the ship sailed on into the night.

There was no stopping the mutineers now. Having disposed of Pigot they turned their attention to the other officers. The officer of the watch, Third Lieutenant Henry Foreshaw, upon hearing cries of 'Murder' coming from below decks, ordered master's mate William Turner to investigate. Turner, however, had fallen in with the mutineers and Foreshaw himself was set upon and slashed at with knives and tomahawks. Foreshaw lost his hand to an axe in the struggle before he and his severed hand were tossed ingloriously into the sea. First Lieutenant Samuel Read was thrown over the side. The Commander of Marines, Lieutenant Macintosh, sick with scurvy in his cabin, was dragged from his bunk and thrown overboard. Second Lieutenant Archibald Douglas was attacked on the quarterdeck by his personal servant, who went at him wielding a hatchet and delivered several blows to his torso. Mortally wounded, Douglas was dragged by his hair to also be thrown overboard.

On a ship of the Royal Navy it was the boatswain who was given the task of administering the lashes, and certainly *Hermione*'s boatswain, William Martin, was high on the list of those to be dealt with by the mutineers. But in addition to his unenviable role as occasional executioner there was another reason Martin's continuing presence would be 'awkward'. His wife Frances was on board. Although it was unusual for an officer's wife to accompany her husband on a voyage it was not unheard of, and captains generally tolerated the practice. Nevertheless, it must have been with some trepidation that Frances Martin boarded a ship with a crew of 170 men, none of whom had been ashore, or seen a woman, for three years.

Although Frances would have kept to herself, one crewmember kept his eye on her. On the night of the mutiny, quartermaster's mate Richard Redman dragged William Martin out of his cabin by his shirt-tails and tossed him overboard. He returned to the cabin where the terrified Frances remained, locked the door behind him and wasn't seen again till morning.

In all, nine of *Hermione*'s officers were murdered that night, including two midshipmen. After several hours debating his fate it was decided midshipman David Casey would be allowed to live, along with the surgeon's mate Lawrence Cronin and the master's mate, William Turner, both of whom had been part of the conspiracy. Others who escaped the slaughter, including carpenter Richard Price, gunner Richard Searle, cook William Moncrief, and *Hermione*'s master, Edward Southcott, did so because they were considered to varying degrees essential in getting the hijacked ship safely to a Spanish port.

HUNTED DOWN

Over the next five days the mutineers sailed *Hermione* 800 kilometres (500 miles) south to the Spanish-controlled port of La Guaira on the Venezuelan coast, founded in 1589 by the Spaniard Don Diego Osorio as a principal hub for the export to Spain of cocoa and other local products. The mutineers knew that the British Navy would come after them in the same way that the *Bounty* mutineers had been relentlessly hunted down. By the time they sighted the Venezuelan coast, *Hermione*'s crewmen had all assumed aliases and agreed to a fabricated version of the mutiny that had them setting Pigot and his officers adrift in a lifeboat in the best traditions of that infamous but by comparison very 'civilised' mutiny of 1789.

But carousing in port after three long years at sea tends to result in indiscretion, and it wasn't long before the truth of what happened on the bloody night of 21 September came out. Five months later five of the mutineers were tracked down and taken from the deck of a French privateer. Four of them received death sentences and were hanged, then gibbeted on a British ship moored in the Haitian port of Mole St-Nicolas. Gibbeting was a practice whereby an executed body was placed in chains and hanged from a gallows or off the side of a high battlement as a public deterrent to others.

On 2 July 1800 seaman John Duncan was found guilty of murder and of turning a Royal Navy ship over to the enemy and was hanged on board HMS *Puissant*. In early July 1801, seamen Adiel Powelson and William Johnson were tried for the crime of being accessories to murder. Powelson was found guilty and hanged. David Forrester, who'd thrown *Hermione*'s purser Archibald Douglas overboard, killed midshipman Smith and admitted to being the one who forced Pigot through his cabin window while still alive, was executed on 1 April 1802. Although it would take another nine years, the Royal Navy with dogged determination brought thirty-two of *Hermione*'s crew to trial, twenty-four of whom were hanged and later gibbeted. This was no mean feat when one considers that in the days and weeks after the mutiny the 170-odd crewmembers fled to every point of the compass, joined the crews of merchant ships from Denmark, America, Spain, and even Britain, signed on to French privateers or simply roamed up and down the South American coast on any one of about a hundred coastal trading ships.

David Casey, the Irishman whose refusal to apologise to Pigot provided one of the primary catalysts for mutiny, was also captured; however, he was acquitted of the charge of mutiny and freed. Richard Redman, the tormentor of Frances Martin, was located serving on a Spanish ship in

1799 and was hanged. Frances Martin survived her ordeal and went to live in the United States before returning to England in 1802 where she organised representations to the British Parliament for the establishment of a widow's pension scheme.

HMS *RETALIATION*

In 1799 a fascinating aside to the mutiny was played out. Understandably reluctant to hand back a perfectly good thirty-two-gun warship to a nation with which they were at war, the Spanish maintained possession of HMS *Hermione*, added several more gunports, renamed the ship *Santa Cecilia*, and left it at anchor in the northern Venezuelan port town of Puerto Cabello. After refusing a request from Sir Hyde Parker, the British naval commander in Jamaica, to return the ship to British hands, a daring raid was organised. Under the command of Captain Edward Hamilton, HMS *Surprise* (ironically, a French corvette captured by the English in 1796 and renamed) sailed into Puerto Cabello under the sights of more than 200 shore-mounted cannon on the night of 25 October 1799, and carried out one of the most daring and successful military incursions in history.

Approaching *Hermione*, whose decks and crew's quarters were packed with over 400 Spanish soldiers, three boats were lowered from *Surprise* and Hamilton, together with 100 sailors and soldiers, cut the mooring lines while others went aloft to set the topsails. By the time the Spanish realised what was happening, it was too late. After a particularly gruesome battle that left almost 120 Spaniards dead and more than 200 prisoners on 'their' boat, *Hermione* was sailed back to Jamaica without the loss of a single British life.

In an attempt to erase the memory of its bloody past, Sir Hyde Parker renamed the ship HMS *Retaliation*. A few months later, on 31 January 1800, it was renamed HMS *Retribution* by the British Admiralty. The former HMS *Hermione*, which would one day become famous as *The Black Ship* in the 1963 book of the same name by British writer Dudley Pope, was finally broken up at the Royal Dockyards in London in June 1805.

‘THE TRAITORS WHOM I COMMANDED REFUSED TO FIGHT; AND NOTHING REMAINS TO ME AND MY BRAVE OFFICERS BUT VAIN RAGE AND THE DREADFUL REFLECTION OF OUR PRESENT SITUATION.’

Rear-Admiral Samuel Story, Batavia Fleet, 30 August 1799

1799

THE *VLIETER* INCIDENT

When the Dutch Republic was overrun by the armies of the French Republic in 1794, the nation's chief executive and commander of its armed forces, Stadtholder William V Batavus, Prince of Orange, was forced to flee in a rather undignified manner in a fishing boat to London, where he established the Government of the Dutch Republic in Exile. The old Republic of the United Netherlands was no more, and in its place was the French puppet state of the Batavian Republic. This new political reality seemed to matter little, however, to the subjects William had left behind, who almost without exception welcomed the French with open arms.

The Batavian Republic was officially proclaimed on 19 January 1795, and in May members of the new state and representatives of the French Republic signed the Treaty of The Hague, which saw 25,000 French troops permanently stationed on Dutch soil, an expensive deployment to be paid for by the Dutch, and the establishment of a mutual defence pact between the two nations.

STIRRING UP REBELLION

In 1799, in an attempt to generate a popular uprising among the Dutch citizenry against their French occupiers, Great Britain and Russia made plans to mount an invasion of the North Holland peninsula. The waters around the peninsula had none of the dangerous shoals that were common along much of the Dutch coast, the area was lightly fortified and defended, and the Dutch Fleet was moored nearby. The fleet had been badly mauled by the British at the Battle of Camperdown in 1797 and had since been engaged in a massive rebuilding program. British Colonel George Don, an expert in espionage, who was involved in the planned land invasion, felt the mood of the Dutch Fleet was such that its crews could well mutiny and turn their ships over to the British rather than risk another disastrous engagement at sea.

This was no idle hope. A squadron of nine Dutch ships, including the sixty-six-gun *Dordrecht* and the sixty-six-gun *Revolutie*, had been surrendered to Britain without a fight at the Battle of Saldanha Bay in the Cape Colony in 1796. During his subsequent court martial the Dutch commander of the squadron, Rear-Admiral Engelbertus Lucas, claimed he was forced to surrender his vessels because his crews, who were opposed to the new republic, were about to mutiny.

With the Dutch Navy's loyalty to the Batavian Republic suspect in the eyes of the Admiralty, Britain was optimistic that its ships might be coerced into mutiny again. In fact, so convinced were the British that Orangist sentiments were still rife that the eldest son of William V, William Frederick, Prince of Nassau-Dietz, Prince of Orange, boarded the invasion fleet so he could greet his father's subjects in person. Loaded onto the eighteen-strong fleet was an assortment of other Dutch émigrés as well as pamphlets and dozens of old flags from the Orangist regime. Efforts to engender a mutiny from within the Dutch Fleet also came from loyalists within the Batavian Republic such as Carel Hendrik ver Huell, a former captain in the Dutch Navy who had been discharged from the service in the wake of the French invasion. Ver Huell was busy contacting other loyalists such as Theodorus Frederik Van Capellen, a former Dutch Navy captain who resigned his commission in the wake of the proclamation of the Batavian Republic. Van Capellen later rejoined the Dutch Fleet and, along with another loyalist captain, Aegidius van Braam, had been given command of a ship-of-the-line in the Helger squadron. History is uncertain, however, whether the two captains encouraged mutiny aboard their vessels prior to the arrival of the Anglo–Russian invasion fleet.

AN UNOPPOSED INVASION

The British Fleet sailed from the mouth of the River Great Stour near Canterbury in Kent, and reached the waters off Texel on 26 August 1799. General Herman Daendels, the commander of the Batavian Republic's land forces, had ordered a string of coastal fortresses along Den Helder, the northernmost tip of the peninsula, to be abandoned and the Batavian Fleet, under the command of Rear-Admiral Story, had withdrawn to the Zuider Zee. Britain put ashore some 7000 troops completely unopposed.

When Story returned with his fleet on 29 August, Orangist flags were flying from the tops of church steeples and over the battlements of Den Helder's coastal fortifications and, just as the British had hoped, the sight of the old colours of the Netherlands and the presence of the British Fleet both excited and terrified Story's crews. The crew of the Dutch flagship, the seventy-four-gun *Washington*, under the command of Van Capellen and with Story himself on board, refused to bed down that evening, convinced the British Fleet would find them in the night and blow them to pieces. Several crewmen, armed with swords and pistols, placed guards on the ammunition boxes. When the commander of the sixtyfour-gun *De Ruyter*, Captain Huis, overheard mutinous talk from two of his quartermasters he was forced to place them in irons. Captain Kolff on the sixty-four-gun *Utrecht* got word to Story that his crew had resolutely refused to fire so much as a single shot in the direction of the British Fleet.

On the morning of 30 August, Story's fleet sighted the British ships off Texel Island off the northern tip of the peninsula, and an intimidating sight it was. The British Fleet, consisting of eleven ships-of-the-line, six frigates and several corvettes, possessed almost twice the firepower of the Dutch Fleet. Story, convinced he needed time to plead with his mutinous crews, decided to send his flag captain, Captain Van Capellen, and the commander of the sixty-four-gun ship-of-the-line *Cerberus*,

Captain De Jonge, in a sloop beneath a flag of truce to Vice-Admiral Sir Andrew Mitchell of the British Fleet to buy some time while he tried to convince his men to fight.

A COUNCIL OF WAR

Signalling to prepare for an engagement, however, only served to harden the mutinous resolve of the ships' crews. When the alarm to attend to stations was sounded on *Washington*, almost the entire crew stated again their determination not to fire a shot in anger. Some even went so far as to extract the cannon balls from the ship's cannon and the cartridges from their rifles and throw them into the sea. By this time every ship in the Dutch Fleet had stated its intention not to fire upon the enemy, with the exception of the fifty-gun ship-of-the-line *Batavier* under the command of Captain Van Senden, whose crew was prepared to follow whatever example was set by *Washington*. Van Capellen and De Jonge then returned from the British Fleet with a letter from Vice-Admiral Mitchell saying that Story could either give up his fleet and join the invasion fleet or face the consequences. He gave Story just one hour to decide what he would do.

A council of war with the captain of every ship in the Dutch Fleet was convened aboard *Washington*. De Jonge, Van Capellen and van Braam all argued in favour of accepting Mitchell's ultimatum, and Story also felt he had no choice but to surrender. Scuttling the fleet was discussed, but it was clear that the crews would not permit it. Story ordered his ships to lower the Batavian flag and declared himself, his officers and his crews to be prisoners of war, which didn't prevent a small group of sailors from the thirty-two-gun frigate *Ambuscade* throwing overboard, against the wishes of their officers, a member of the crew who oddly enough preferred to fight the British whatever the odds. The flags of the Republic were brought down from mastheads and torn up by the mutineers. Skirmishes broke out on several ships between those wishing to surrender and those few still with a sense of loyalty to the Batavian Republic.

Prince William Frederick could scarcely conceal his delight and insisted on being ferried to every ship in the captured fleet to address their crews, who cheered him wildly. The Dutch crews were removed to British vessels and prize crews from the British Fleet boarded the Dutch ships and sailed them back to England. Five ships deemed unable to make the trip remained with volunteer crews loyal to the deposed Orangist regime and were sailed to England a few months later.

TRIED *IN ABSENTIA*

Story had surrendered 632 guns and more than 3700 men to the British, the second time in three years that a Batavian naval fleet had been handed over to the British without a fight. It was a shameful incident and a court martial was convened on 8 October to seek the punishment of those responsible. This was largely theatrical, as almost all the accused had been taken back to England and could be tried only if they returned to Dutch shores on *parole*. When Captain Connio of the brig *Gier* and Captain Kolff of the *Utrecht* returned, they were condemned to death. Kolff escaped back to England, but Connio was executed on 27 December 1799. Captain De Jonge on his return escaped a charge of treason but was convicted of dereliction of duty and forced to undergo a humiliating ritualistic dismissal in a mock execution in which a sword was waved menacingly above his head.

The 1802 Treaty of Amiens brought a temporary halt to the war between Britain and France, and it was hoped this might lead to Story, Van Capellen, van Braam and Kolff returning to the Batavian Republic to face trial. When it became obvious they intended to stay in England, the Batavian Republic established a High Military Court and tried them *in absentia*. They were found guilty of dereliction of duty, cowardice and treason, and declared to be devoid of honour. Beheading at the guillotine would be Story's punishment should he ever return, and the others would end their days in front of a firing squad.

Story went to live in Germany and settled in the northwestern town of Cleves not far from the Dutch border. He protested his innocence until his death in 1811. Van Capellen, van Braam and Kolff were all eventually rehabilitated when Prince William Frederick returned to the Netherlands in 1813 and accepted the title Sovereign Prince William I.

'IF WE DO NOTHING, WE BE KILLED. WE MAY AS WELL DIE IN TRYING TO BE FREE AS TO BE KILLED AND EATEN.'

Sengbe Pieh

'DEAR FRIEND, WE WANT YOU TO KNOW HOW WE FEEL. MENDI PEOPLE THINK, THINK, THINK. NOBODY KNOW WHAT WE THINK, THE TEACHER HE KNOW, WE TELL HIM SOME. MENDI PEOPLE HAVE GOT SOULS ... ALL WE WANT IS MAKE US FREE.'

Letter to John Quincy Adams from Kali, one of the four captured Mendi children

1839

THE *AMISTAD* MUTINY

In July and August of 1839 scattered reports began to appear in newspapers along America's Atlantic seaboard of a long, black, two-masted schooner that was moving in a northeasterly direction towards New York City, paralleling the coast in a suspicious zigzag pattern and said to be crewed by men of dark and 'savage' appearance.

The mysterious vessel was not flying any recognised flag, leading many to suspect it might be a pirate ship that had sailed north from the Caribbean in search of plunder. In spite of several unsuccessful attempts at boarding the vessel by officers of passing ships, no one was able to confirm its purpose, or its intended destination. It was a small vessel, built to transport sugar cane and supplies to the many plantations that dotted Cuba's coastline. Its first owner named it *Friendship*, but when later purchased by a Cuban Spaniard it was renamed *La Amistad*.

In the early hours of 26 August, on Montauk Point on the eastern tip of Long Island, two men hunting birds were approached by four black men who had come ashore out of desperation, in the search for food and provisions and anyone who might be able to aid them in their attempt to navigate their way across the Atlantic to Africa. The two men, Henry Green and Peletiah Fordham, were led to a coastal headland from which they could see *La Amistad* moored a mile offshore, and were made to understand that if they agreed to supply the passengers of the schooner with sufficient food and water for a long voyage back across the Atlantic, they would be rewarded with a portion of the treasure that was being carried on board.

In a longboat on their way out to *La Amistad*, Green, Fordham and the Africans were apprehended by the surveying brig USS *Washington*, whose crew boarded the vessel at gunpoint and ordered everyone below decks. The US Attorney-General ordered an immediate investigation on board *Washington* but there was much confusion over whether or not a crime had been committed, or by whom, as well as several unresolved issues regarding jurisdiction. The ship was eventually towed to New London, Connecticut, where its desperate passengers were incarcerated in a county gaol in New Haven on charges of piracy and murder. It was only then that the astonishing story of *La Amistad* and the plight of those who had sailed in it for sixty-three days in the hope of achieving an unlikely freedom began to unfold. In a few short weeks this unremarkable schooner would become the most recognised ship in America, and those sailing on it would be lifted out of obscurity and bondage to becoming the toast of New York and living symbols of humanity's universal right to self-determination.

SLAVE TRADING

La Amistad's story had had its genesis months earlier in the jungles of West Africa when Sengbe Pieh, a rice farmer and the son of a local chieftain, was captured on the upper reaches of Sierra Leone's Gallinas River, about ten days' march from the coast, and taken to the notorious slave island of Lomboko. There he was held for two months along with hundreds of other kidnapped men and women from the surrounding Gbandi, Kissi and Kono tribes before being herded into the lower decks of the Portuguese slave ship *Tecora*. Walking the upper reaches of the Gallinas River was a dangerous practice in the 1830s, its consequences vividly reflected in the name of a Mendi man who was also taken while walking a road in the region and who would go on to become one of the chief interpreters in the *Amistad* trial. His name was Kaw-we-li. Translated, it meant simply 'war road'.

The practice of slavery had, by the 1830s, become ingrained into almost every strata of West African life. The need for slaves in the Americas and the Caribbean had become so great that individual roadside abductions alone could not keep pace with demand, and the paths from freedom to slavery became far more varied. An African from the Mendi country might be threatened with being sold to slavers as punishment for a crime such as adultery, or even be sold to a family member as a means of paying off a debt. One of the *Amistad* Africans was sold to his uncle by his own family to pay for a coat before being captured by soldiers and taken to Lomboko.

Lomboko was a large masonry compound built on an island off the Gallinas coast by the infamous Spanish slave-trader and former sugar merchant Pedro Blanco, who had been trading in slaves since 1822 when he arrived from Cuba on his ship *Conquistador*. Lomboko was synonymous with misery, deprivation and the end of the lives they had known for tens of thousands of Africans. They were also held in open-air cells known as slave sheds or 'barracoons', flimsy, high-walled structures built on the many low-lying islands near the mouth of the Gallinas River.

ACROSS THE OCEAN TO CUBA

In April 1839, 600 Africans, mainly young healthy men, were crammed into the cargo bay of the brig *Tecora* for the treacherous two-month voyage across the Atlantic Ocean to Spanish-controlled Cuba. The *Tecora* had a clipper-shaped hull and was built for speed and manoeuvrability. Its half-height decks were purposefully constructed for the transportation of slaves, designed to cram as many human beings as possible into spaces that were not high enough to allow a person to stand. Slave ships would sometimes lie hidden among the delta islands of the Gallinas River for up to three months to avoid being captured by fast-sailing patrol ships from Britain, where slavery was banned. Without notice, the captives would be marched from the barracoons and forced into large wooden canoes to be ferried hurriedly to slave ships moored offshore, where they were manacled with iron collars and chained to the floorboards.

By the time *Tecora* slipped undetected past patrolling English ships into Havana Harbour two months later, over 200 of the original 600 captives had perished. As the ship approached Havana its captain ordered the survivors on deck, where they were cleaned, clothed and given a final meal. Ashore, they were transferred to a complex of roofless barracoons constructed between the city's main avenue and the offices of the island's governor. Two Spanish plantation owners, Pedro Montes and Jose Ruiz, purchased fifty-three slaves from the new shipment, including four children from another vessel, for US$450 each. Although Cuba was a signatory to treaties that were intended to prevent the importation of slaves, once they were brought illegally to shore there was little that could be done to prevent them being fraudulently traded and sold under the guise of being Cuban-born. Ruiz and Montes gained passports for their illegally purchased slaves by presenting the Captain-General's office with false documents claiming they were Cuban-born, or 'ladinos'.

The next day the prisoners were transferred to the schooner *La Amistad* to be taken to the sugar plantation of Jose Ruiz outside the small town of Puerto Principe, 500 kilometres (300 miles) down the coast. In a damning indictment of the captives' perceived value, the expensive silks, calicos, glassware and china that *La Amistad* was also carrying were insured for a total value of US$40,000, whereas the lives of the fifty-three Africans were calculated to be worth just US$20,000, or US$377 per person.

The US-built *La Amistad* was not a purpose-built slave ship but a schooner designed primarily to transport sugar cane in coastal waters. It measured just 20 metres (65 feet) in length, which meant its unwilling passengers could only be brought up from the pungent, airless storage area below in very small groups for exercise and to be fed. Conditions on board were beyond harsh. The slaves were joined together in a series of iron collars in the stifling heat of the lower decks, and anyone caught consuming more than the allotted share of water was flogged.

REVOLTING INSENSITIVITY

Although these slaves dragged from their families, held in chains for weeks on end, and taken to a world they did not know had already ample reasons to mutiny, the incident that is generally perceived to have ignited the revolt was little more than one person's appalling insensitivity.

Shortly after *La Amistad* left Havana Harbour on 28 June, the cook began to taunt the slaves with actions designed to convince them they were to be cooked and eaten at the end of the three-day journey to Puerto Principe. In full view of all the captives he mimicked cutting his own throat before pointing to some nearby barrels of meat, an action clearly designed to give the impression that the captives' future was to be cut short with a barbaric massacre. The terrified prisoners, despite being from a variety of tribal backgrounds and without a common language, were able to make themselves understood and rallied behind Sengbe Pieh, a natural leader who had begun to formulate a plan of escape.

Two days into the journey the weather began to deteriorate and it was estimated the journey would now take four days rather than three. Rations were cut, and anyone caught taking more than their allotted portion was flogged, and had their wounds smothered in vinegar and gunpowder. On 30 June, Pieh loosed his shackles and those of the others with a nail he had smuggled below decks, and led an assault on the crew. Armed with long-bladed steel cane knives, the slaves quickly overwhelmed and killed the captain and the ship's cook but were unable to prevent two crewmen from fleeing in one of the longboats. The ship's owners, Montes and Ruiz, were restrained after Montes was found hiding below decks wrapped up in one of *La Amistad*'s sails. The navigator, a Spaniard named Montez, was also spared, and told to steer a course for the west coast of Africa. During the day he had little choice but to keep *La Amistad*'s bow pointed squarely to the east. At night, however, he managed to steer northwest in the hope of sailing into American coastal waters and making good an unlikely escape. After spending several weeks navigating the waters surrounding the Bahamas but with the 'mutineers' too fearful of going ashore for provisions lest they be apprehended, *La Amistad* finally emerged from the Bahama Channel and entered the swift northerly current of the Gulf Stream, which took it past the southern slave states of Georgia and the Carolinas and into the waters off New England. Off the eastern tip of Long Island, Sengbe Pieh made the decision to land a small party of men to search for food and for anyone who might be able to assist them in their journey home to Africa.

IN US HANDS

When Lieutenant-Commander Thomas Gedney of the USS *Washington* boarded *La Amistad*, drifting aimlessly off the coast of Long Island on

26 August, its sails in tatters, its inhabitants weary and supplies of food and water desperately low, only forty-three of those on board when the ship sailed from Havana were still alive. Jose Ruiz claimed Sengbe Pieh's real name was the very Spanish-sounding Joseph Cinqué, in the hope that the leader of the revolt would not be recognised as a recently imported slave, which would make Ruiz guilty of violating an 1820 agreement banning the importation of slaves into Cuba.

On the morning of 27 August, Sengbe Pieh and the other 'mutineers' were brought to New London aboard the USS *Washington* and taken to the admiralty court in New Haven, Connecticut, where they were imprisoned on charges of piracy and murder. It is still a matter of conjecture just why Gedney chose to take the slaves to Connecticut, where slavery was still legal, rather than to New York, a free state. The likely reason was that only Connecticut would legally be in a position to consider any possible salvage rights to the US$40,000 worth of goods in *La Amistad*'s hold.

Meanwhile the plight of the captives had captured the American imagination. On 2 September, barely a week after their arrival, as if to demonstrate New York's capacity to mount a show before the paint had barely dried on its props and even before a way had been found to communicate with its star protagonists, a play entitled *The Black Schooner—or the Pirate Slaver Amistad*, sub-titled 'The Procession of the Doomed', had its opening night in New York's Bowery Theater. In a week of packed houses it took a record US$1,500; at the same time the good citizens of Connecticut were paying 12 cents each just to catch a glimpse of the incarcerated Africans. Lithographs of Sengbe Pieh by the sketch artist James Sheffield sold widely. Pieh and his countrymen were becoming big business.

The story of Sengbe Pieh soon became the story of *La Amistad* itself. He proved a rallying point for the other prisoners, carrying with him an air of intensity and magnetism. By the time the trial had concluded the American people had developed an unprecedented degree of fascination with him that was reflected in the *New London Gazette*, which described him as possessing an intelligent countenance and uncommon composure, and the *Herald of Freedom* which wrote he was a man with a gentle, magnanimous countenance who looked more like a sage than a warrior.

According to eyewitness reports the prisoners were treated well. The men were dressed in cotton shirts and trousers and were even permitted onto New Haven's green, under supervision, for periods of exercise. The children of *La Amistad*, a boy and three girls aged between ten and twelve, so enamoured themselves to their captors that they were taken in a series of buggy rides by the county sheriff and various 'hardened' gaolers were seen to have enjoyed themselves immensely. The children were given their own room in the county gaol and during the trial would only be called upon as witnesses, and only then as a last resort.

A CELEBRATED LEGAL CASE

Meanwhile Ruiz and Montes were doing all they could to avoid being found guilty of illegally importing Africans into Cuba. In an interview published in the *New York Herald* on 9 September, Ruiz claimed he first saw the slaves working in fields on the outskirts of Havana and at the time made no inquiries as to where they might have come from, but added they were 'clearly' Cuban-born. Much of the trial to follow would turn on the validity or otherwise of this claim.

The defence attorney for the accused was the Connecticut lawyer Roger Sherman Baldwin. Born in New Haven in 1793, Baldwin was raised in a fervently abolitionist household whose father was a founding member of the Connecticut Society for the Promotion of Freedom. He graduated from Yale Law School in 1811, was admitted to the bar in 1814, elected a member of the Connecticut State Senate in 1837 and again in 1838, and agreed immediately to join the defence when asked to do so by the abolitionist Dwight Janes.

On 19 September 1839, the US Circuit Court at Hartford was filled to capacity for the first day of the trial. A mood of jubilation and expectancy had been growing for weeks across Connecticut and in neighbouring New York in the lead-up to what would become one of the most celebrated cases in US legal history. Engravings and sketches of Sengbe Pieh/Joseph Cinqué and *La Amistad* were selling out on street corners. Pro-abolitionist newspapers proclaimed God had initiated the incident to hasten the demise of slavery, while pro-slavery newspapers like the *New York Herald* claimed the abolitionists were trying to turn the accused into 'saints'.

The legal complexities of the *Amistad* trial overwhelmed the Circuit Court of Judge Smith Thompson. Lawyers for the two hunters who encountered Pieh and his men on the beach on Long Island claimed they were entitled to salvage rights on the vessel and a percentage of the ship's stores. Attorneys for Ruiz and Montes claimed that since slavery was legal in Spain the slaves should be returned to their purchasers. The government of Spain was demanding *La Amistad* be returned to Cuba. There were even suggestions that the slaves could be released and placed in the protective care of the US President, Martin Van Buren. In the end, with a confused jury constantly emerging from the jury room to ask for clarification and direction on innumerable points of law, Thompson chose to dismiss the case on jurisdictional grounds, happy to leave it all for the District Court to unravel.

On 2 January 1840, with the trial about to reconvene in the District Court in New Haven, Connecticut, the US Secretary of State John Forsyth ordered the naval vessel USS *Grampus* to lie at anchor in New Haven Harbor ready to transport the prisoners back to Africa should the trial end in their acquittal. The trial began on 8 January, and was presided over by Judge Andrew T. Judson who, a few years earlier, had taken an anti-constitutional stance by refusing permission to a young white woman named Prudence Crandall to open an all-black academy for girls near his Connecticut home. Judson blocked the application on the grounds that it violated a state law which discouraged any activity that would increase the migration of blacks into Massachusetts. The abolitionists, wary of Judge Judson's apparent predisposition for denying African-Americans basic human rights, had secretly chartered a schooner that was moored in an undisclosed location and had been made ready to whisk Sengbe Pieh and his comrades to Canada should the decision of the court not go their way.

There were few more-exciting places to be in America in the early days of January 1840 than New Haven. In the District Court of Judge Andrew T. Judson. Baldwin and the other members of the defense team reiterated time and again that the two Spaniards Ruiz and Montes did not possess any legal claims over the Africans and that the Africans had been, and should now be considered to be, free men. Law students from Yale Law School refused to leave the room, even during long recesses, because of the certainty they would lose their seats, every last one of which was filled by people representing every conceivable segment of American society, sitting in awe of impassioned defences of personal liberty that were cheered by abolitionist sympathisers amid Judson's continual calls for order.

SENGBE PIEH'S TESTIMONY

Everyone waited breathlessly for the testimony of Sengbe Pieh, and they were not disappointed. On 8 January, Pieh recounted to the court every fateful incident in his five-month journey from a jungle road in Africa to a New Haven courtroom. At the conclusion of his lengthy testimony and wrapped only in a blanket, he sat on the floor of Judson's courtroom and chillingly recreated, for a hushed and expectant audience, the posture he was forced to assume in the darkness and squalor of the Portuguese slave ship *Tecora*. The court adjourned on 11 January with Judson stating he would make his decision known within the week. The abolitionists would ideally have wanted a precedent-setting judgment repudiating the institution of slavery and affirming that all slaves in the slave states of the south were free. In reality, however, they knew such a pronouncement would never come from the lips of a District Court judge, and certainly not from the lips of Andrew T. Judson. But Judson was to prove he was far more than the pro-establishment mouthpiece the abolitionists had painted him.

On the morning of Monday, 13 January Judge Judson announced to a packed courtroom that the men who had mutinied against their captors and committed murder were now free men. Judson determined they were not the property of the two Spaniards who purchased them, that they were free to return to their homes in Africa, and, furthermore, that their murderous actions were born solely from a desire to return to their homes and their families and so they would not be extradited to Cuba to face charges of piracy and murder. Judson gave an order placing them in the care of President Martin Van Buren and called upon him to organise their safe passage back to Africa.

JOHN QUINCY ADAMS

President Van Buren became worried that complying with Judson's determination could jeopardise his popularity with southern voters, and chose to appeal the decision to the US Supreme Court. With five of the nine Supreme Court justices being southerners and, worse, slave owners, Lewis Tappan and his defence team began to envisage the prospect of defeat being snatched from the jaws of victory and so in October 1840 approached former President John Quincy Adams in the hope he would help plead the defendants' case. By this time the trial had become something of a media circus. Even Adams himself was quoted as referring to the melee of reporters that had swollen New Haven's population as 'that public raree show'.

Looking back over the momentous life of John Quincy Adams and with the benefit of hindsight, it should really be no surprise that the seventy-four-year-old juror, scholar and former President made himself available to argue the abolitionist cause at such a crucial juncture in history. He had been a constant observer of many of the significant events of his country, ever since witnessing the Battle of Bunker Hill as an eight-year-old from Penn's Hill with his mother Abigail in 1775. Three years later he travelled to France with his father John Adams, when Adams senior was made US Commissioner to Paris, and in 1781 travelled with his father to Russia when the United States Government began courting Russian diplomatic recognition.

John Quincy Adams received his Masters degree from Harvard in 1790, was appointed US Consul to the Court of Prussia in 1796 and on his return to Massachusetts in 1802 was elected to Congress. His oratorical skills saw him attain the position of Boylston Professor of Oratory and Rhetoric at Harvard in 1805, and he was a key member of a carefully selected core of diplomats sent to Europe to help negotiate an end to the War of 1812. He became Secretary of State under President James Monroe in 1824 and was elected the sixth President of the United States later that same year, serving only one term. In 1832 he became the first ex-President in the nation's short history to be re-elected to Congress after leaving the Oval Office. This was the man Tappan knew he had to have in his corner. Even though he was seventy-four years old and partially deaf, Adams had become in the eyes of the average American 'Old Man Eloquent', and it was this eloquence, combined with a scholarly mind and intimate knowledge of the rights and implications inherent in the Declaration of Independence and the US Constitution, that would sway the southern justices and help deliver an historic verdict.

A LEGAL AND MORAL VICTORY

As the trial approached, Adams filed a series of persuasive briefs with the court, and when the trial began on 22 February 1841, he was ready. He argued passionately for the instant acquittal of the defendants, with his overriding arguments flowing directly from the Declaration of Independence, a copy of which hung above the judges' heads. His arguments spanned almost nine hours over two days and relied not on legal precedent, of which there was none, but on universal, inalienable rights and the ineffable laws of nature common to all that ensure freedom to people everywhere regardless of colour, race or religion.

In the wake of the historic 8–1 vote on 9 March that ruled the defendants had been 'unlawfully kidnapped' and would be 'dismissed from the custody of the court', Chief Justice Joseph Story wrote to his wife that Adams' arguments 'were extraordinary for their power, their bitter sarcasm, and dealing with topics far beyond the records and points of discussion'.

The now free Africans were taken voluntarily to the town of Farmington, Connecticut, to begin discussions on how best to raise funds for their return home. In May they took centre stage in New York's Broadway Tabernacle to describe to the crowd, which numbered in the several thousand at 50 cents a head, their capture and subsequent revolt—also demonstrating their newly acquired skills in the speaking and reading of English. On 18 August the Union Missionary Society was formed at a gathering at the Hartford Congregational Church, attended by a representation of the *Amistad* captives, and decided that its first goal would be to establish a 'Mendi Mission' in Sierra Leone. Three months later, on 27 November thirty-five of *La Amistad*'s survivors departed New York Harbor aboard the barque *Gentleman* for the two-month voyage home, accompanied by the Reverend James Steele, who would be the spiritual head of the new mission.

In January 1842 the remaining survivors of the *Tecora* and *La Amistad* at last returned home. They had made headlines around the world and brought much-needed attention to the fledgling abolitionist movement in the United States and England. Their unlawful and abhorrent abduction from the jungles of West Africa hastened the demise of the slave trade in America and resulted in a legal and moral victory twenty-one years before Abraham Lincoln's historic 1863 Proclamation of Emancipation, issued in the midst of the American Civil War.

‘... AND OF THOSE COMMITTED TO OUR CHARGE ... THEY SHOULD BE PUT TO DEATH IN A MANNER BEST CALCULATED AS AN EXAMPLE, TO MAKE A BENEFICIAL IMPRESSION UPON THE DISAFFECTED.’

Written statement, Council of Officers, USS *Somers*

‘THREE MEN, IN A TIME OF PEACE, WERE THEN HUNG AT THE YARDARM, MERELY BECAUSE, IN THE CAPTAIN’S JUDGMENT, IT BECAME NECESSARY TO HANG THEM.’

Herman Melville, *White-Jacket*, 1850 (referencing the ‘*Somers* Affair’)

1842

MUTINY OR MURDER? THE USS *SOMERS* AFFAIR

Philip Spencer was born on 28 January 1823 in the town of Canandaigua in upstate New York. His father, John C. Spencer, the son of the eminent Chief Justice Ambrose Spencer, graduated from Union College in Schenectady, studied law in New York's state capital of Albany, and was admitted to the bar in 1809. He was elected to the US Senate in 1824 and appointed Secretary of War by President John Tyler in 1841. There were few more-privileged families in the United States into which the young Philip could have been born.

Unfortunately Philip Spencer didn't possess the academic drive or the patriotism of his father, nor did he possess a stable personality. He was withdrawn from Hobart College in Geneva, New York, after three years of exhibiting little capacity for academia, and was enrolled in Union College, but quit that institution as well and fled to Nantucket to sign on as a seaman on a whaler. Before he was able to embark, however, his father convinced him that if he must go to sea, a better life could be had as a commissioned officer in the navy than as an ordinary seaman on a series of whaling voyages that often lasted up to two or three years. John Spencer then used his influence as Secretary of War to arrange for his son to join the crew of what was regarded as the most powerful ship in the US Navy, the seventy-four-gun USS *North Carolina*. The appointment didn't go well.

A TROUBLESOME DRUNK

Midshipman Spencer began to drink heavily and was dismissed from the ship's company after a series of brawls in which he assaulted one of its officers. He was then assigned to the frigate USS *John Adams* but, having become involved in another fight while the ship was in the Brazilian port of Rio de Janeiro, was charged with dereliction of duty and drunkenness. In the wake of that incident a chastened Spencer offered his resignation, which was rejected pending his transfer to the frigate USS *Potomac* for the voyage back to the United States—where a man of lesser parentage would have faced certain court martial. *Potomac* sailed into Boston Harbor on 31 July 1842, and only John Spencer's quick intervention prevented the formal arraigning of his disgraced son. Instead of a dishonourable discharge the troublesome Spencer was assigned to the position of acting midshipman on the brig USS *Somers*, about to sail on its maiden Atlantic voyage to the coast of West Africa.

When the *Somers* sailed out of New York on 13 September 1842, it's hard to imagine anyone failing to be impressed with its immaculate straight lines. Its captain was Alexander Slidell Mackenzie, a commander of US squadrons (fleets) from the Mediterranean and the Atlantic to the West Indies and the Pacific, where he provided naval protection to US whaling fleets. He had been promoted to the rank of commander in 1841 and when he wasn't at sea found the time to author several books, including the biographical *The Life and Times of Commodore Stephen Decatur*.

With *Somers* designed primarily to provide training for naval apprentices in the absence of a land-based naval academy, the average age of the crew was very young, mid-teens mostly, and although Spencer was only eighteen years old he was seen by the cadets as relatively experienced, albeit someone with a chequered history. His undiminished contempt for authority, and his father's position, however, combined to produce in him a complete disregard for naval discipline and for the consequences of breaching it.

Mackenzie, like Spencer, was not without connections. His brother, John Slidell, was a US Senator and his sister was married to the Commodore of the US Navy, Matthew Perry. Mackenzie was a disciplined naval veteran of twenty-seven years' standing, and well aware of the circumstances surrounding Spencer's dismissal from his two previous postings. He openly disapproved of the special treatment afforded Spencer because of his father's position, and ordered the cadets not to associate with him.

A DISCONTENTED CREW

Somers sailed towards the coast of West Africa via Portuguese-held Madeira, Tenerife and Puerto Praia in the Cape Verde Islands, where it searched in vain for the eighteen-gun sloop *Vandalia* for which it was carrying a series of dispatches. Living conditions were especially cramped in the tiny vessel and the food, even by naval standards of the day, was appalling. Acting midshipman Spencer was spurned by the other officers despite being given his own cabin, and often found himself in the company of the youthful, impressionable and increasingly disgruntled crew in the lower decks. He began to talk about how a black flag might look flying from the topmast, and how the ship would fare as a pirate vessel, and repeatedly referred to Mackenzie as a 'damned old granny'. The discontent of the crew was enhanced by the supplies of alcohol and tobacco that Spencer had managed to smuggle aboard, by the taunts and bravado of a man whose privileges saw him act as though he were immune to naval discipline, and by Mackenzie's harsh methods of command.

On 10 November, after two months at sea, *Somers* dropped anchor in the Liberian port of Monrovia where Mackenzie learned that *Vandalia*, which had been in port for several days, had already sailed for America. The following day *Somers* set sail for the US Virgin Islands in the hope of meeting up with *Vandalia* on the island of St Thomas. It was on the way to St Thomas that Captain Mackenzie and Lieutenant Guert Gansevoort, an aristocratic Dutch career officer and the only other commissioned line officer on board, first heard rumours of mutiny.

MUTINOUS INTENTIONS

On the evening of 26 November Mackenzie was informed by the purser's steward, James Wales, that Spencer, along with two suspected conspirators, boatswain's mate Samuel Cromwell and seaman Elisha Small, had made plans to throw the officers and anyone loyal to them overboard, seize control of *Somers* and live a life of piracy in the Caribbean. Hardly able to believe what he was being told, Mackenzie ordered Gansevoort to Spencer's cabin where Spencer was found intently studying a map of the Caribbean. A search of his cabin uncovered a list, written in Greek, of those seamen it was felt could be counted upon to crew the ship in the wake of the mutiny, a smaller list of so-called 'unwilling', and a damning sketch of *Somers* flying a black flag. Those marked with the word 'certain' included Wales, Cromwell, Small, and a man noted as Edwards, although the ship's manifest showed no one by that name on board. Spencer was arrested, taken to the ship's quarterdeck, and placed in double irons.

Under interrogation Spencer admitted to having asked about the accuracy of *Somers*' chronometer, a timepiece used to calculate latitude. He also confessed to telling Wales of his plans, but insisted he did it as a joke to make a fool of Wales and never intended to turn those plans into reality. 'I may have told him so, sir, but in a joke,' Spencer said to Mackenzie. Unfortunately for Spencer, Mackenzie failed to share his sense of humour.

The following day, Cromwell and Small snapped the main topgallant mast when they swung too hard on a brace in an attempt to set some studsails. Mackenzie immediately saw this as an attempt to free Spencer and promptly had the two men placed in irons alongside him. Mackenzie and Gansevoort had clearly been spooked by Spencer's mutinous intentions and were not going to take any chances—suspicions abounded. When a group of seamen appeared on the quarterdeck to replace the damaged topgallant mast, Gansevoort drew his pistol in a panic and aimed it at them, fearing it was an attempt to free the prisoners. When two of the crew arrived late for a mid-watch muster on 29 November they too were manacled, along with two others suspected of complicity. Seven of the crew of 120 now sat huddled in chains on the quarterdeck.

A DARK CHAPTER

Somers was just 30 metres (100 feet) in length, small in comparison to most other brigs, and an increasingly agitated Mackenzie became concerned about not having the option of sequestering the prisoners away from the rest of the crew and so preventing further dissent. On 30 November he called for a meeting of the ship's officers and asked them to provide a written statement on what should be done. Their response provided the foundation for one of the darkest chapters in US naval history.

Written on a single sheet of paper and signed by all seven officers, the statement acknowledged that Spencer and certain co-conspirators had plotted to engage in mutiny and throw the captain, his officers and anyone else loyal to them overboard. As *Somers* was still two weeks away from any US port, and with the officers unable to gauge the level of sympathy the mutineers might still have among the crew, it was decided that the only course of action to maintain the safety of the ship, its officers and its loyal crew was to remove the threat by hanging the ringleaders Philip Spencer, Samuel Cromwell and Elisha Small. Making an example of them, it was hoped, would snuff out any remaining insubordinate impulses.

> The punishment of death, or such other punishment as a court martial may adjudge, may be inflicted upon any person in the naval service—
>
> 1. Who makes, or attempts to make, or unites with any mutiny or mutinous assembly or, being witness to or present at any mutiny does not do his utmost to suppress it or, knowing of any mutinous assembly or of any intended mutiny, does not immediately communicate his knowledge to his superior or commanding officer ...
>
> ARTICLE 4:1
> *Articles for the Government of the United States Navy*

On the morning of 1 December, Mackenzie ordered three ropes be slung over the *Somers*' main yardarms, two to starboard and one to port, and at 1.45 pm the crew was ordered topside to witness the first ever hangings aboard a US naval vessel.

The starboard ropes were placed round the necks of Philip Spencer and Elisha Small, while Samuel Cromwell was positioned on the port side. Petty officers, armed with pistols and cutlasses, were placed at strategic points on the deck to maintain order. The nation's flag was raised, three cheers rose from the assembled crew, and hoods were placed over the heads of the accused. At 2.15 pm, to the accompanying sound of cannon and a roll of drums as required by naval protocol, those crewmen selected for the task wrapped their hands around the ropes hoisted over the yardarms and ran across the quarterdeck, pulling the three men high into the air. The crew, boys mostly, were then reminded of the consequences of violating the Articles of War, and as if to reinforce the point the bodies were left to swing from the yardarm until the 3.30 watch, when they were cut down and given over to the crew to be prepared for burial. At 6.30 that evening, with the mutineers' bodies and whatever weights could be found sewn neatly inside their hammocks, and with all the ship's lanterns lit, the three corpses were committed to the cold, dark waters of the Atlantic Ocean.

MUTINY OR MURDER

After sailing on to St Thomas in yet another unsuccessful attempt to rendezvous with *Vandalia*, Mackenzie set sail for *Somers'* home port of New York, arriving there on 14 December. The captain immediately organised for a naval clerk to go to Washington DC with a full report of the incident before ordering the transfer to the USS *North Carolina* all of those suspected of either being supportive of or in sympathy with the mutineers.

On 28 December 1842, a court of inquiry was convened aboard USS *North Carolina*, presided over by Commodore Dallas of the Pensacola Navy Yard, Commodore Jones of New York, and the commander of the Home Squadron, Captain Charles Stewart. Their brief was a simple one: to determine whether the actions of Captain Alexander Mackenzie had been an appropriate response to the threat. To, in effect, ask and answer the simple question: 'Was it mutiny, or was it murder?'

Initially there was general acceptance in the press that Mackenzie had taken the only course of action available to him, an acceptance summed up in an editorial in the *New York Herald* on 8 December, which read in part: 'We can hardly find language to express our admiration of Mackenzie and his officers for their resolute application of naval discipline.' The support however, was short-lived. The unprecedented action of hanging suspected mutineers on a US naval ship at sea without trial had generated public debate, in no small part due to the high political office held by the father of the alleged ringleader. The question 'Was it mutiny, or simply murder?' was soon asked in the press, and on every street corner. Certainly Spencer was guilty of, at the very least, injudicious speech. Everybody knew that even to murmur to another crewmember of one's predilection towards mutiny was to invite imprisonment and eventual court martial. There was no such thing as being 'a little mutinous'. But to be denied a fair trial, the opportunity to argue in one's own defence? It was a worrying precedent.

The prevailing legal opinion of the day was that technically the captain of a US Navy vessel did not possess the authority to unilaterally order a court martial while at sea, which meant therefore that the council of officers which Mackenzie ordered be formed had no status to act as a court. The statement by the officers of the USS *Somers* claimed, however, that they were forced to act as they did because they felt the ship and its officers were in imminent and extreme danger. So, regardless of whether or not their recommendations had legal merit, their unanimous support for the death penalty certainly buttressed the uncompromising action Mackenzie had taken. In mitigation of the mutineers' behaviour, however, according to eyewitness accounts from members of the crew, floggings were a common occurrence during the voyage, as was the preaching of vitriolic sermons extolling the men to work. Morale had been at rock bottom.

'NOT PROVEN'

On 20 January 1843 the court of inquiry exonerated Mackenzie. To safeguard himself and give him immunity from any further prosecution, Mackenzie then requested a full court martial, and after two months of deliberation, on 31 March, the court handed down its findings. The charge of murder came back 'not proven' by a vote of 9–3, the charge of oppression was also 'not proven', this time by a vote of 8–4, and on the issue of illegal punishment the result was 'not proven' by a vote of 12–nil. Further charges of 'conduct unbecoming an officer' and 'cruelty and oppression' towards the crew were dismissed out of hand.

The other prisoners suspected of complicity were eventually released without charge. Despite avoiding any findings of culpability, the incident effectively ended Mackenzie's naval career. In 1846 President James Polk dispatched him to Cuba to serve out the remainder of his military tenure as an artillery commander. Mackenzie died two years later.

Lieutenant Guert Gansevoort went on to command the USS *John Adams* in America's war with Mexico, and was eventually promoted to commodore in what became a distinguished naval career.

In the end, of course, there was no mutiny aboard the USS *Somers*. There was, however, a questionable suspension of the normal rules of law, with those accused denied the opportunity to defend their actions, a right guaranteed every American citizen by the Bill of Rights and the US Constitution. Since the prisoners had already been secured in chains, they surely could have been kept under confinement until the ship made landfall in a US port.

ROMANCES OF A HEEDLESS BOY

Philip Spencer's father, John C. Spencer, Secretary of War, certainly thought so, and was furious at Mackenzie's rush to judgment. Although *Somers* was weeks away from arrival in New York it was only fourteen days' sail from St Thomas where the prisoners could have been handed over to US authorities and tried according to US law. Mackenzie did little to maintain his rapidly eroding reputation when he admitted privately to friends over dinner that he felt Spencer would evade justice if brought to trial because of his father's position and influence, suddenly taking on the appearance of judge, jury and executioner. Secretary of War Spencer wrote in the Washington *Madisonian* that his son's deeds were nothing more than the 'mere romances of a heedless boy,' and initially pushed to have Mackenzie brought to trial for murder in a civil court. But his subsequent court martial made that impossible. Spencer, however, wasn't free from criticism himself, pilloried mercilessly in the press for using his influence to keep his son in the navy and for providing him with immunity from naval discipline that only made more likely the events that led to his eventual execution.

The case attracted the attention of academics and lawyers from across the country. The celebrated author James Fenimore Cooper (*The Last of the*

Mohicans and the popular *Leatherstocking Tales*) called Mackenzie a murderer and a tyrant. In rebuttal, the lawyer Richard Henry Dana Jr. (author of *Two Years Before the Mast*) spoke out in support of Mackenzie's actions in an open letter to newspapers in Boston and New York, likening a mutiny to an accident which, once it has been recognised as approaching, should be subject to any measure deemed necessary to prevent its occurrence. 'Must they [captains] then wait the onset and its chances?' Dana asked. He also argued that the tiny brig simply was not big enough to ensure the prisoners were sufficiently separated from the rest of the crew and that guarding them effectively would have been all but impossible. The ship was in fact so small, Dana argued, that 'you feel as though half a dozen resolute conspirators could have swept the decks and thrown overboard all that opposed them before aid could come from below'.

In the late 1880s Herman Melville, author of *Moby-Dick* and brother-in-law of Mackenzie's second-in-command, Lieutenant Guert Gansevoort, wanted source material for a mutiny for his new book *Billy Budd*, and organised for the case of the USS *Somers* to be re-examined. After poring over the court transcripts Melville concluded that although Mackenzie failed to act according to the strict interpretation of the prevailing statutes and 'according to the customary form of law' by transporting the mutineers to a US port to await trial, he should not have been blamed for the decisions he made. Melville, an experienced sailor himself, believed that Mackenzie should be given the benefit of the doubt, taking into account the pressure of the situation and the limited options he saw being available to him.

In a political reaction to the incident aboard USS *Somers*, the decision was made to end the use of 'training ships' and to begin the construction of the nation's first naval academy, which was established on 10 October 1845 at Annapolis, Maryland. This ensured that young, impressionable cadets would never again be trapped on board a US Navy ship and subjected to the incitements of a mutinous and desperate crewmember.

‘TEXAS HAS YET TO
LEARN SUBMISSION TO
ANY OPPRESSION, COME
FROM WHAT SOURCE IT MAY.’

**Sam Houston, twice President
of the Republic of Texas**

1842

MUTINY ON THE TEXAN SCHOONER *SAN ANTONIO*

In 1824, still basking in its victory over Spain in the War of Independence three years earlier, the Mexican Republic ratified its new constitution. The new nation was to be a representative republic with a bicameral parliament and Roman Catholicism as the state religion. One of the new nation's nineteen states was an arid expanse north of the Rio Grande River, Coahuila y Tejas (the departments of Coahuila and Texas).

The Department of Tejas was a sparsely populated region first settled in 1822 by the Old Three Hundred, a group of highly literate and industrious Anglo-Protestant settlers who fought their own war of independence with Mexico in 1835–36. Their struggle ended with General Sam Houston's victory over the forces of Mexico's General Antonio Lopéz de Santa Anna at the Battle of San Jacinto, and resulted in the establishment of the Republic of Texas on 2 March 1836.

A NAVY FOR TEXAS

One of the key initiatives that paved the way for independence was the formation of the Texas Navy in January 1836. With Mexico obstinately refusing to recognise the legitimacy of the new republic, a military presence was necessary to prevent a Mexican blockade of the Texas coastline and keep open vital supply lines to the United States of America. Four schooners were purchased specifically for the task at hand: *Liberty*, *Brutus*, *Invincible* and *Independence.* They were sleek, highly manoeuvrable and could each carry up to ten cannon, but by mid-1837 all four schooners had either been run aground, lost at sea or repossessed by disgruntled creditors.

In 1838 the Texas Congress authorised the financier Samuel Williams to go to Baltimore and purchase the fledgling republic another fleet. Despite the loans organised by the Congress falling through en route, Williams was able to stitch together sufficient bond money from various benefactors to order a sloop, two brigs, three schooners and a single-wheeled paddle-steamer. The three schooners *San Antonio*, *San Bernard* and *San Jacinto* arrived in Galveston in the summer of 1839, followed in October by the brig *Wharton*, and in December by the fleet's flagship, the twenty-gun, 610-tonne (600-ton) sloop *Austin* and the paddle-steamer *Zavala.* In April 1840 the last of its big ships, the 406-tonne (400-ton) brig *Archer*, arrived, and Texas had a navy again.

The new fleet was placed under the command of twenty-nine-year-old Commodore Edwin Moore, a decorated lieutenant and fourteen-year veteran of the US Navy who despite his length of service felt his chances of promotion through its officer-laden ranks were slim. He decided to move to Texas and was immediately given the rank of commodore in what was now officially called the Second Texas Navy, and chose *Austin* as his flagship. One of the new schooners under his command was the sleek, 173-tonne (170-ton) *San Antonio.* Launched in 1836 and commissioned into the Texas Navy on 7 August 1839, *San Antonio* was a typical two-masted schooner constructed in the Baltimore shipyards of Schott and Whitney and affectionately known as a 'Baltimore Clipper'. Like its sister ships *San Bernard* and *San Jacinto*, it boasted four 12-pound cannon and a 12-pound pivot cannon, and carried a complement of thirteen officers and between sixty-five and seventy sailors and marines.

For most of 1840 and into 1841 most of *San Antonio*'s time was spent in various unremarkable ways, patrolling the waters off the Texas coast and helping suppress and apprehend Mexican smugglers. In September 1840 it joined the fleet off the coast of Mexico's Yucatan Peninsula and in October was ordered to return the Texas diplomat Judge James Treat to Galveston after his failed attempt to seek recognition of Texas from the Mexican government.

On 4 July 1841 *San Antonio* began a three-month survey of the Texas coastline in order to make it easier for commercial ships to safely navigate their way in to Texan ports, and in December 1841, along with *Austin* and *San Bernard*, sailed to Sisal on Mexico's Yucatan Peninsula, returning to Galveston on 31 January. The schooner's activities, though dull, were nevertheless routine and not unexpected. When it sailed to New Orleans in February to collect provisions and recruits and to return survivors from the shipwreck of the American vessel *Sylph* that had run aground off the Alacranes Islands, the unexpected occurred. The possibility of mutiny, seemingly without any real provocation or cause, became a blood-soaked reality.

DISPATCHING THE ACTING COMMANDER

In New Orleans on the night of 11 February 1842, *San Antonio* was lying at anchor in the Mississippi River with most of its senior officers, including its commander, Lieutenant Seeger, ashore. It was wisely anchored offshore to prevent desertions and with its sailors and marines confined below decks. A number of the crew, however, began to indulge in the alcohol that had earlier been smuggled aboard with the help of a local fisherman. A request by Sergeant of Marines Seymour Oswald to the officer in charge of the deck, Lieutenant M. H. Dearborn, to be allowed to go ashore was denied, with Dearborn explaining that no officer present possessed the authority to permit shore leave. Already sporting a history of insubordination, the intoxicated Oswald refused to return below decks and continued to argue.

The ship's acting commander, Lieutenant Charles Fuller, came up from his cabin and ordered Dearborn to arm the marine guards even though their commander was the cause of the disturbance. Oswald got hold of a hatchet and suddenly lunged at Fuller. During the fierce struggle that ensued Fuller was felled by a bullet from a pistol in the hand of a young marine named Benjamin Punipelly. After collapsing on the deck, Fuller was immediately set upon, stabbed with cutlasses and bayonets repeatedly and beaten with muskets while two midshipmen threw themselves over his body in a valiant but unsuccessful attempt to save his life. Whether Fuller was killed by the shot or in that savage attack cannot be said.

With the remaining officers taken below and locked securely in the wardroom, it was only a dearth of experienced sailors that prevented Oswald and his fellows from following the established pattern of the mutineer and sailing *San Antonio* to a new life as a privateer in the pirate-filled waters of the Caribbean. Instead, he and several members of the crew took the comparatively inglorious option of taking to the water in *San Antonio*'s lifeboats and heading for shore. Their bid for freedom would be short-lived, however. The captain of the US Revenue Cutter *Jackson* had heard the shot that felled Lieutenant Fuller and had drawn alongside *San Antonio*. He pursued the boats, captured thirteen of the mutineers, and gave them over to local authorities.

TRIAL AND RETRIBUTION

On coming aboard again, Lieutenant Seeger faced an awkward predicament. *San Antonio* was a small vessel, only 20 metres (66 feet) in length, which made the safe separation and detention of a group of desperate mutineers almost impossible. Seeger chose instead to take two of them back to Texas for trial, and for the remainder to spend the next twelve months incarcerated in a New Orleans gaol awaiting their extradition.

The two mutineers who were returned to *San Antonio* on the night of the mutiny were court-martialled on board on 14 March 1842. One was found not guilty and the other sentenced to a hundred lashes. Both remained as members of the crew, only to die some months later. *San Antonio* was lost at sea in October 1842 after having been dispatched to Campeche on the Yucatan Peninsula to raise funds for the then-financially strapped Texas Fleet. The loss of the schooner also robbed the coming court martial of most of its witnesses to the mutiny.

The prisoners in New Orleans were at last handed over to Commodore Moore on the flagship *Austin* on 15 April 1843, more than a year after the mutiny, and a court martial was convened at 1 pm the following day. Of the thirteen held in New Orleans, only eight were court-martialled on *Austin*. The State of Louisiana refused to extradite three of them. Samuel Oswald had escaped custody and was never heard of again, and Benjamin Punipelly, who fired the shot that felled Lieutenant Fuller, had died in custody. Those who were left were charged with a range of offences including murder, mutiny, attempted murder and desertion.

Presiding over the court were Commander John Lothrop, Methodist minister Cyrus Cummings, second in command Lieutenant Alfred Gilliat Gray, Lieutenant J. Lansing and *Austin*'s chief surgeon, Thomas Anderson.

Ordinary seamen John William, Edward Keenan and William Barrington were each sentenced to a hundred lashes. Barrington, one of those most implicated in the affair, should have considered himself exceptionally fortunate. During the hearing of evidence one of *San Antonio*'s officers admitted that Barrington had given him notice that some of the crew had been talking of mutiny. This admission almost certainly was what spared Barrington from the hangman's noose. Barrington received his hundred lashes on 22 April.

On 25 April, James Hudgins, Isaac Allen, Antonio Landois and William Simpson were found guilty on all charges. At noon the following day the four were hanged from the yardarm. Prayers were offered over each body before they were committed to the ocean. The eighth prisoner was boatswain Frederick Shepherd, who had turned informant and provided the court with the evidence necessary to convict the others. He was acquitted and released, but died soon afterward in a battle on the Yucatan Peninsula.

Another member of the crew, Joseph Shepherd, told the court that the mutiny was not the spontaneous affair it had at first appeared, that in fact a group of men from *San Antonio* and its sister ship *San Bernard* had been talking about taking over both vessels from as early as January 1842. It was thought that *San Antonio* could be sold to the centralist government in Mexico City and *San Bernard* sailed to the Caribbean where it could operate as a privateer. His claims were not pursued, however, as most of the men he implicated had perished with the loss of *San Antonio* in October 1842.

FIRST AND ONLY MUTINY

The *San Antonio* mutiny was the first and only mutiny in the history of the Texas Navy, surprising perhaps considering that the bankruptcy of the republic in its ten years of existence meant its sailors were not always paid, were forced to wear substandard uniforms and to endure particularly bad food. Yet despite being outgunned and poorly funded, *San Antonio* and the Second Texas Navy successfully harassed the larger ships of the Mexican Navy for three years, keeping them focused on defending their own coastline and helping to maintain the sovereignty of the young republic. The mutiny was a very small blemish in an otherwise proud period in Texan history.

On 1 May 1845, with the push for Texan statehood gaining in popularity, the United States Congress passed a resolution that paved the way for the Texas Navy to be incorporated into the US Navy. The Lone Star state's navy officially ceased to exist on 29 December 1845 when US President James Polk signed a joint resolution admitting Texas to the Union as its twenty-eighth state.

Lieutenant Charles Fuller, the only officer of the Texas Navy killed by his own men, was buried in Girod Street Cemetery, New Orleans' first Protestant cemetery. The inscription on his headstone reads:

SACRED TO THE MEMORY OF
CHARLES F FULLER, LIEUTENANT, TEXAS NAVY,
WHO FELL IN THE EXECUTION OF HIS DUTY
IN SUPPRESSING A MUTINY ON BOARD
THE SCHOONER OF WAR *SAN ANTONIO*,
11 FEBRUARY 1842

The Sons and Daughters of the Republic of Texas arranged in 1955 to have his body re-interred, and Charles Fuller now lies at rest in the Texas State Cemetery in Austin, Texas.

‘I SHALL PUT DOWN MY RIFLE WHEN I NO LONGER HAVE TO LIVE LIKE A CORPSE.’

Afanasy Matyushenko, sailor, *Potemkin*

‘I’VE REPEATEDLY TOLD YOU, AND I SHALL NOT REPEAT MYSELF AGAIN, OF WHAT’S IN STORE FOR SAILORS WHO FORGET DISCIPLINE. YOU WILL BE HANGED.’

Ippolit Gilyarovsky, commander, *Potemkin*

1905

THE MUTINY OF THE RUSSIAN BLACK SEA FLEET AND THE BATTLESHIP *POTEMKIN*

By early June in 1905 the crews of the Russian battleship *Potemkin* (full name *Kniaz Potemkin Tavritchesky*) and the rest of the Black Sea Fleet had all heard the horrifying news. As if the war with Japan hadn't been going badly enough, Russia's Baltic Fleet, which had just spent eight months steaming around the world in the hope of ending the Japanese blockade on their garrison at Port Arthur on the Manchurian coast, had been all but annihilated by the Japanese Combined Fleet.

When the first shots were fired in the Russo-Japanese war in February 1904 the Russians had believed that the Japanese were poor fighters, that all Russia needed to do to win was to 'throw our caps at the enemy, and they will run away'. But the war had proved a disaster for Russia, and taken the nation to the brink of bankruptcy. Its troops were ill-equipped, woefully underfunded and betrayed by an archaic and out-of-touch leadership. Now all eight battleships of its Baltic Fleet, as well as three cruisers, five destroyers and numerous auxiliary vessels, lay at the bottom of the Tsushima Straits and almost 5000 Russian sailors were dead. Of the forty-two ships in the Baltic Fleet, only six managed to flee the carnage. The Battle of Tsushima in May 1905 lasted just four hours. It was the Russian Navy's Armageddon.

A PIVOTAL YEAR

The year 1905 was a year of discontent in Russia. On 22 January some 200,000 workers and their families marched on the Tsar's residence, the Winter Palace in St Petersburg, to deliver a list of grievances and much-needed reforms, only to be fired upon by the Imperial Guard. Conservative estimates put the number killed at over a thousand. Widespread political and social unrest, strikes, mutterings of revolution and revolt among the peasantry, and calls for political reform soon spread to every corner of the empire. The government, its coffers almost dry, began cancelling armaments contracts, forcing factories to lay off hundreds of thousands of workers.

Hoping to quell the unrest, Tsar Nicholas II issued the October Manifesto, a document designed to appease those calling for change by promising various civil and religious freedoms as well as the freedom of assembly and a broader participation in the Russian Parliament, the Duma. It was a year of political and social gain for the fledgling Social Democrats, with Vladimir Lenin later to claim that 1905 had been the dress rehearsal for the Bolshevik Revolution of October 1917.

It would also prove to be a pivotal year for the crew of the battleship *Potemkin*, though it wasn't the destruction of a Russian armada or the misery of Russia's 100 million peasants that led to their act of insurrection. Nor was it the demands for religious freedom, the calls for the establishment of a representative parliament, or the increasingly brazen appeals for an end to the generational autocracy of the Tsars. The crew of *Potemkin* had a much more immediate and pressing issue to deal with. Their meat was riddled with maggots.

Unlike other navies, where it was common practice for officers to dine with their enlisted men, Russian officers never ate with their crews. The navy's leadership, unlike that of the army, had remained intensely aristocratic, with nine out of every ten students at St Petersburg's Naval Cadet School drawn from the nobility and bringing to their new commands all of the aristocracy's inbred indifference to the wellbeing of the peasant.

At the turn of the twentieth century the lifestyle of the sailors in the Russian Navy bordered on the barbaric. They enjoyed a miserly six hours of free time a month and were forced to live in quarters not much better than those reserved for cattle. They were forbidden to ride city trams or patronise restaurants or go to the theatre. They were not allowed to walk in public parks, many of which boasted statues honouring the sacrifice of their fallen comrades. In the Black Sea port of Sevastopol, enlisted men were only permitted to walk down one side of certain designated streets. The sailors' treatment amounted to a virtual reintroduction of serfdom, supposedly eliminated more than forty years earlier with the issuing of Alexander II's Emancipation Reform of 1861. For the average sailor in the Russian Navy of 1905, living a hellish existence below decks in the bowels of vessels collectively referred to as 'iron monsters', emancipation was little more than a fancy piece of bourgeois trickery. They were serfs by another name.

The supply of fresh food was also a constant source of criticism and something it would have behooved *Potemkin*'s supply officer Makarov to have kept in mind. In the late afternoon of 12 July 1905, in the company of junior surgeon Dr Golenko, two cooks and a small number of sailors aboard *Potemkin*'s torpedo boat escort *Ismail*, he went ashore in the port city of Odessa, Russia's third-largest city, to buy meat.

On its maiden voyage from Sevastopol, *Potemkin* was anchored offshore from Odessa in the waters of Tendra Bay. Odessa, the home city for Russia's Black Sea Fleet, was known as the city of Catherine the Great, her Imperial dream. It was her vision, embodied in a decree of 1794 that transformed it from a sleepy Tartar fishing village into a city that looked almost more European than Russian, with wide, tree-lined avenues and architecture more reminiscent of Vienna or Prague than Moscow.

Odessa was one of the world's great melting pots, a city built upon trade and commerce, its shops stocked to overflowing with exotic goods from across the world. It was also a city in the grip of fear and uncertainty. Almost a third of Odessa's population was Jewish, and for months rumours had been circulating that Jewish revolutionaries had been smuggling guns into the city and were planning to assassinate as yet unnamed city officials. Workers' strikes had been causing unrest all year and this particular afternoon was no exception, with the military governor, General Semyon Kakhanov, a hero of the 1877–78 Russo-Turkish war, deciding he'd once again dispatch his crack regiment of Cossacks to restore order. Makarov, who had come ashore for no other reason than to buy supplies, had walked into a city in crisis. Gunshots rang out through the stifling humidity of a typical June evening. Workers were being arbitrarily arrested in the streets. The city was an angry, discontented mix of Social Democrats, Mensheviks, Bolsheviks, anarchists, Social Revolutionaries and liberals, with seemingly no one in control. All things considered, it was not a good night to be out.

RIDDLED WITH MAGGOTS

When the lights went out just after 9 pm after an attack on the Sevastopol electrical supply, *Potemkin*'s small group had already spent an hour hemmed in by crowds of protesters, hearing calls for an end to Tsarist rule and workers encouraging armed rebellion. Makarov's usual nerve deserted him. Normally he liked to shop around for the best price. He liked to negotiate, to beat down the seller and walk away with a bargain. But this was not a night for haggling. Makarov decided he'd purchase the very first carcasses he saw. Market price would do.

Makarov located a butcher in the city's Greek quarter prepared to sell them 450 kilograms (1000 pounds) of meat, but one of the sailors commented that the meat appeared to be infested with maggots. By now thoroughly rattled, Makarov uncharacteristically rebuked the sailor, threatening to arrest him if he spoke up again. The meat was paid for and hauled back to *Ismail* through the hot, humid streets.

The next day, 13 June, began much like any other for the officers and crew of *Potemkin*. Reveille was called, as usual, at 5 am. Hammocks were rolled up and sailors made their way to the upper decks to wash themselves and be led in their Orthodox prayers by the ship's priest, Father Parmen. Then followed a breakfast of black bread and tea, after which the scrubbing of the ship began. It was while scrubbing down the decks that a sailor noticed an unusual smell and followed its source to the meat that had been brought on board the previous night. A group of sailors soon gathered and close inspection made it obvious the meat was riddled with maggots. Over cries demanding that the rotten meat be thrown overboard, Captain Yevgeny Golikov sent Chief Surgeon Sergei Smirnov on deck to talk to the disgruntled crew. The situation immediately worsened.

Smirnov cut a section of meat from a carcass, held it to his nose, and declared it to be fresh. When the sailors, aghast, inquired if he couldn't see the maggots in front of his eyes, Smirnov replied that once they were washed off and the more putrid sections of meat cut away the carcasses would be fine. The sailors were enraged. Captain Golikov assigned a watch on the meat and ordered the name of any sailor who approached the meat to be recorded.

This was not the first time that the issue of rotten meat threatened mutiny on a Russian naval vessel. In July 1903 on the heavy cruiser *Berezan* the crew was a hair's breadth away from open revolt over the serving of tainted meat in their borscht. Over the course of a single afternoon the crew refused to perform their duties until the issue of the tainted meat was resolved. Tense negotiations resulted in fresh meat being served and the sailors' concerns addressed. The action on *Berezan* never amounted to the technical definition of a mutiny, but it came close.

The officers of *Potemkin* were far closer than they realised to seeing how a few hundred maggots could do more to incite a crew to violence than the combined exhortations of all of Russia's revolutionaries. A petty officer reminded the crew that the besieged troops in Port Arthur were forced to eat dog meat to survive. 'So this is Port Arthur then?' came the reply.

STIRRING THE CREW TO ACTION

Every ship in the Russian Fleet had its sprinkle of revolutionaries always looking for an opportunity to sow dissent, and *Potemkin* was no exception. Afanasiy Matyushenko was born into a peasant family in the Ukrainian village of Dergachi in 1879. As a former peasant who loathed the aristocracy and would often share with other disgruntled sailors sad stories of hardship and exploitation, Matyushenko saw the maggot-ridden meat as a perfect catalyst to stir the crew to action. One of his collaborators was artillery quartermaster Grigory Vakulenchuk, who'd been illiterate when he enlisted but had studied hard and become well informed and politically astute. Matyushenko was impatient and wanted to take control of *Potemkin* immediately. Vakulenchuk urged caution, convincing him to wait for the crews of others vessels to join with them. A hasty meeting was arranged in the torpedo room to discuss what to do next.

It was agreed they would wait. Vakulenchuk, who along with Matyushenko and A.M. Petrov of the training ship *Prut*, and with the help of the Russian Social Democratic Labor Party (RSDLP), had formed the revolutionary Tsentralka, an association of revolutionary sailors whose leadership had already chosen 21 June for the initiation of a fleet-wide rebellion. Vakulenchuk convinced the impatient Matyushenko that the maggots would only get bigger and suggested instead a boycott of the meat. The planned assault on Odessa, which Tsentralka hoped would ignite a Russian revolution, was only six days away. Now was not the time for unilateral action.

The Russian Naval Command had long been aware there were subversive elements within the Black Sea Fleet. Revolutionary pamphlets and newspapers were found circulating among the crews in 1900, with Social Democratic groups first appearing in the Black Sea cities of Sevastopol and Kerch in 1902. Tsentralka was formed over the winter of 1903–04.

Tsentralka had planned their mutiny well. Knowing the Black Sea Fleet would likely follow the lead of the flagship *Rostislav*, it was decided that the mutiny would begin there. The moment the *Rostislav* mutineers signalled they were in control of the bridge, crews on other ships would act. Timing and discipline would be their keys to success. Any unilateral action, any deviation from this carefully laid plan, would end in disaster. The message to the increasingly angry and agitated crew on *Potemkin* was to curb their anger, to be patient. Revolution was coming soon enough.

A LESSON THEY WILL NEVER FORGET

Back on deck, however, in the heat of another stiflingly hot June day, the problem at hand was only getting greener. Second in command under Golikov, Commander Gilyarovsky, who was well known for his hatred of enlisted men, went on deck at lunch and saw the borscht still steaming in its barrels. On being assured by the cook that the meat was of good quality Gilyarovsky went into a rage, demanding to know why the sailors were not eating their borscht. The sailors, by this time emboldened and resolute, shouted back that if he liked it so much perhaps he should eat it himself. Unable to contain his fury, Gilyarovsky went to the wardroom where the officers were enjoying a maggot-free lunch and demanded that the crew be taught 'a lesson they will never forget'. Captain Golikov, aware of the presence of revolutionaries within the fleet, was careful not to over-react and cautiously ordered a roll call on the quarterdeck.

Golikov, flanked by his officers, appeared before the crew and promised to send a sample of the borscht to his commander in Sevastopol for examination. Then he pointed to the yardarm, reminded the crew of the ultimate price of insubordination, and demanded to know who had incited their act of defiance. In an attempt to weed out the ringleaders, Golikov asked those willing to eat the borscht to step forward. A few did, but most continued their steadfastness. It was only when a contingent of armed marine guards were ordered on deck that the first few rows began to waver and step forward. Some, however, refused to surrender and retreated to the relative safety of the rear gun turret as others broke ranks and took what cover they could find. The inexperienced marine guards, sympathetic to the crew's dilemma, held fast to their weapons. Gilyarovsky screamed an ineffectual order to make a list of those who had broken rank. Golikov stared down from the capstan, witnessing the mutiny of his crew in silent astonishment. The battleship *Potemkin* was about to do far more than merely leave in ruins the carefully laid plans of the revolutionary Tsentralka. It was about to enter the pages of history.

'SO IT'S MUTINY THEN, IS IT?'

With Vakulenchuk, Matyushenko and a hundred others taking refuge behind the gun turret, Gilyarovsky, refusing to be intimidated, said, 'So it's mutiny then, is it?' and ordered a tarpaulin brought on the deck. If there was going to be a firing squad there was no point in staining the deck with the blood of a few dozen mutineers. The timid Golikov was willing to give his zealous second in command all necessary latitude to regain control of the ship.

The significance of the tarpaulin was not lost on the crew. Vakulenchuk and Matyushenko knew the time for revolution had come. They advanced towards Gilyarovsky, encouraging other sailors to join them. There was now no going back.

Vakulenchuk and Matyushenko raced below deck to the armoury, overpowering its guards and seizing a number of rifles and pistols. By this time other revolutionaries were spreading throughout the ship, assuming control of vital infrastructure. The radio room was overrun. The sea cocks, which could be opened to bring the ocean rushing into the lower decks should Golikov give the order to scuttle the ship, were secured.

Back on deck the stalemate continued. The marine guards had still not acted, defying an order from Gilyarovsky to shoot. When Vakulenchuk and Matyushenko re-emerged on the quarterdeck a young stoker named Nikishkin grabbed a rifle from a guard, pointed it into the air, and pulled the trigger. In that moment the conditioned obedience of the peasant sailors, and the chain of command that represented structure, order and all that stood in the way of anarchy and murder, was sacrificed to revolution.

Gilyarovsky, who despite many other things could never be accused of cowardice, at this point instinctively thought that if he could kill Vakulenchuk there might still be some hope of quelling the rebellion. He charged at the revolutionary and fired his rifle in Vakulenchuk's chest. Vakulenchuk fell to the deck and was taken below decks to the infirmary. Many of the officers who weren't killed or injured in the crossfire that followed seemed unable to comprehend what was happening, just standing where they were. Matyushenko shot Gilyarovsky as he stood by the ship's railing, walked over to the hated commander and shot him again before dumping his body into the cold waters of the Black Sea. Captain Golikov, realising he had lost control of his command, retreated to the presumed safety of his cabin, as did several of his officers. Dozens of armed revolutionaries now stood resolutely on *Potemkin*'s quarterdeck and began to spread out across the ship.

Lieutenant Kovalenko, who had long harboured revolutionary sympathies, remained in hiding lest he be gunned down. Junior Lieutenant Vakhtin, attempting to flee by jumping overboard, was gunned down as he left his cabin. Other officers rushed from their cabins and jumped into the Black Sea, only to become easy targets for the revolutionaries as they flailed about in the choppy waters in full uniform. Lieutenant Grogiriev was shot several times and killed. Another lieutenant was killed as he attempted to reach a torpedo boat moored nearby.

Golikov, who preferred to scuttle *Potemkin* rather than allow it to fall into the hands of revolutionaries, then ordered Junior Lieutenant Alexeev into the magazine to fuse its mines. Only minutes away from initiating a catastrophic explosion, Alexeev was apprehended and brought before Matyushenko, pleading for his life to be spared. The least despised of the ship's officers, and seen by some as possessing a kind of kindred spirit, Alexeev was stripped of his insignia and allowed to go.

Smirnov, the hated chief surgeon, had been dragged alive from his cabin with his body covered in stab wounds. There was talk that he had tried to commit suicide, that a shot was reportedly heard to have come from inside his cabin before the locked door was battered down. The sailors who had hold of him were overheard taunting him, telling him to get his teeth into the meat he had tried to force them to eat, before his body was ingloriously thrown overboard.

With the death of Gilyarovsky and the apparent disappearance of Golikov there was one last, futile attempt to restore order and fill the vacuum left by those officers who by this time were either dead or up to their necks in the waters of the Black Sea. Lieutenant Tomm, the torpedo officer, appeared on the quarterdeck, sidearm drawn, and yelled above the gunfire and pandemonium to the men to drop their weapons. This extraordinary display of courage resulted in a brief lull in the shooting and allowed Tomm to issue an invitation to Matyushenko to talk things over in the hope of preventing further bloodshed.

With weapons drawn, the two men disappeared behind the aft gun turret. Matyushenko later confided to a comrade that he had offered to spare Tomm's life if he would remove his epaulettes, to which Tomm replied that Matyushenko hadn't given him the epaulettes and therefore had no right to ask them to be removed. A few moments later two shots were heard,

Tomm emerged, and was cut down by a barrage of gunfire. Matyushenko, following, ordered his body thrown overboard. The authority of the mutineers was now complete and the ship was theirs, but there was still one person unaccounted for. Had anyone seen Captain Yevgeny Golikov?

'WHERE'S THE CAPTAIN?'

Shouts of 'Where's the captain?' rose up across the ship and it wasn't long before Golikov was dragged from his cabin dressed in only a shirt, singlet and underwear. He was a sorry figure but not despised and hated. The crew's anger had always been directed at Gilyarovsky, and with his death had gone much of their lust for vengeance. However, such were the circumstances and passions of the occasion that it would only take a shout from one disgruntled revolutionary to incite the shedding of more blood. The recently reprimanded seaman Sirov, reminding the others that Golikov had earlier pointed to the yardarm and threatened to hang them all, pushed forward with a small group of men and took the captain to the rails. Sirov shot Golikov in the head with a single bullet from his service revolver and threw him overboard. Now the mutineers had a ship to run, and almost immediately there were decisions to be made. The first concerned the captain and crew of the torpedo boat *Ismail*, anchored just a few metres away, who had seen and heard everything.

Lieutenant Pyotr Klodt von Yurgensburg, *Ismail*'s captain, was a forty-one-year-old Swede who should never have been in the services. A perfect example of everything that was wrong with the Russian Navy's approach to officer recruitment, von Yurgensburg spent twenty minutes watching events unfold on *Potemkin* instead of doing what he should have done, starting his vessel's engines and setting out on the eight-hour trip to naval headquarters in Sevastopol. With *Ismail*'s top speed a spanking 25 knots, it would have been impossible for the much slower *Potemkin* to give chase. Now it was too late. To make matters worse, when von Yurgensburg belatedly gave the order to weigh anchor the anchor buoy became entangled with the mooring line. Attempts to cut the boat free failed but von Yurgensburg, now in a complete panic and ignoring cries of surrender from his crew, believed he could still fashion an escape and ordered his engines full ahead.

On board *Potemkin*, Matyushenko ordered his gunners to open fire on *Ismail* with its 47 millimetre (2 inch) guns. At such close range it wasn't long before a shell tore through the torpedo boat's funnel. Realising he was just a few well-aimed shots away from oblivion, von Yurgensburg surrendered, *Ismail*'s crew was brought aboard and the torpedo boat was manned with some of *Potemkin*'s crew. The mutineers had gone from what officers regarded as nothing more than 'beasts of burden' to being the proud owners of two Russian naval vessels. And it all took just thirty minutes.

Not all the crew of *Potemkin* considered themselves mutineers, and it was up to Matyushenko and the other ringleaders to convince the holdouts to join them. Matyushenko gave what many recalled as a stirring speech, reminding the crew of the tyranny of the state, that other ships would soon join them, that they would not be acting alone. Nikishkin spoke of the need for the ship to be governed by elected officials, that the sailors, as long as they remained on the ship, would never again have to suffer the humiliation of imposed rule. Members of the crew would be elected to a sailors' committee that would be similar in structure to the local committees found in peasant villages, which many of them would already have been familiar with.

Though the mutiny had been a success, *Potemkin*'s crew, ironically considered the most loyal of all the crews in the Black Sea Fleet, was composed largely of raw recruits with no experience of command. Matyushenko was concerned that they might find it difficult to accept someone from the ranks as captain, and at a meeting in the admiral's stateroom put forward the unexpected proposition that a captain be selected from the group of officers now under guard. After some initial opposition an open ballot was held and Ensign Alekseyev was elected. Prior to the outbreak of war with Japan, Alekseyev had been in Russia's merchant fleet, and was not regarded with the level of disdain the crew reserved for *Potemkin*'s career officers. Ten petty officers were also selected. And so, with a crew of over seventy, it was decided that the following day they would sail the most powerful weapon to fall into the hands of anti-government forces in modern Russia right into Odessa Harbour.

As the crew ran down the flag of the Tsar and raised the red flag of revolution, Grigory Vakulenchuk died from his wounds. His body was taken to the ship's chapel and, following Russian Orthodox tradition, encircled by candles. Once they arrived in Odessa he would be given a hero's burial. On the night of 14 June, *Potemkin* and *Ismail* entered Odessa and Vakulenchuk's body was laid at the base of the city's famous Richelieu steps. The following day thousands of citizens made their way to the dock to see the ship that symbolised the nation's struggle for freedom and equality and to talk with its crew. Radicals from the RSDLP boarded *Potemkin* and together with the Sailors' Committee agreed that the two vessels would remain where they were and await Tsentralka's coming fleet-wide mutiny.

On 15 June, when riots erupted in the streets of Odessa, *Potemkin* resisted pleas to open fire on the city. Over a thousand people lost their lives that night and the port facilities were badly damaged. The next day, on the way back from Vakulenchuk's funeral, three *Potemkin* sailors were killed by loyalist soldiers and in retaliation *Potemkin* fired three shells into the city. On the same day Tsar Nicholas II received news of the mutiny—and noted in his diary: 'I simply do not believe it.'

RETAKE OR SINK IT

By now the fact that the pride of Russia's Black Sea Fleet was in the hands of mutineers had captured the nation's imagination. Although it succeeded in taking attention away from the numerous strikes and revolts that were occurring elsewhere in the country, it was obvious that such a potent symbol of Russian military might must not be allowed to remain in the possession of armed men calling for an end to Tsarist rule. Nicholas immediately ordered a taskforce under the command of Junior Flagman Vishnevetskii to retake *Potemkin*. And if he couldn't retake it, sink it.

The taskforce sailed from Sevastopol and *Potemkin* confronted it head-on. This was to be Matyushenko's great gamble, to win over the support of the fleet's crews with one astonishing, never-to-be-forgotten act of courage. *Potemkin* approached the taskforce head-on, not with guns blazing but in an extraordinary act of silent defiance. It cruised between the ships of Vishnevetskii's fleet, splitting it in two. Cheers were heard from the fleet as the sailors eyeballed the mutineers on *Potemkin*'s decks and vice versa. *Potemkin*, with hundreds of guns aimed at its sides and superstructure from a distance that would have made it impossible to miss, could have been blown out of the water. But nobody fired a shot. Inexplicably, everyone lost their collective nerve. Not even Vice-Admiral Krieger on the bridge of *Rostislav*, with one of *Potemkin*'s guns pointing directly at him, issued the order to fire. The fleet commanders maintained order. Matyushenko's bold gamble had failed.

'ROMANIA! ROMANIA!'

Only some of the crew of the battleship *St George* mutinied—a rather half-hearted and ill-conceived action, as it quickly became clear the majority wanted nothing to do with such an act of defiance. Thus, instead of joining *Potemkin* the ship was run aground on the shoals just out from Platonovsky Wharf. Sailors were thrown off their feet as the giant ship lurched to a halt, and the crew subsequently surrendered to the authorities.

The beaching of *St George* spelled the end of any thoughts Matyushenko had of shelling the city, forcing the surrender of the city's military governor, General Kakhanov, and igniting revolution. The sudden loss of conviction on the part of the *St George* mutineers was seen as nothing less than treason by those on board *Potemkin* and had a devastating effect upon morale. Many now wanted to sink the ship. Others wanted to sail to naval headquarters in Sevastopol and surrender. Several courses of action were shouted back and forth across *Potemkin*'s decks, but eventually one demand overwhelmed the others to grow into a deafening chant, 'Romania! Romania!'

Romania had a proud tradition of independence from the Tsars and its monarch, King Carol I, had a reputation for protecting civil liberties. Matyushenko saw sailing there as akin to retreat, but to shell Odessa would undoubtedly result in heavy loss of life, and how could he justify this to an unsophisticated crew whose only motivation was that they had been acting in the best interests of Russia's impoverished underclass? It was agreed they would sail to the Romanian port of Constanza, take on fresh supplies, and reassess the situation. Matyushenko tried to buoy the spirits of the crew, claiming this would give them the time they needed to plot their next move. Perhaps Tsentralka had captured the naval base at Sevastopol. Perhaps revolution had spilled over in the streets of Odessa and was spreading to other Russian cities even as they spoke.

Potemkin and *Ismail* arrived in Constanza on 19 June and were met by the port commander, Captain Nikolai Negru. Although he treated the revolutionary leaders cordially, Negru denied their request for provisions, which included over 406 tonnes (400 tons) of coal and 200 kilograms (440 pounds) of machine oil, as well as food and water for its crew of over 700, until permission to do so came from the government in Bucharest. When word finally came that the Romanian Government would only release provisions to the mutineers if they surrendered the ship, Matyushenko was incensed, especially after having shown the Romanians every courtesy and offering to pay for their supplies in rubles. The ships put to sea once more.

After being denied supplies at the Crimean port city of Theodosia and refusing to resort to piracy by boarding Turkish coal ships bound for Constantinople, the mutineers returned to Constanza on 25 June and surrendered to Romanian authorities. The Romanian Government returned *Potemkin* to the Russian Navy and in October 1905 it was renamed *Panteleimon.*

Despite the mutiny achieving worldwide notoriety, the truth is that *Potemkin* was never central to the plans of the Social Democrats, and not at any stage was there any coordination between the ship and the revolutionary groups in Odessa. Its mutiny was born of spontaneity, sparked by rotten meat on a ship crewed by enlisted peasants who had few if any political aspirations. Demonstrating their ambivalence, in the wake of the mutiny few showed any devotion to the politics of revolution by joining the ranks of the RSDLP or its affiliated groups. Over 600 members of the crew chose to stay in Romania. Others, including one of the mutiny's ringleaders, Joseph Dymtchenko, fled to Argentina, about as far away from Russia as one could get.

Matyushenko remained in Romania but was lured back to Russia in 1907 with a promise of amnesty. On his return he was immediately arrested and hanged. Ivan Beshoff, sailor and former chemistry student, escaped to London and eventually in 1913 to Ireland. He settled in Dublin where he established a fish and chip shop. Thought to be *Potemkin*'s last survivor, he died in October 1987 at the age of 102.

‘GENTLEMEN, THIS IS AN HONEST REVOLT!’

Ruy Barbosa, Brazilian senator

‘IT IS NOT EASY TO ASCERTAIN THE TRUTH ABOUT MUTINIES.’

Lieutenant-Commander C. Drage, ‘Some Modern Naval Mutinies,’ 1928

1910

BRAZIL'S *REVOLTA DA CHIBATA*: 'THE REVOLT OF THE WHIP'

The boatswain takes the instrument out of its green baize bag as the prisoner is led across the quarterdeck to the gangway exit. His wrists are lashed to the railing's brass eyebolts and his ankles to a grate on the deck below. The prisoner's shirt is removed and the ship's surgeon steps forward to make certain the punishment won't be 'excessive'. The ship's complement of officers and enlisted men, caps in hand, stand assembled as solemn and silent witnesses to the application of naval discipline as the captain cautions his boatswain to do his duty lest he suffer the same fate. Thin strips of cord begin to come down upon the man, peeling the skin from his back.

Until the mid-nineteenth century the use of the whip had been the most common method of maintaining discipline at sea, and despite the sure testimony of sailors who would have gladly queued up to justify its measured use to maintain discipline and hence their own individual safety, the public's acceptance of its overuse at the hands of sadistic captains was fast running out. France ended the practice during its Revolutionary Wars (1792–1802). Herman Melville's novel *White-Jacket* contained a chapter on flogging so damning that in January 1905 his publishers made sure a copy of the book was sent to every member of Congress. Despite Melville's vivid description shocking the American public, it would be another twelve years until a Congressional vote finally saw flogging abolitished. Britain suspended rather than abolished flogging in 1881, and Royal Navy ships continued to carry cat-o'-nine-tails on board as a visible deterrent until 1906, when their use was ended once and for all by Royal decree.

By the end of the nineteenth century there was widespread acceptance by the legislative bodies in the Western world that stripping a man's flesh from his bones as a deterrent to others was a barbaric act that had no place on a modern ship of war. But old prejudices die hard.

DISREGARD AND CONTEMPT

The Brazilian Republic, like most other Western governments, was not devoid of altruistic intentions. It unconditionally outlawed slavery with the adoption of the *Lei Áurea* (Golden Law) on 13 May 1888, and followed that with the abolition of corporal punishment in the navy in 1889. Unfortunately, the end of the use of force as a disciplinary tool was virtually ignored by the entrenched officer corps, who refused to believe it was possible to keep order in the ranks without the threat of violence. This belief in the use of force proved so prevalent that the following year a Correctional Company was formed to administer naval discipline, and the whip was reintroduced.

The officer corps of the Brazilian Navy had its roots deep in the nation's aristocratic past. For over a hundred years a regulation required a candidate for officers' school come from either Portuguese or Brazilian nobility, and the elitist attitude towards serving in the navy wasn't limited to the upper classes. Even among the poor and the working class it was unheard of for a Brazilian national to volunteer to serve as an enlisted man. The enlisted ranks were made up almost entirely of former slaves and 'mulattos', people with either one dark-skinned parent or descendants of mixed bloodlines. The ethnic make-up of the Brazilian Navy in the early years of the twentieth century indicates that more than half its ranks were made up of Afro-Brazilians and one in three were mulattos. Just one in ten represented indigenous or Brazilian nationals, though the majority of these were either criminals or orphans dragooned into the navy the moment they were of age. Even before the establishment of the republic in 1889, Brazil's armed forces were considered as little more than a mere depository for the poor, the criminal and the oppressed; so-called 'recruitment' was seen as a form of punishment, military service usurped as a means of rehabilitation.

In the first half of the eighteenth century Portuguese Brazil imported more than 800,000 slaves from the west coast of Africa and from Mozambique—more than were sent to the United States during the same period, and their descendants proved ideal fodder for the crewing of the nation's warships, on which they were required to serve for a minimum of fifteen gruelling years. In the same way the aristocratic Russian officer corps' treatment of its enlisted men as little more than slaves in sailors' uniforms resulted in the mutiny on board the battleship *Potemkin* in 1905, so too was the pervasive disregard and contempt shown by generations of Brazilians towards Afro-Brazilians and mulattos, both within the military and in the wider community, to have consequences of its own.

Unfortunately, an objective appraisal of the uprising is almost impossible due to the almost complete lack of primary source material from the mutineers. Everything we know of the events of 20–24 November 1910, comes from accounts written by the military and political establishment—accounts which offer no insights into precisely what motivated those in charge of the rebellion to take the actions they did. The Revolt of the Whip has an embarrassing lack of anecdotes, of incidental observations, of the sort of cataloguing of the small, personal dramas that so illuminate and give depth to the accounts of other contemporary insurrections like the *Potemkin* mutiny in Odessa or the rebellion of the Austro-Hungarian fleet at Cattaro Bay in 1918. The face of the uprising, a young helmsman named João Cândido Felisberto, never wrote his own account of what happened and was only interviewed on the subject many years later, his memory of events by then dimmed by time and his own advancing years.

PUBLIC FACE OF THE MUTINY

Cândido was born in 1880 in Brazil's southernmost state of Rio Grande do Sul, a region with as much in common with Uruguay and the pampas of Argentina as it has with Brazil. His parents were former slaves, and João's prospects were bleak. Guaranteed his freedom upon reaching maturity in accordance with the 1871 *Law of the Free Womb*, he left home at the age of thirteen in 1894 to study in a naval apprentice school, where he learned to read. Three years later he was sent to the English port of Newcastle upon Tyne for two years to await the completion of Brazil's newest and most powerful dreadnoughts, *Minas Geraes* and *São Paulo*. During this time he witnessed firsthand the living conditions and personal liberties enjoyed by the average English sailor and the tireless efforts of Britain's trade unions in their quest for better pay and conditions for its workers.

It is ironic that the two dreadnoughts, which for a brief moment propelled Brazil into the ranks of the world's most modern and best-equipped navies, were used almost before their paint had dried as tools to demonstrate to the world the inequalities of Brazilian society. Newspaper caricatures depicted the prized vessels growling at the republic, like angry dogs that had turned against their masters.

A determination had been brewing among Brazil's sailors for more than two years to stage an armed response to the continued use of the whip, with the preferred date for action being the anniversary of the monarchy's overthrow on 15 November 1889. Seaman first class Cândido, who would become the public face of the mutiny, was tired of living a life of virtual slavery, and living in fear of the dreaded whip. He knew, however, that to maximise any chance of mounting an organised response a lightning rod was needed to ignite the simmering rage of the fleet's sailors, rather than settling on a specific date. The rebels needed to be patient and act in the wake of the next flogging. He knew they would not have long to wait.

On 16 November 1910, an Afro-Brazilian sailor named Marcelino Rodrigues Menezes was led shackled onto the quarterdeck of *Minas Geraes* and viciously lashed 250 times. His crewmates, among them João Cândido, were forced to watch. The flogging was in contravention of the Articles of War, which allowed for a maximum of twenty-five lashes per person per day. Cândido immediately began to organise a response, and by the evening of 22 November he had been joined by the crews of *Minas*

Geraes and *São Paulo*, the light cruiser *Bahia*, and the coastal defence vessel *Deodora*. The crew of the cruiser *Republica* left their posts and transferred to the undermanned *São Paulo*. Almost 2500 sailors from a total of just over 5000 stationed in Rio de Janeiro had promised to join the revolt.

That evening the French cruiser *Duguay-Trouin*, at anchor with other foreign ships well out of earshot of the rebellious Brazilian Fleet, had put on a sumptuous dinner for João Batista das Neves, the captain of *Minas Geraes*, whose evening took a turn for the worse when he attempted to board his ship around 10.30 pm. Confronted by a group of armed mutineers, das Neves refused to back down and together with a small number of fellow officers forced his way on board, only to be overwhelmed, bayoneted and killed.

Unlike the mutiny on the *Potemkin*, this was not a politically inspired rebellion. There were no overtones of class warfare or demands for an overhaul of the country's governmental and political structures, and all the commandeered ships continued to fly their national flags alongside the red flag of rebellion. Nevertheless fifteen to twenty sailors were killed that first evening. As for the fleet's officer corps, apart from das Neves and one of his fellow officers the only other recorded death was that of a junior lieutenant, Mario Alves de Souza, on the scout cruiser *Bahia*. Most of the remaining officers were forced at gunpoint to leave their ships, while several British engineers who had remained with *Minas Geraes* and *São Paulo* since they sailed from England were kept below decks as hostages.

THE MUTINEERS' DEMANDS

Later that evening Cândido gave orders for the four rebel ships to sail across Guanabara Bay and fire their guns to signal to other ships in the fleet that the mutiny had been initiated. He also ordered a communiqué sent to the Brazilian President to make him aware of their demands, which included an end to corporal punishment, the honouring of legislation to increase wages, better food, a decrease in the number of hours worked and the retirement of officers considered incompetent.

President Hermes Rodrigues da Fonseca, eighth president of the Brazilian Republic, had just returned to the Palácio do Catete from a night at the opera when a telegram was received signed on behalf of the crews of the rebel ships, which in addition to the above demands included the chilling ultimatum: 'We do not want the return of the *chibata* (lash). This we ask the President of the republic and the Minister of the Navy. We want an immediate response. If we do not receive such a response, we will destroy the city and the ships that are not revolting.'

Fonseca not only pointedly refused to reply to the mutineers' demands, he immediately ordered that all future communiqués not be released to the public. When it became apparent that no response from the government would be forthcoming, Cândido ordered the ships to fire upon the city, though he was careful to stress the gunners should avoid any populated areas. Only a few shots were actually fired, and were directed into unpopulated areas. A government representative, José Carlos de Carvalho, was permitted on board the rebel ships to negotiate their surrender and assess the claims of the mutineers. After Carvalho was satisfied that the ships were in responsible hands, Cândido insisted he be shown the lacerated back of Marcelino Rodrigues Menezes. Carvalho was profoundly shocked, and immediately organised Menezes' transfer to a naval hospital in the city. Later, in a personal meeting with President Fonseca, he described the seaman's back as resembling 'a mullet sliced open for salting'.

Carvalho had acquitted himself well in treating the mutineers and their claims with respect and ordering the repatriation of Menezes. Although he was aware the Senate was in the process of debating a possible amnesty he made no mention of this to the mutineers, allowing the Senate time to refine and ratify the proposal. Naval authorities, meanwhile, were furious with Carvalho for even deigning to meet with the rebel leadership and began to make plans to take back the ships by force. Fonseca, with the navy insisting on the use of force and the Senate moving towards a negotiated settlement, refused to rule out either approach, and he also refused to speak to the rebels while they still had the guns of the fleet pointing at the citizens of Rio de Janeiro.

AN OFFER OF AMNESTY

On the evening of the 23 November, after the mutineers received a telegram warning that a small force of destroyers loyal to the government was preparing to attack the rebel ships, the decision was made to sail out of Guanabara Bay and take refuge in the open sea before sailing in formation into the bay the following morning. By mid-afternoon on 24 November, word had leaked back to the mutineers that the Senate was preparing an offer of amnesty and that widespread sympathy for their plight was beginning to mount. The mutineers certainly had some powerful allies. Senator Ruy Barbosa, known as the 'Eagle of The Hague' for his tireless contribution to the 1907 Hague Peace Conference, was particularly vocal in his push for a diplomatic solution, speaking in support of the mutineers. He also spoke eloquently on the Senate floor of the evils of slavery and how its continuing presence in the armed forces and in society, although no longer sanctioned by the state, was a continuing drain on Brazil's moral and economic development. He also took the opportunity to poke fun at the navy's commanders, who in one breath claimed their dreadnoughts were unsinkable and in the next were formulating plans to end the mutiny by sending destroyers into Guanabara Bay to, presumably, sink them.

With the amnesty legislation progressing quickly, the navy knew it was running out of time to mount an attack, which they believed was the only way to restore its credibility and rapidly eroding pride. Warships still loyal to the government included the cruisers *Rio Grande do Sul* and *Barroso*, and several destroyers and torpedo boats. Officers would assume all the combat roles and together they would challenge the rebel ships and force their surrender. Unfortunately for the navy, the loyal ships needed to replenish their stores of shells, and to reach the munitions depot on Boqueirão Island would have to first sail past the rebel fleet, right in the line of fire of twenty-four 12 inch guns. In any case, by the 24 November Barbosa would be putting a final Bill abolishing the use of corporal punishment to Congress within the next forty-eight hours. It seemed to the mutineers that they had, in fact, won an historic and relatively bloodless victory.

A PYRRHIC VICTORY

The next day, 25 November, the mutineers agreed to hand over the rebel ships and surrender if new commanding officers were appointed, and that the new commander of *Minas Geraes* be Captain João Pereira Leite, the celebrated former Brazilian journalist and Court of Appeals judge.

On the evening of 26 November the rebels lowered their red flags and the commandeered ships were handed back to representatives of the Brazilian Navy. In just four days the mutineers had succeeded in igniting the nation's conscience, their actions proving a catalyst for eventual change in the treatment of the navy's mulatto and Afro-Brazilian sailors. Undeniably they had won a great victory, and that evening they received permission to go ashore. Their initial euphoria at the passage of the amnesty legislation and senatorial speeches promising change was, however, for those sailors involved, a pyrrhic victory. Just two days after their surrender a presidential decree authorised the Minister of the Navy to dismiss without a court of inquiry anybody he felt was a threat to discipline. Was it possible that their 'victory' was nothing more than the response of a government that recognised it had little choice but to accede to the requests of desperate men who had dozens of 12 inch guns trained on the capital?

A few weeks later, on 10 December, a small, unrelated revolt by a few sailors broke out at a munitions depot on Ilha das Cobras (Cobras Island) and aboard the warship *Rio Grande do Sul.* The depot was besieged by government troops, and one of those arrested was João Cândido. Cândido, whose bravery and heroism in the November revolt earned him the nickname the 'Black Admiral' in an editorial in the *Diário de Noticias*, was arrested, tortured and thrown with eighteen others into a cell barely large enough for one person. Sixteen of the eighteen died of suffocation before the weekend was out. Cândido was one of the two who survived.

THE MOST COVERED-UP MUTINY IN HISTORY

The Navy High Command, concerned at the prospect of presiding over a force in which half of the enlisted men were former mutineers, took the opportunity afforded them by the second revolt to dismiss hundreds of sailors under new laws enacted in the aftermath of the November revolt. Many who had been enjoying the amnesty in Rio were suddenly arrested, imprisoned and tortured, including more than 200 sailors who were herded into the lower decks of the steamer *Satelite* and taken without trial up the Amazon River into oblivion. Those who were not executed on the voyage were made to work as slaves on rubber plantations and never heard from again. The amnesty proved to be a short-lived victory.

Within weeks prisons were filled with the rebels, and in the coming months over 1200 were dispersed to their homes across the length and breadth of Brazil, in a desperate attempt to prevent the possibility of unified action. The military elite and their sympathetic legislators had managed to exact their revenge. Brazil's warships were re-crewed. Although the actions of João Cândido and others did ultimately lead to better pay and conditions for the navy's mulatto and Afro-Brazilian conscripts, as far as the military were concerned those whose actions proved a catalyst for change would have nothing to do with the birth of the 'new' Brazilian navy.

In years to come, several revisionist accounts of the incident were written by military historians who questioned the mutineers' threat to shell the capital, claiming that most of the warships' primary guns, particularly on the two dreadnoughts, were either disabled or for whatever reason could not be fired, thus calling into question the mutineers' ability to control a ship of war in the absence of officers. In response to this, a statement issued by the British engineers held hostage during the revolt claimed that the guns of *Minas Geraes* were in perfect working order, that the ships were professionally sailed and maintained, and that it was only due to a sense of honour and desire to avoid bloodshed on the part of the rebels that the guns of Brazil's mightiest ships of war were kept as silent as they were. They knew it was never meant to be a Russian-style revolution, that all the mutineers wanted was respect and the basic rights of citizenship.

In another attempt to discredit and silence the telling of the story from the mutineers' point of view, João Cândido was assessed by a group of navy doctors in April 1911, declared to be mentally ill and committed to a state mental institution. A declaration of mental incompetence was all that was needed to prevent him from testifying in the upcoming naval tribunal.

These attempts to discredit the mutineers were typical of how the government and the military succeeded in smothering the incident through the imprisonment, torture, dispersal and elimination of those involved. The media suffered decades of bullying and intimidation whenever it tried to present an objective account of the revolt. In 1934 the journalist and satirist Aparicio Torelly managed to have published only two articles of a proposed ten-article indictment of the role of the government and military before he was kidnapped and beaten by a group of naval officers. Other writers were forced to use pseudonyms. The result is that even today there is a paucity of material within Brazil and even fewer accounts in English.

The Revolt of the Whip remains to this day the most covered-up mutiny in history.

‘WE ARE ALL EQUAL,
WE ARE ALL CITIZENS.’

Anton Grabar, mutineer, *Sankt Georg*

‘BLOOD MUST FLOW IN EVERY REVOLUTION, AND IT IS ALL THE SAME TO ME IF I AM HANGED TODAY OR TOMORROW.’

Franz Rasch, boatswain, *Sankt Georg*

1918

THE CATTARO MUTINY

By the winter of 1918 the dual monarchy of Austria-Hungary was fast becoming little more than a remnant of a once-proud empire that at its peak spread across 650 thousand square kilometres (almost a quarter of a million square miles) of Central Europe. In the closing decades of the nineteenth century, from present-day Slovakia and the Czech Republic to the Balkan states, including Bosnia, Serbia and Croatia as well as parts of Poland, Romania and even northern Italy, the 50 million people under the rule of the Austrian Habsburgs and the Hungarian Magyars were citizens of a European power the equal of Germany, France and Russia.

In the years prior to the outbreak of World War I, however, the empire's influence was on the wane. In 1913 territory was lost to Serbia in the Second Balkan War and nationalist fervour in Italy saw the return of lands conquered by the Habsburgs to Piedmont. The Austro-Hungarian armed forces, drawn from a vast ethnic and tribal diversity, lacked the cohesion common to the other great European powers. And whereas the Triple

Entente of France, Great Britain and Russia had increased military spending threefold over the previous thirty years, the Austro-Hungarian Empire had not even managed to double its own spending over the same period.

In alliance with Germany against the Triple Entente, World War I (1914–18) proved a disaster for Austria-Hungary. In 1914 the empire lost over 200,000 men in a bungled attempt to retake lost Serbian territory. Then in 1916 over a million of its soldiers were killed in Russia's lightning Brusilov Offensive, which swept through Ukraine all the way to the base of the Carpathian Mountains. The offensive broke the spirit of the Austro-Hungarian army and fuelled a spirit of discontent throughout the empire's armed forces.

A DETERRENT ONLY

At the outbreak of the Great War in 1914 the Austro-Hungarian navy was based in the Adriatic port towns of Pola (present-day Pula in Croatia) and Cattaro (present-day Kotor in Montenegro). In the years leading up to the war the navy was busily transforming itself from what was essentially a modest coastal defence force into a respectable deterrent, consisting of three Radetzky-class pre-dreadnoughts, nine battleships, almost twenty destroyers and a small submarine fleet. Despite some early action against coastal targets in northern Italy, the navy's fleet commander and later its grand admiral, Anton Haus, saw his ships primarily as a 'fleet in being', with its true strength lying in its deterrent effect. The presence of a large number of armed warships along Austria's Adriatic coast certainly made the consideration of any coastal assault by land forces of the Triple Entente problematical. Haus was criticised for this 'policy of idleness' by his German ally, but his cautious approach was supported by the Habsburg rulers of the empire, who saw no point in risking their smallish fleet in engagements with numerically larger forces.

Haus died of pneumonia in February 1917. His policy was continued by his successor, Maximilian Njegovan, and resulted in the empire's battleships and dreadnoughts, with a few exceptions, spending the last twelve months of the war tied to their moorings in their Adriatic ports, amply protected from predatory fleets by the presence of submarines easily able to patrol the restricted waters of the northern Adriatic.

This is not to say that the Austro-Hungarian Navy was without its losses. In October 1917 a small group of Slovakian sailors mutinied and after barricading their officers in their cabins turned their commandeered torpedo boats over to the Italian Navy; two months later Italian torpedo boats known as MAS boats sank the ageing Monarch-class battleship *Wien* in Pola Harbour. Even so, by the winter of 1918 it had been a mostly tedious and morale-sapping four years for the sailors of the Austro-Hungarian Fleet. But idleness wasn't the only constant in their lives.

HURRA-RAFE

In addition to a persistent lack of direction and purpose there were persistent shortages of almost everything, including clothing and, most particularly, food. By January 1918, the reductions in bread and meat rations had become intolerable, resulting in the mass singing at meal times of a song known as the *Hurra-Rafe* ('hurrah-shouts'), once a song of greeting, turned into a song of protest. The *Hurra-Rafe* would sometimes spread from ship to ship, resulting in thousands of sailors joining in a spontaneous fleet-wide, though overtly peaceful, protest. In late January a series of strikes threatened to bring industrial production in the empire to a standstill. Strikes crippled the Daimler aircraft factory in Wiener Neustadt, the Skoda factory in Pilsen, the shipyards in Trieste, and on 22 January Prague and most of the region of Bohemia ground to a halt under a general strike. Slovakian calls for a Slavic state began to be heard. Even submarine technicians went on strike. Fleet sailors were becoming involved in street riots and being beaten by their own militia. The structures and threads that held the empire together were beginning to unravel.

DISCIPLINE PROBLEMS AND INSURRECTION

Meanwhile, in the Gulf of Cattaro the unsympathetic officer corps provided their crews with little in terms of recreation apart from occasional shore leave into Cattaro, which was not one of the more exciting of the Adriatic ports. Disciplinary issues were spreading throughout the fleet, particularly on the big ships, where large complements of ethnically mixed conscripts made it difficult to build a sense of camaraderie. Discipline was a particular problem aboard the armoured cruiser *Sankt Georg*, the flagship of the fleet's Fifth Division, whose only taste of anything resembling a battle was a brief sortie in May 1917 that failed to result in so much as a shot being fired when approaching Allied ships failed to engage the vessel and turned for home. It had been a long, tedious and frustrating war for the nation's sailors, and something had to give. On the morning of 1 February 1918, the crew of *Sankt Georg* decided their days of idleness were over.

The Cattaro Mutiny began aboard two of the largest ships that had mostly been at rest while the rest of Europe was at war, SMS *Sankt Georg* and another armoured cruiser, SMS *Kaiser Karl VI*, though it was *Sankt Georg* that was the centre of the unrest. As the officers of *Sankt Georg* sat down to lunch, they were taken by surprise when a group of armed sailors emerged from below decks. They shot and wounded an executive officer and a petty officer, broke into the armoury and released the prisoners in the brig to join their act of insurrection. Cries of support began to erupt from other vessels of the Fifth Division as the angry mob spread across the *Sankt Georg*, ransacking the officers' quarters, sounding the air-raid sirens, igniting signal flares and firing celebratory rifle shots indiscriminately into the air.

A red Austrian signal code flag, no doubt chosen as an overt show of solidarity with the Bolshevik uprising in Russia just a few months earlier, was run exuberantly up the foremast. A small orchestra on board began to play the 'Marseillaise', the revolutionary anthem of the French. The topography of the fjord-like bay that surrounded Cattaro amplified the mutinous cacophony that, despite the wounding of a few officers, seemed to observers to have the air of a celebration rather than being the result of simmering, class-ridden tensions or the years of inhumane treatment that had characterised the mutiny on the Russian battleship *Potemkin* in 1905. The Cattaro Mutiny seemed an almost joyous event, with no real malice and lacking in political rhetoric. One officer was even reported to have remarked: 'Well, it's better they behave like this than go and do something worse.'

The mutiny was to last three days, and despite the seizing of arms, the mood of the mutineers was perhaps best illustrated by the fact that the Austro-Hungarian flag continued to be flown alongside the red flag of protest and was saluted twice a day. The mutineers were keen to show that their actions should not be interpreted as challenging the authority of the state, even making it clear to the arrested officers that should an enemy attack be launched they would not hesitate to relinquish control of the ship to its officers.

TRYING TO BROKER A SETTLEMENT

After permitting the wounded to be transferred to the hospital ship *Africa* the spontaneous nature of the mutiny was then evidenced in a sudden scramble to select someone from the mutineers' midst to negotiate their grievances with their superiors. The *Sankt Georg*'s acting boatswain, Franz Rasch, a former member of the revolutionary Social Democrats, led a contingent to the naval barracks in nearby Kumbor, where Sub-Lieutenant Anton Sesan of the Naval Air Service agreed to return with them to the ship and address the crew. Sesan, twenty-five years old and a recent recruit from the merchant marine, spoke to the crew in Italian, Croatian and German, talking them out of taking the ship to Malta and handing it over to the Italian Navy, then suggesting the ship's officers be locked in their cabins so he could have time to perhaps broker a settlement between the men and the government. He had taken the mutineers' side.

The submarine depot ship *Gäa*, a handsome former German steamer crewed by reservists with ties to the Social Democrats and the trade union movement, became the administrative centre of the mutinous fleet. *Gäa* and *Kaiser Karl VI* had both sent men to *Sankt Georg* to assess the situation, and meetings aboard the depot ship had resulted in the establishment of a sailors' committee that would be responsible for presenting a list of grievances to their superiors. The mutinous fervour released on board *Sankt Georg* had spread to other ships, including the cruiser *Kaiser Franz Joseph I*, the battleship *Monarch*, and *Kronprinz Erzherzog Rudolph*, a coastal defence vessel that had spent the entire war bobbing up and down at its moorings in Cattaro Bay. *Kronprinz Erzherzog Rudolph* was now seen to be readying to prevent ships not willing to join the mutineers from steaming out to sea.

Not every crewman in the fleet shared the mutineers' defiant spirit. The German and Austrian submarine fleets based in Gjenovic refused to join the mutiny, and an offer was even made by Commander Ackermann, one of the submarine group's officers, to torpedo *Sankt Georg* and *Gäa* although this was dismissed in favour of negotiation. Even on *Sankt Georg* the telephonists pointedly refused to relay a message to headquarters in Pola advising of the mutiny and encouraging other ships to join their cause. The crews of the light cruisers *Helgoland* and *Novara*, which had seen repeated action in the Straits of Otranto fighting the Allied blockade and whose officers commanded a healthy respect, were also not easily influenced, though the ships' commanders were to admit privately in the days after the mutiny that maintaining crew loyalty had been a near thing.

When the captain of the destroyer *Csepel* saw the red flag flying over *Sankt Georg* he positioned his vessel off the mutinous ship's starboard beam and was in the process of swinging his torpedo tubes round with a view to blowing it out of the water when he received orders to return to dock.

The captain of the dreadnought *Helgoland*, Erich Heyssler, also considered training his torpedoes on *Sankt Georg*. But *Sankt Georg* had its guns trained on the dreadnought—any move to fire on the mutinous vessel could have disastrous consequences for both sides. Taking an educated guess that its presence wouldn't incite his own crew to mutiny, Heyssler decided instead to hoist the red flag on *Helgoland*. With the red flag flying from the foretop and the imperial ensign still raised at the stern, Heyssler was conveying a message of sympathy if not solidarity, and managed to diffuse a potentially calamitous situation.

'WHAT WE WANT'

In the evening of 1 February a list of demands, unambiguously titled 'What We Want,' was scrawled on a piece of paper delivered by representatives of the sailors' committee to Rear-Admiral Hansa, who was detained on board the *Sankt Georg*. Reflecting many of the same moral and social concerns found in the famous 'Fourteen Points' speech of US President Woodrow Wilson to the US Congress made just a few weeks earlier on 8 January 1918, the broad political demands of the mutineers included:

- the demobilisation of Austria-Hungary's armed forces and the creation of an all-volunteer militia
- political moves towards a comprehensive peace settlement with France, Russia and Great Britain

- self-determination for the disparate regions under the yoke of Habsburg rule
- an end to all political and economic dependence on foreign powers (notably Germany)
- moves to create a genuinely democratic and representative government.

Demands pertaining to their own personal needs included:

- an end to inappropriate exercise programs due to their state of malnutrition
- an increase in daily rations including extra tobacco
- shore leave to be increased in both frequency and time spent ashore
- all officers' kitchens to be shared with enlisted men
- an end to the censorship of personal mail.

The sailors took the opportunity to reassert their loyalty to the Emperor and reminded their admiral that their actions should be seen as more akin to a demonstration than a revolution. Hansa replied that although he had no authority to address their political demands, he promised he would look at their requests for better food and extended periods of shore leave. In turn the sailors gave their word they would continue to behave in a gentlemanly fashion.

As the sun went down on the waters of the gulf that night, searchlights from garrisons and gun emplacements on shore and from the ships themselves were trained on the surrounding mountains and the vessels of the fleet, both loyal and mutinous, were bathed in a luminous, silvery light. Echoing a tradition that became famous during the American Revolution, small bonfires known as *feux de joie* ('fires of joy') were being lit on the decks of the warships and songs echoing hope and even patriotism rose into the night. Choruses were returned from soldiers on shore. It was an extraordinary night, a night of unbridled optimism where anything seemed possible.

FROM COHESION TO DISARRAY

The mutiny certainly seemed to be exceeding everyone's expectations. There had been minimal bloodshed, clear lines of communication had been established between the crews of the rebellious ships and their commanders, and there was every hope the situation might be resolved without the sort of overwhelming military response which the world's great navies generally reserved for its mutineers. On land, however, the perspective was very different, and by early morning on the following day ominous signs were emerging that the brief window of civility and compromise was fast being closed.

At 7.30 on 2 February Hansa again met with representatives of the sailors' committee, which was now led by *Sankt Georg*'s boatswain Franz Rasch and his self-appointed deputy, Sub-Lieutenant Anton Sesan. Hansa advised them that they had until 10 am to return to their stations, and that if they did so he would attempt to gain a pardon for all those involved, with the exception of those who had initially fired upon the *Sankt Georg* officers.

In the face of this ultimatum the cohesion and coordination that had characterised the mutineers and the sailors' committee began to unravel. Nobody appeared to be in charge and meetings fell into disarray, with one of the committee members likening the atmosphere to that of a 'coffee-house' rather than a committee.

Meanwhile Baron Stefan Sarkotic, commander of land forces in Sarajevo, had ordered thousands of troops from across Montenegro and Bosnia to make for Cattaro Bay. Oskar von Guseck, the uncompromising commander of the harbour's armed forces, had already been busy deploying his troops throughout the Gulf of Cattaro and had issued an ultimatum of his own. If the sailors had not resumed their duties by 2 pm he would order his shore artillery and the German U-boats to open fire on *Sankt Georg* and *Gäa*, despite the latter's lower decks being filled to overflowing with the fleet's reserve store of torpedoes. At 10.15 am von Guseck issued orders to his soldiers to prevent any sailors from coming ashore, and began the evacuation of civilians in preparation for the coming bombardment.

CRUMBLING RESOLVE

At 1.30 pm, *Kronprinz Erzherzog Rudolph* defied an order to remain at its station in the outer gulf and began to sail towards the middle of Cattaro Bay; it was immediately fired upon by von Guseck's artillery, and a sailor was killed. The effect of this exchange was instantaneous. The resolve of the mutineers started to crumble as fears of an impending counter-revolution swept through their ranks; the ships began to lower their red flags of protest. The first to do so was the cruiser *Novara*, whose commander, Captain Prince Johannes von und zu Liechtenstein, told his crew that anyone who wished to abandon the vessel could do so. Within twenty minutes almost 150 men, nearly half of the ship's complement, had either jumped into the water or scrambled into its lifeboats. *Helgoland* raised steam and made for the relative safety of the inner harbour, closely followed by torpedo boats, destroyers, and other ancillary vessels. Crewmembers aboard *Gäa* who had opposed the mutiny disarmed the ship by removing the firing pins from its guns.

Everywhere they looked it must have seemed to the mutineers they were being abandoned. On board *Sankt Georg*, however, the crew held fast. Franz Rasch informed Hansa he would remain a prisoner until negotiations on their list of grievances were concluded, claiming to have 'the entire navy' still with him, a grandiose statement that bore little resemblance to reality. In the early hours of 3 February, Captain Heyssler of *Helgoland* took matters into his own hands, telling *Sankt Georg* that unless it surrendered and made its way into Cattaro's inner harbour by 10 am, it would be sunk.

LOWERING THE RED FLAG

The final straw came with the arrival of the Third Battle Division and its three pre-dreadnought battleships, *Erzherzog Karl*, *Erzherzog Friedrich* and *Erzherzog Ferdinand Max*, each of which boasted four 9.4 inch (24 cm) guns and thirty-four slightly smaller guns of varying sizes, overwhelmingly greater than the firepower on *Sankt Georg*. The battle group had been dispatched from Pola the previous day, but despite their approach the mutineers aboard *Sankt Georg* remained optimistic, aware of the recent political unrest in Pola and hoping that when the battle group sailed into sight it would be flying red flags. When only battle flags were seen, the last of the mutinous ships surrendered. *Kaiser Karl VI* lowered its red flag after dark on 2 February and at 9 am on 3 February, after a public show of hands the crew of *Sankt Georg* lowered their red flag. Franz Rasch went below decks on *Sankt Georg* and turned himself over to Rear-Admiral Hansa. Sub-Lieutenant Sesan, who had earlier come to the conclusion the mutiny was doomed to fail and gone ashore, escaped over the Adriatic to Italy.

On the morning of 7 February more than 800 seamen from over twenty vessels were taken ashore for questioning. Of the 392 who were charged, almost half of whom were either Slovakian or Croatian, 348 were acquitted. On 10 February four of the mutineers' inner circle—Anton Grabar, Franz Rasch, a Croatian sailor named Brnicevic, and Jerko Sizgoric, the latter accused and found guilty of shooting *Sankt Georg*'s captain—were found guilty of treason and taken to a prison under the foundations of one of Cattaro's forts. The following morning they were marched one by one to a churchyard in the nearby village of Skaijari and executed by firing squad.

UNDERLYING CAUSES OF DISCONTENT

That same day an emissary from Emperor Charles, Admiral Archduke Charles Stephan, arrived with a brief to examine the underlying causes of the mutiny and suggest possible remedies. He interviewed many officers and enlisted men and came to the conclusion that the ageing officer corps, many of whom he had served alongside in years gone by, could do with some revitalising. He also uncovered countless examples of abuses of privilege.

The reasonably representative split of nationalities involved in the uprising certainly goes a long way to discounting ethnicity as a primary cause of the revolt, with far more basic concerns such as poor conditions, inadequate rations, low morale and the non-egalitarian lifestyle of officers providing the fuel for discontent. Liechtenstein, the commander of *Novara*, even went so far as to refer to the sailors' demands as 'sensible'.

The issue of the availability, quality, equitability and distribution of food was a primary cause of discontent, and examples abounded of officer privileges raising the ire of enlisted men. The admiral of the Fifth Battle Division had had a motor launch converted so his wife could hold water-borne tea parties. Rear-admirals regularly hosted lavish lunches and dinners with their families, and to add insult to injury stayed on shore with them overnight. Kitchen staff whispered about the fine food served at banquets and told crewmembers how they'd overhear officers raising their glasses and toasting to the continuation of the war at the same time that the sailors' bread rations were being cut to 18 ounces (500 g) a day. Officers were also permitted to travel into the hinterland and purchase whatever food they liked at significantly lower prices than were being asked in port.

In an attempt to quell ethnic tensions the fleet's commander, Maximilian Njegovan, was relieved of his command and replaced by Miklos Horthy, a friend of the Emperor. *Sankt Georg* and *Kaiser Karl VI* were stripped of their armaments and converted into accommodation ships. Rear-Admiral Hansa was promoted to Vice-Admiral in March 1918 and left the service altogether the following September. The navy used the Cattaro Mutiny to rid itself not only of an ageing officer corps but of many of its old and obsolete ships as well.

Significantly, the mutiny had a lasting effect on the navy's commanders, reminding them that the strength of a nation's armed forces lay not in the destructive power of its weapons but in the enlisted men who made up its ranks. Erich Heyssler, the captain of *Helgoland*, put it best when he later wrote:

> *... something fundamental was gone, the atmosphere of trust and security in which we had been brought up and had spent our entire service years, had been shattered. The fact that the raw, physical power of an army is actually in the hands of ordinary soldiers and that these, if tested too hard, could be swayed to revolutionary ideas, driven to stupid, idiotic notions and even to treachery, this would never have entered the mind of an officer strictly disciplined to service life.*

Few mutinies in history set up so many hurdles in the way of coming to a true understanding of its causes. The mind-numbing mix of nationalities involved, and the differing perspectives from which accounts were written in its aftermath, take time and patience to unravel. Villains became heroes, and heroes, villains. Franz Rasch, disgraced and executed for treason, became a socialist hero in the new Yugoslavia. Miklos Horthy, not even present during the three days of the mutiny, received the politically motivated title 'butcher of Cattaro' in post-World War II communist Hungary.

Perhaps the most exhaustive and accurate account is the work of the Czech historian Richard Plaschka, who together with colleagues at Vienna's Eastern and Southeast Europe Institute brought together various Slavic and German texts, with attention primarily on the sailors themselves and the events that led to their extraordinary act of defiance.

‘NOBODY WANTED A REVOLUTION, WE JUST WANTED TO BE TREATED MORE LIKE HUMAN BEINGS.’

Willy Weber, convicted mutineer

‘I HAVE NO LONGER A NAVY.’

Kaiser Wilhelm II, November 1918

1918

THE WILHELMSHAVEN MUTINY

The Great War had been an inglorious and frustrating period for the officers of Germany's Supreme Naval Command. Separated from the strategic shipping lanes of the Atlantic Ocean by the gauntlet of the English Channel, with Britain's warships and submarines patiently waiting at anchor should they decide to sail by, the surface ships of the German High Seas Fleet were always destined to do little more than patrol the strategically insignificant waters of the North Sea.

With the exception of inconclusive sea battles at Heligoland (1914), Dogger Bank (1915) and Jutland (1916), and a few other engagements that were really nothing more than skirmishes, Germany's warships had spent most of the war holed up in the German Bight, watching helplessly as the British Imperial Fleet continued to grow in influence and firepower, and seeing their own importance as a tactical force dwindle to the point of irrelevance. Only Germany's submariners could look upon their fleet with any sense of pride. Their increasing effectiveness in the sinking of American and British merchant shipping in the Atlantic in the early months of 1917 threatened to starve Great Britain of food and supplies and forced America's entry into the war on 6 April 1917.

Despite its size the High Seas Fleet, sometimes referred to disparagingly as the 'Kaiser's Navy,' was nothing more than a costly exercise in national pride instigated by Kaiser Wilhelm II, who treated it much like a child would treat a mechanised plaything, a product of his own vanity. This was a reality that wasn't lost on its enlisted men, who were considerably more sophisticated than their forebears in the age of sail, a mix of skilled craftsmen and technicians with increasingly refined political sensitivities and increasingly resentful of the navy's ambivalence towards reforming the officers' corps with its inbred Prussian aristocratic traditions. When a policy of 'inactivity' was pursued after the stalemate at Jutland the fleet became little more than a floating museum, setting the stage for the sort of dangerously low morale that can only come from quarantined idleness.

GROWING FRUSTRATION

By 1918 the navy was well aware of the poor morale and lack of discipline among its sailors, but did nothing to alleviate the problem. The best commanders had been transferred to the U-boat arm, and those who were left seemed unable to quell the discontent.

Advances in battleship design in the decades leading up to the Great War did nothing to alleviate the conditions of inferiority imposed on the enlisted men, or their physical separation from their officers. In the days of sail officers had spacious quarters aft while their crews endured the cramped spaces of the fo'c'sle, but at least they were separated by only 30 metres (100 feet) or so, the length of the ship. In the modern German dreadnoughts and battleships the enlisted men, often numbering 800 or more, were crammed into the aft section while forty or so officers lived in comparative comfort forward, and now they were separated by roughly 120 metres (400 feet) of engine rooms, boilers and magazine compartments. The sailors' sense of isolation and the accompanying opportunities for groups of disgruntled men to meet and air grievances had never been greater.

OPERATIONS PLAN #19

In the final months of the war, without consulting either Kaiser Wilhelm or the Reichstag, Admiral Frank von Hipper, Admiral Reinhard Scheer and the German Supreme Naval Command decided on a plan they hoped would salvage their navy's battered pride. Operations Plan #19 called for one last, mighty action. The German Navy's Battle Cruiser Squadron would make a series of daring raids along the mouth of the Thames and at the same time its High Seas Fleet would bombard Allied positions in northern France. Then the two fleets would combine, await the arrival of Britain's Imperial Fleet, and engage it in the English Channel regardless of the odds. It was argued the German Fleet would somehow be able to sustain itself while far from home and in the face of the overwhelming numerical superiority of an enemy navy ably reinforced from bases just a few nautical miles to the north. It was suggested that (perhaps with a dash of providence thrown in) an unlikely German success might lead to some concessions at the negotiating table and win Germany a more honourable peace.

When Operations Plan #19 was announced to the High Seas Fleet at anchor in Kiel on 29 October 1918, it was immediately seen for what it was—a suicide mission. The officer corps, already aware of it, was flushed with expectations of a final, apocalyptic battle and apparently unconcerned at rumours that the fleet would be sacrificed if necessary. Several officers holding parties the previous night had been overheard proposing toasts using phrases such as the 'death-ride of the German navy'. The 80,000 sailors of the fleet were, understandably, far more sombre in their appraisal. They were well aware that negotiations to bring an end to the war had been in progress for several weeks and could result at any time in the announcing of an armistice. No enlisted man wanted the honour of being remembered as one of Germany's last official casualties of the Great War, sacrificed in a dubious attempt to resuscitate the pride of a failed navy.

Many sailors had already made plans for the rest of their lives and hadn't waited for the mutiny that now seemed inevitable to draw unwanted attention to themselves. Desertions had increased apace in the months leading up to the announcement of Operations Plan #19, and many private homes in Wilhelmshaven and the nearby port town of Schillig had become safe houses. Sailors sold their uniforms and were clothed in civilian attire by sympathetic civilians who then organised safe passage throughout the country. Given the conditions that saw the emergence of deserters on a large scale and of the shore-based network that helped them, what is surprising is not that a mutiny erupted at Wilhelmshaven and Kiel in November 1918, but that it hadn't occurred much earlier.

REVOLUTION AND INSUBORDINATION

The first crews to mutiny were those of the dreadnoughts SMS *Thüringen* and SMS *Helgoland* of the First Navy Squadron. They disabled the engines, smashed navigation lights, and locked a number of their officers in their cabins. Stokers on *Helgoland* doused the fires in the boilers, making it impossible for the ship to sail, and one of its stokers, Ernst Wollweber, later claimed to be the first sailor to raise the red flag, the symbol of revolution. The crews of the battlecruisers SMS *Von der Tann* and SMS *Derflinger* refused to return to their ships after a period of shore leave. Acts of insubordination were reported from the battleships SMS *Kaiserin*, SMS *Kronprinz Wilhelm* and SMS *Konig Albert* of the Third Navy Squadron.

Not every vessel in the High Seas Fleet was so disposed to protest and revolution, however. The crews of the torpedo boats, which didn't suffer from the low morale and the politics of the workers' groups that were common throughout the larger ships, swung their torpedo tubes round and took aim at SMS *Thüringen* and SMS *Helgoland*, forcing their mutinous crews to give themselves up and resulting in the arrest of over a thousand men.

Elsewhere, choruses of 'down with Kaiser Wilhelm' began to echo from the decks of other rebel ships. Vice-Admiral Hugo Kraft, commander of the Third Navy Squadron, took his ships out into Heligoland Bight in an attempt to separate his men from the contagion of revolt, and in the process was able to identify several dozen revolutionary ringleaders from the battleship SMS *Markgraf*. Kraft had them imprisoned at Holtenau on the Kiel Canal before organising their transfer to various military prisons in Kiel the next day. On the evening of 1 November a delegation of sailors from the Third Squadron met in Kiel's Union House and demanded their release and the freeing of the crews of *Thüringen* and *Helgoland.* When local police shut the meeting down, this only inflamed emotions and led to plans for an even larger gathering.

SPREADING REVOLT

On learning of the revolt, Admiral von Hipper immediately cancelled the planned assault in the English Channel and, in an attempt to diffuse the mutiny, ordered the First Navy Squadron to the mouth of the Elbe River, the Third Squadron to remain in Kiel, and the Fourth Squadron to Wilhelmshaven. However rather than containing the revolt, this had the effect of spreading it from one end of Germany's coastline to the other.

On 2 November Karl Artelt and Lothar Popp called for a gathering of sailors at Kiel's drill ground. Popp was born in Bavaria in 1887, ran away from home at the age of sixteen, and joined Germany's Social Democratic Party (SPD) in 1912. It was Lothar Popp and Karl Artelt, the founder of the Kiel Soldier's Council and a worker in one of Kiel's torpedo factories, who emerged as leaders of the revolt and who together confronted government troops sent to put down the revolt and convinced them not to take action.

At 10 am on the morning of 3 November, workers at Kiel's torpedo factory and the Germania shipyards downed their tools. At the drill ground, placards and slogans reading 'Frieden und Brot' ('Peace and Bread') could be seen above the heads of sailors and civilians alike. This was not just a protest born of the mutiny that was unfolding. In April 1917 more than 300,000 factory workers in Berlin had gone on strike over a reduction in the bread ration, and similar strikes had followed in many other cities across the nation. The war was turning Germany into a country unable to feed its own people. Although the mutinies at Kiel and Wilhelmshaven began as a response to a suicidal order, the country's descent into poverty and deprevation provided ideal platforms for socialist revolutionaries to stand up and offer solutions to a populace tired of sacrifice and war.

FROM REVOLT TO OPEN REBELLION

At the drill ground in Kiel, a naval sub-lieutenant under orders not to permit the demonstration to go ahead unwittingly provided the spark for revolution by ordering his unit to fire into the crowd. Seven demonstrators were killed and several dozen were wounded, and what had begun as a protest soon grew into open rebellion. On the following day, in defiance of the government, a Soviet-style Workers & Soldiers Council was established in Kiel, and over the next four days the entire fleet turned to a state of open revolt. Right across the fleet the flag of the Kaiser was lowered and replaced by the red flag of protest.

The revolt spread so quickly that by the afternoon of 4 November the base commander at Kiel, the Kaiser's brother Crown Prince Heinrich, was forced to disguise himself and flee in a truck through crowds of people openly asking one another 'Will the fleet sail?' and calling for an end to the war. By early evening all the imprisoned sailors had been released, and the port and city of Kiel were firmly in the hands of tens of thousands of mutineers and factory workers.

Anyone in authority who represented the old regime was a target. In Bremen thousands of sailors roamed the streets in commandeered vehicles, singing songs of freedom and revolution. A Bremen police officer asked a group to stop riding on the outside of a city tram and was beaten to death where he stood. Officers slow to hand over their pistols to mutineers in the streets were set upon. Dead rats were thrown through police station windows. The revolution ignited by the mutineers was spreading throughout the country.

Wilhelmshaven fell to the mutineers on 6 November and over the next three days the unrest spread all the way to Berlin. Hamburg, long a melting pot of socialist sympathisers, already had Bolsheviks embedded in City Hall. Bremen and Lübeck followed. Bavaria in the south proclaimed itself a republic, forcing the abdication of King Ludwig III. As the unrest continued, swallowing up Germany's towns and cities, socialist workers' committees were established to restore order. Admiral Scheer confided to the Kaiser that his beloved navy could no longer be relied upon to follow the command's orders. This was followed by an ultimatum from the Commander-in-Chief of the Western Front, Wilhelm Groener, to the Kaiser: 'If you won't abdicate, the best thing for you to do is shoot yourself.'

Within forty-eight hours the Kaiser had fled to safety in the Netherlands. The sailors of the German Fleet had brought to an end the era of the German monarchy and in so doing gave pause to governments everywhere who for centuries had understood all too well the potential for revolution that a properly orchestrated and timely mutiny could wield.

‘THE ONLY ENEMIES ARE YOUR OWN OFFICERS.’

André Marty, mechanic, French destroyer *Protet*, 23 April 1919

1919

THE FRENCH BLACK SEA MUTINY

Within two years of the rise to power of Vladimir Lenin and his Bolshevik Social Democrats in Russia's October Revolution of 1917, forces opposed to their rule had formed a loose confederation known as the White Army and had organised themselves into regional militias, determined to continue the fight against communism. In the northwest, former Russian World War I prisoners of war were turned into an army with German assistance; in Siberia, units hastily brought together to fight during World War I turned their guns on their new communist government and advanced towards Moscow from the east; in the south there was a loose alliance of various anti-Bolshevik forces fighting throughout the Crimea and Ukraine.

In an effort to lend assistance to the White Army and to destabilise if not overthrow the new communist leadership, France intervened militarily in the Crimea and Ukraine in late 1918. During World War I the Allies had loaned Russia vast amounts of military hardware; now, with the new Russian Government signing a pact with Germany, the Allies feared it all might find its way into German hands. Whether this was just a pretext or not is open to debate but, for better or worse, the French became embroiled in the Russian Civil War.

French ambitions in the region had all the hallmarks of pre-war colonial expansionism, with hopes high in Paris that there would not only be a political and military defeat of Bolshevism but also the establishment of a French sphere of influence that would result in economic and strategic benefits. But the French military campaign had proved a disaster. The White Army was not the 'national army' the French thought it was and the morale of its volunteer soldiers was poor. In early 1919 the combination of an unexpectedly hostile local population, an inability to unify the region's anti-Bolshevik movements, difficulties with logistics and supply, and a disciplined, well-organised enemy saw Bolshevik forces cross the vital Perekop Isthmus, the gateway to the Crimea, on 6 March. The Crimean Government fell on 8 March and by 14 March Bolshevik troops were at the outskirts of Sebastopol. Odessa had been evacuated, and the French were being brutally reminded of the many pitfalls to be encountered when a government decides to interfere in another country's civil war.

SINGING A REVOLUTIONARY SONG

By now it had become clear to General Louis Franchet d'Espèrey, commanding the French forces from his headquarters in Bucharest, Romania, that Sebastopol could not be defended. This decision enraged Vice-Admiral Jean-François-Charles Amet, the commander of France's Second Naval Squadron, whose guns, including those of his flagship, the battleship *France*, and the battlecruiser *Jean Bart*, had only days earlier held off a Red Army advance on Sebastopol. Amet believed he could continue to hold the city indefinitely with support, and he might well have been able to argue the case if he wasn't distracted by events much closer to home.

On Saturday, 19 April *France*'s boiler crews were issued with orders to begin coaling the following day, Easter Sunday. Later that afternoon hundreds of sailors assembled on the forward deck and voiced their refusal to coal on Easter Sunday. Later that evening, without warning, almost 200 sailors began to mutiny on shore. The uprising quickly spread to the crews of *France* and *Jean Bart*, who joined with their fellow enlisted men on shore in singing the 'Internationale', the song of the French Revolution that by the late nineteenth century had become the working classes' anthem worldwide. Crewmen ran wildly through the ships, smashing lights, ripping telephones off walls, and hurling insults at bewildered officers. At an assembly on *France*, crew delegates presented a list of demands to Vice-Admiral Amet, who struggled to make himself heard above the noise of the mob. Unable to address their grievances in the midst of what he later called an act of collective madness, Amet retired to his cabin. Outside the protests began to fade, and Amet hoped that a good night's sleep would restore some calm and that the issues, whatever they were, could be addressed with clear heads in the morning and the incident promptly put behind them. But it wasn't going to be that easy.

FED UP SAILORS

On the morning of 20 April, Easter Sunday, on the decks and in the corridors of *France* and *Jean Bart*, the protests began anew and soon spread throughout the fleet. On both ships the red flag of sedition and protest was run up the masthead, although on *Jean Bart* the popular commander succeeded in having the flag lowered before personally tearing it to shreds. The officers on *France*, however, were facing a more militant situation. An entire section of the ship had come under the control of its crew, which refused an order from Amet to prepare to sail to Constantinople (present-day Istanbul). The ship's delegates then advised the Vice-Admiral that *France* would not sail anywhere unless the rest of the fleet sailed with it. The delegates were giving the orders, and Amet had a mutiny on his hands.

The men of France's Second Naval Squadron were tired, disillusioned, war weary, and had just endured a particularly harsh winter made all the more unbearable by a lack of warm clothing. Fighting ashore also meant fresh food had been difficult to obtain, and a constant stream of strikes by Russian dockyard workers meant the French sailors were often called upon to load and unload their own supplies. There was also the apparent irony that France was supporting a rag-tag army fighting the Bolsheviks'

'Red Army', which less than six months earlier had been allied with France in the war against Germany.

Following victory in one war, the French were now embroiled in a deeply unpopular conflict a long way from home, which few enlisted men understood and even fewer cared about. Although supplies of food and clothing had improved in the weeks leading up to the mutiny, the sailors were fed up with the long, slow rate of demobilisation after the Armistice of November 1918 and wanted nothing more than to simply turn the bows of their ships towards home. World War I had been little more than four years of frustration for the crews of France's large warships. Kept in port away from marauding German submarines, never seeing the German surface fleet that was kept at bay in the far-away North Sea by the might of Britain's Royal Navy, they'd seen little action and spent most of the war idling away their days behind defensive steel netting.

SUPPORT FOR REVOLUTIONARIES IN THE FRENCH NAVY

There was an undeniable level of support for the Russian revolutionaries in the enlisted ranks of the French Navy, with many sailors seeing the White Army volunteers they were there to assist as arrogant and ineffective fighters who lacked the purpose and commitment of their Bolshevik adversaries. Five months earlier, when Russian revolutionaries were in Odessa, French sailors had refused to fire on them. Sailors on shore leave mixed with ordinary Russians who overwhelmingly supported the Bolshevik cause, and had been subjected to Bolshevik propaganda from the day they arrived, in the leaflets they were handed and in the places where they drank. France had had its revolution, they were told. Let us Russians have ours. Then there was the propaganda coming from France itself, with communist leaders such as Marcel Cachin claiming parliamentary debates were undermining the French commitment in the Crimea and calling into question the legitimacy and desirability of continuing the conflict.

HOME TO FRANCE

So it should have come as no surprise when, on the afternoon of 20 April on the streets of Sevastopol, sailors whom Amet had allowed to go ashore in an effort to defuse tension aboard his ships took part in demonstrations in support of the Bolshevik cause, joining the crowd in demanding an end to Allied interference in the country's internal affairs. A Greek military detachment allied to the French forces opened fire on the demonstrators, killing two civilians and wounding six French sailors, one of whom, a crewmember from the pre-dreadnought battleship *Vergniaud*, later died.

Meanwhile Vice-Admiral Amet was being ferried from ship to ship in an attempt to prevent his squadron from descending into full-scale mutiny. Although Saturday's refusal to coal the boilers provided on obvious trigger for the mutiny and suggested spontaneity, the simultaneous appearance of delegates on numerous ships in the fleet indicated the uprising may have been premeditated. There was a commonality in the delegates' behaviour and in the themes of the speeches they gave to their respective crews. It was a mutiny orchestrated not by long-serving ratings who one might think had been worn down by years of inaction, but by recently acquired recruits from the industrial heartland of France, men like André Marty, whose left-wing political views were suddenly provided with an ideal stage on which to flourish.

The mutiny was akin to a strike on a factory floor. There would be no bloodshed and ships' delegates made certain the day-to-day maintenance of each vessel continued. Their principal demand was that the ships return to France, a demand that gained strength in the wake of the shootings on shore. This had incensed the crew of *France* in particular, who demanded an explanation of why soldiers from a nation allied with France would take aim at their shipmates. Within two weeks the Ministry of Marine in Paris gave them their wish. When Vice-Admiral Amet agreed to take a number of the vessels from the Second Squadron to France, the mutiny ended.

For the average sailor this was all they ever really wanted, but for the socialist revolutionaries at the heart of the mutiny there had been hopes of initiating an uprising similar to that at Wilhelmshaven in October 1918, when the revolt of the German Baltic Fleet led to the overthrow of the Kaiser and the establishment of a socialist government. Ringleaders such as André Marty may have entertained visions of sailing their ships into the port of Marseilles and igniting a nationwide revolution, but their dreams only isolated them from their own crewmembers who, having not even seen so much as a French port in over a year and a half, wanted nothing more than to return to their loved ones and resume their lives.

'... THE LAST BOAT HAVING BEEN HOISTED IN I GAVE THE ORDER TO "LET GO AFT" WHEN SIMULTANEOUSLY BY TELEPHONE FROM THE ENGINE ROOM I RECEIVED A COMMUNICATION THAT THE STOKERS ON WATCH HAD LEFT THE BOILER ROOMS.'

Captain Cumberlege, 'Letter of Circumstances', June 1919

1919

HMAS *AUSTRALIA* MUTINY

Not all mutinies are murderous, bloody affairs. A mutiny is merely a refusal to obey the order of a superior officer and can range in scale from an angry mob throwing a captain overboard to a sailor refusing to pick up his cap. Often they involve no violence and are the product of relatively mundane grievances. Such a broad definition means that occasionally a mutiny might come and go and barely rate a footnote in the pages of history. But even the smallest of mutinies are extraordinary events in the life of a ship and its crew—like the mutiny on board HMAS *Australia* in June 1919.

HMAS *Australia* was an 18,800-tonne (18,500 ton) Indefatigable-class battlecruiser launched in England in 1911 and commissioned as flagship into the Royal Australian Navy (RAN) in 1913 at a time when the Australian Navy, and the country itself, was still in its infancy. Only thirteen years had passed since Queen Victoria signed the *Commonwealth of Australia Constitution Act*, which allowed the six British colonies to unite to form the Commonwealth of Australia on 1 January 1900. Its navy was little more than an extension of the British Royal Navy (RN), with most of its command roles and appointments still being awarded to RN officers. Less than half of *Australia*'s complement of 820 were regarded as 'Australian'.

HEADING FOR HOME

Accompanied by the light cruiser HMAS *Sydney*, *Australia* sailed from Portsmouth Harbour in July 1913 and arrived in Sydney in the early hours of 4 October to a rapturous reception. The most powerful warship in the Pacific, HMAS *Australia* was more than just another battlecruiser. It was the country's first capital ship and a powerful symbol of the nation's growing maturity and self-reliance, representing the casting-off of the shackles of British colonial rule. It was envisaged as the nucleus of a new Australian fleet that would include heavy cruisers, destroyers, submarines and auxiliary craft. Its passage into Sydney Harbour resulted in an outpouring of nationalistic pride never before seen. And in the eyes of the thousands of people who lined the foreshore to see the ship come in, its crew could do no wrong.

In 1914, at the outbreak of World War I, all RAN ships, with the consent of the Australian Parliament, were transferred to the British Admiralty. *Australia* was dispatched to Great Britain's China Station before being sent to Rosyth in Scotland to patrol the North Sea as part of the Second Battlecruiser Squadron. Five months after the end of the war, *Australia* finally set sail for home from Portsmouth Harbour on 17 April 1919. Its commander was an Englishman, Captain Claude Cumberlege RN. Receiving his new commission only a week prior to departure, Cumberlege had previously been in command of Australian warships and was regarded as an unflappable and capable commander, always calm in a crisis and with a refreshing lack of pomp, which appealed to the 'larrikins' in the lower decks.

The voyage home took HMAS *Australia* to Gibraltar, Malta, down the Suez Canal to Aden on the Arabian Peninsula and Ceylon (present-day Sri Lanka). Normally sufficient shore leave would be considered prudent on such a long trip, but the sailing schedule was so tight that only a few hours' leave was possible in Gibraltar and Malta. Then in Aden, to compound the increasing ire of the crew, only officers were permitted ashore; not only that, but the following day they permitted themselves an officers-only party. Tensions between officers and crew were beginning to simmer.

AN UNHAPPY CREW

Australia had been away from home for four and a half years when it arrived back in the Western Australian port of Fremantle on 28 May 1919 to take on coal and restock depleted stores. The crew did manage a few days of shore leave but were looking forward to four additional days already promised them. The stokers were particularly eager for a break. Stokers were required to be on hand should a ship need to make steam in a hurry, and as a consequence often had far shorter periods of leave than the rest of the crew.

A hectic schedule of 'welcome home' appearances intervened, however, and preparations to again put to sea began on Sunday, 1 June. On hearing the news that the additional shore leave had been cancelled, around a hundred enlisted men gathered on the quarterdeck in the shadows of gun turret P, refusing to disperse until they could speak to their captain. Cumberlege, after listening to their grievances, gave a veiled warning that their request to remain in port for a few more days seemed to him more like a demand. The crew then asked whether it would be possible to delay their departure by just a day, to give them an opportunity to entertain friends from shore on board. Cumberlege replied that the forthcoming series of appearances that had been scheduled made it impossible to delay their departure. Although unhappy with what they had heard, the crew broke ranks without incident.

Not long afterwards Commodore John Saumarez Dumaresq, commander of the Australian Fleet, was piped aboard and Cumberlege gave the order for the ship to let go its moorings. Steam was being raised in the boilers and the crew was lining the forecastle. Everything seemed in readiness for an on-time departure until Cumberlege received some unexpected news from the engineer commander—the stokers had abandoned their posts and refused to return. Without stokers to keep the boilers at full steam, *Australia* wouldn't be going anywhere. One of those stokers was Dalmorton Rudd, who had taken to alcohol after the death of his wife in 1918. Rudd was awarded the Distinguished Service Medal in 1917 for bravery during the attack on the German submarine pens at Zeebrugge, but was later demoted after a violent incident.

Cumberlege immediately assembled his officers and petty officers, together with enlisted men drawn from other areas of the ship, and ordered them to the engine room to begin restoking the boilers. *Australia* once again built up steam, and departed an hour later. An immediate investigation saw twelve junior sailors arrested, of whom seven received sentences of ninety days after having pleaded guilty to the relatively minor offence of 'failing to use their utmost exertions to suppress a mutiny'. The ringleaders were remanded for court martial on arrival in Sydney.

JOINING IN A MUTINY

A court martial was convened aboard the cruiser HMAS *Encounter* in Sydney Harbour on 20 June 1919. It consisted of Commodore J.C. Glossop RN from the cadet training school HMAS *Penguin*, District Naval Officer Captain F.H. Brownlow RAN, Commander F. Brabant RN of HMAS *Australia*, Captain J. Robbins of HMAS *Encounter* and Commander H. Feakes RAN of the clipper HMAS *Tingara.*

The mutiny's five accused ringleaders were stokers Dalmorton Rudd and his brother Leonard, stoker William Macintosh, and two ordinary seamen, Kenneth Patterson and Wilfred Thompson. They were all charged with 'joining in a mutiny not accompanying violence'.

During testimony a series of simmering grievances surfaced that suggested perhaps the action, as spontaneous as it may have been, could have been a long time coming. *Australia* saw very little action during the war years. Its patrols in the North Sea were mostly tedious affairs, and at one stage it was even used in experiments to test the feasibility of deploying shipborne aircraft. There were also several outstanding issues regarding pay, and lingering discontent over a paucity of leave during its time in Great Britain.

The events leading up to the mutiny were few and relatively straightforward. In the wake of Cumberlege's refusal to delay the ship's departure a number of the crew, including Dalmorton and Leonard Rudd, had gone below decks with black silk handkerchiefs tied round their faces and through a mix of intimidation and persuasion convinced the stokers to abandon their posts. All five of the accused pleaded guilty and their convictions, based on the provisions of the British *Naval Discipline Act* of 1866, were relayed to the Naval Board on 25 June. Two mutineers were given sentences of twelve months, but Dalmorton, Leonard and a third able seaman were sentenced to two years' imprisonment with hard labour in Goulburn Gaol and dismissed from the service.

CALLS FOR LENIENCY

The reaction of the public to the sentences was one of outrage fuelled by continuing pacifist sentiments in the wake of the horrific Australian losses suffered in the trenches of Europe and on the beaches of Gallipoli. There was also a deep sense of resentment that an Australian court martial had been forced to operate under the auspices of a foreign piece of legislation in determining the guilt and punishment of the accused. Demands for leniency began to be made, not only in the press and on the street but also on the floor of the Australian Parliament, where the Opposition made vigorous calls for the government of Prime Minister William 'Billy' Hughes to intervene and impose clemency. Opposition Members of Parliament sought legal opinions on the possibility of mounting an appeal, and even some of the government's own backbenchers lent their support for clemency. In the Senate the incident was referred to as 'that so-called mutiny', and the sentences as nothing short of 'savage'.

With the RAN still operating under the auspices of the British Admiralty, the findings were sent to London for review and on 10 September, despite the Admiralty agreeing that the sentences were appropriate, it was suggested that due to the mutineers' relatively young age perhaps time served could be halved. The government bowed to mounting public and political pressure and, to the ire of the Naval Board, whose members were incensed that the government had chosen to meddle in its internal affairs, reduced the sentences of the five men, setting 20 December as the earliest date of release for the two seamen given twelve-month terms and 20 June for the release of the other three.

Pressure, however, continued by the families of the accused and by Members of Parliament, forcing the Australian Government to send a telegram to the Secretary of the Colonies in London on 6 November asking whether all five prisoners could be released before Christmas. The following week a reply granting the request was received, and it was announced all five men would be released on 20 December 1919—provided, of course, that the navy agreed to sign the release warrants.

A WORRYING PRECEDENT

Commodore Dumaresq was incensed the government went behind the navy's back in its application to the Admiralty, concerned that such flagrant disregard for naval procedures and public lack of support could lead to a further erosion of discipline and authority. If enlisted men could cite the Australian Government of all things as being at odds with the navy's own interpretations of its disciplinary code of conduct, where would it end? It was a worrying precedent.

On 14 December, Rear-Admiral Sir Percy Grant RN resigned in protest and six days later, on 20 December, the day of the mutineers' early release, so did Commodore Dumaresq. The two officers withdrew their resignations on 13 February 1920 after a government notice stating that the original sentences had been 'proper and just' was posted throughout the fleet. But the temporary resignation of the two highest-ranking officers nevertheless soured relations between the navy and the government for years to come.

Although the incident on board *Australia* on 1 June 1919 faded from the consciousness of the nation soon after the release of the five 'mutineers', the question 'Was it mutiny or not?' refused to go away. The emerging Australian tradition of egalitarianism, of the worker and his boss sorting out their differences toe to toe in a relatively classless society, was a powerful social truism. Australians, perhaps as a result of their colonial beginnings and an inherent disregard for authority, were largely of the opinion that an 'Aussie' had the right to confront his boss and, if necessary, simply refuse to work if he felt so inclined, and to be able to demonstrate this inalienable right on a workshop floor, a shearing shed or even on the quarterdeck of one of His Majesty's warships.

The navy, not surprisingly, had a different view. Direct orders had been disobeyed. Traditions were ignored in the manner in which the crew approached their captain. All five of the accused had several years of navy service behind them and could not claim ignorance of the gravity of their actions or of their inevitable consequences. On joining the service they had been read the Articles of War relating to mutiny. The encouragement of others to join their actions, their threats of intimidation towards their fellow crewmembers, their disregard of navy protocol and the *Naval Discipline Act* of 1866 left nothing more to be said. It was mutiny. Every step they took. Mutiny.

In the end, the mutineers on HMAS *Australia* were lucky. Lucky the navy chose to try them under the lesser charge of 'taking part in a mutiny' rather than the more serious charge pertaining to 'ringleaders of mutinies', which they all undoubtedly were, and which carried the death penalty. They'd been done a favour by their British commanders, who'd realised there was little to be gained in punishing them to the full extent of the law for something that was likely a momentary lapse in judgment, a bloodless folly fuelled perhaps by alcohol (although the official records are silent on this), but in any case an act that was not deserving of swinging back and forth at the end of a rope.

‘ON THE WHOLE IT WAS
GOOD MEN GONE WRONG.
ALL THE SHIPS QUICKLY GOT
BACK INTO APPLE-PIE ORDER ...’

**Austen Chamberlain, First Lord of the Admiralty,
27 September 1931**

1931

THE INVERGORDON MUTINY

By December 1930 the Great Depression had devastated not only the economic but also the social fabric of Great Britain. Countless thousands languished in homelessness. Unemployment had more than doubled to 2.8 million, representing more than 20 per cent of the workforce, and the manufacturing sector was in turmoil with demand for British-made goods having all but collapsed—exports had fallen in value by 50 per cent.

On 11 September 1931, following a meeting of the Committee on National Expenditure in July and amid mounting pressure from Britain's banks to drastically slash spending, the newly elected Labour government of James Ramsay MacDonald responded to what the Prime Minister called 'the full force of an economic blizzard' by initiating a series of initiatives which included cuts to unemployment benefits and the slashing of public spending and public sector wages. These moves were deeply unpopluar—many traditional Labour supporters refused to support the measures.

INFURIATING CUTS

Almost hidden amid the committee's sweeping recommendations was a proposed 10 per cent pay cut to all naval officers and enlisted men. At first glance this seemed an entirely reasonable response to what were desperate economic times, but a closer examination of the breakdown of the cuts infuriated the fleet's enlisted men.

There had been a gradual improvement in living conditions in the Royal Navy since the end of the Great War in 1918, although able and ordinary seamen were still poorly paid and could scarcely afford a drop in salary. Rates of desertion had fallen significantly. There were fewer incidents of summary punishment and court martials, and with warship technology becoming increasingly complex there was a greater need for educated, trained crews. The creation in 1921 of the canteen cooperative, the Navy, Army and Air Force Institutes (NAAFI), saw food at last being prepared by trained cooks. These changes however, though welcome, were mostly incremental, some might even say grudging. It was warship and gun design, ship propulsion and battle tactics that dominated the agendas of Admiralty meetings in the post-World War I period, not the state of morale in the lower decks.

In the months leading up to the revolt rumours were rife that some sort of cut was being considered. The *Daily Express* predicted in an editorial on 5 September that a reduction of 10 per cent across the board for all those in the employ of His Majesty's government, and the day after the budget speech on 10 September Scotland's *Daily Record* reported that all enlisted men should prepare themselves to return to the levels of pay they were receiving in 1925. For those on the lower decks of Britain's naval vessels news of the cuts must have fallen like a sledgehammer and made it seem as though all the gains in living conditions and the awarding of sundry benefits over the previous ten years had amounted to little more than window dressing.

An admiral's pay was cut by 7 per cent, a lieutenant-commander's by 4 per cent. But if you were an able seaman your rate of pay went down from 4 shillings a day to just 3 shillings, a drop of 25 per cent. If you were unfortunate enough to be an ordinary seaman your rate of pay would plummet from 2 shillings and 9 pence to just 2 shillings a day, a drop of more than 30 per cent. Enlisted men were about to revert to the pay levels of 1925 at a time when the average weekly rent for a room in an English naval town was 11 shillings a week. Take that away from the new weekly wage for an ordinary seaman of 14 shillings, and there was barely enough left for food.

Sailors with families were hit hard. The Royal Navy had refused to recognise the financial burdens that accompanied marriage until the outbreak of World War I in 1914, and it wasn't until 1926 that naval widows were able to draw a state pension. Even in 1930, married enlisted men had to be over the age of twenty-five to be eligible to receive the newly legislated marriage allowance. To supplement their meagre incomes, sailors on Britain's warships with the responsibility of wives and children had for years run unofficial small businesses known as 'Dhoby firms'. For married sailors in particular to be told they had to sacrifice a quarter of their wages for an indeterminate period to help pay for a financial crisis that was precipitated on the other side of the Atlantic in the boardrooms and banks of Wall Street was, simply, unacceptable. Rents were high in England's naval towns and good accommodation was hard to find. Reductions in sailors' wages would have repercussions. Families would be evicted. Furniture would be repossessed. Children would go hungry.

A MONUMENTAL BLUNDER

On Friday, 11 September, the day that the cuts were announced, Britain's Atlantic Fleet sailed into Cromarty Firth, a deepwater inlet of the North Sea north of the Scottish town of Invergordon, to prepare for its annual autumn exercises. There was no greater concentration of firepower anywhere on the planet. The battleships HMS *Repulse*, HMS *Valiant*, HMS *Warspite*, HMS *Malaya*, various heavy cruisers, the fleet's flagship HMS *Hood* and HMS *Rodney* were all there, along with sundry heavy cruisers, minesweepers and support vessels. *Rodney* alone had nine 41-centrimetre (16-inch) guns, the recoil from which would rock the iron giant in the water. Vast and imposing though it was, *Rodney* was meant to be even bigger, its aft section having been cut and its hull hastily shortened when international treaties limiting the size of battleships came into force during its construction.

With the commander of the Atlantic Fleet, Admiral Michael Hodges, in a Portsmouth hospital suffering a severe bout of pleurisy, command had fallen to Rear-Admiral Wilfred Tomkinson, former commander-in-chief of the Mediterranean Fleet, who first heard of the cuts via a BBC radio broadcast on the evening of 10 September as the fleet was sailing north. Only officers' wardrooms had radios, and Tomkinson, perhaps feeling burdened by his new command and the coming exercises, failed to break the news to his crews. To compound matters further, a letter from the Admiralty detailing the cuts officially had been addressed not to Tomkinson but to Michael Hodges in Portsmouth.

The following morning, Friday, 11 September, after the fleet had berthed, the enlisted men first learned of the cuts not from their superior officers or from the Board of the Admiralty, but from the *News of the World* and the front pages of Britain's newspapers, brought on board by columns of bewildered seamen who had gone ashore in Invergordon to pick up their mail and do a little shopping. The Admiralty had failed to give its own officers adequate warning and therefore any opportunity to prepare the enlisted men for the coming shock. Tomkinson did not receive the details of the cuts until the evening of 12 September, when he arranged for them to be posted the following morning. The handling of what was always going to be an extremely delicate situation had been nothing short of a monumental blunder.

REFUSING ORDERS TO PUT TO SEA

On Sunday, 13 September, in and around the shore canteen in Invergordon groups of confused and angry enlisted men gathered and were heard to burst into occasional renditions of the famous song of insurrection, 'The Red Flag'. The political overtones subsequently ascribed to these 'canteen meetings' were mostly a result of crewmembers with links to the Communist Party opportunistically attempting to portray the Invergordon mutiny as a political grassroots class struggle rather than the apolitical show of force which it was.

As far as the average Royal Navy rating was concerned the confirmation of the size of the cuts, to say nothing of the inequity involved, represented far more than just a loss in pay. It was a betrayal. The realisation that there needed to be a united response to the cuts came not from groups of political ideologues on shore leave but from a series of relatively uncoordinated and spontaneous meetings held below the decks of the Atlantic Fleet, where the downing of tools combined with a general refusal to put to sea was quickly settled upon as the most appropriate and least violent form of protest. It was also decided that the moment to initiate the action would be when the big ships *Rodney*, *Valiant* and *Hood*, and the just-arrived flagship of the fleet, HMS *Nelson*, were poised to put to sea for exercises on the morning of Tuesday, 15 September.

The call to refuse orders to put to sea spread through the fleet like a bushfire and on the morning of 15 September only three ships, the heavy cruisers *Norfolk* and *York*, and the battlecruiser *Hood*, were able to report full musters. Even the Royal Marines, normally brought in to quell disturbances and keep order, but who also happened to be on the same pay rate as an able seaman and subjected to the same cuts, joined with the protesters.

Crews on *Hood* and *Nelson* refused to carry out anything more than routine harbour duties; those aboard *Rodney* and *Valiant* refused orders to prepare the ships for sailing. As the mutiny began to spread the crews demonstrated their solidarity by assembling on the decks and cheering. Officers warned the mutineers that they wouldn't get any further 'than the end of a rope', but the revolt had a momentum of its own now and could not be stopped. *Valiant*'s anchor crew refused to weigh anchor, an act that brought cheers from the crews of the ships moored around it. Stokers on the heavy cruiser *Norfolk* refused to enter the engine room. Most of the stokers of the heavy cruiser *Dorsetshire* simply refused to report for duty. Fifty stokers from the cruiser-minelayer *Adventure* were missing. At 9.16 am Rear-Admiral Tomkinson sent a telegram to the Admiralty stating that four of the vessels in its Atlantic Fleet had failed to put to sea. The mutineers had achieved their aim. Four of Britain's mightiest ships of war had been forced to remain at anchor in Cromarty Firth.

NO SCAPEGOATS

Unfortunately Tomkinson proved to be the last man the Admiralty should have chosen to negotiate a crisis with 12,000 enlisted men. When it came to establishing rapport with the lower ranks he was a disaster, admitting to 'never being a popularity Jack' with those below deck and being steadfastly of the opinion that those officers who tried to ingratiate themselves with enlisted men did more harm than good. The only product of excessive familiarity between an officer and an enlisted man, according to Tomkinson, was an erosion of discipline and authority. It was hardly surprising that no instances ever came to light in the official records of Tomkinson making any real effort to intervene, or of using the power and influence of his position to prevent the crisis from developing.

With the big ships still at anchor, the fragmentary nature of the mutiny began to surface. There was growing uncertainty as to what to do next, and even a fundamental dispute as to whether it was a mutiny at all, with many enlisted men and officers preferring to think of it as nothing more serious than an industrial strike that just happened to have occurred on Royal Navy ships rather than on the workshop floor. Fred Copeman, a twenty-four-year-old able seaman on HMS *Norfolk*, recorded in his journal: 'The mutiny was a spontaneous, commonsense form of strike action. It wasn't planned.' This isn't to say that strong personalities didn't begin to emerge on individual ships. There were firebrands like Willie Ryder and Alfred Fowler on *Rodney*, and Arthur Harwood on *Nelson*, but they were not part of a larger executive and very likely did not even know one another. They were lightning rods for the disaffection of their own crews certainly, but little more than that. Lists of the men involved compiled by ships' officers in the aftermath of the revolt failed to highlight any ringleaders. Nobody stood out. There were no organisational structures to target, no scapegoats to make examples of.

Subsequent events seem to bear out Copeman's claim of spontaneity. With so many ships involved, coordinating unified action became almost impossible. Beyond the galvanising act of preventing the ships from sailing it appeared that little thought had been given to what should come next. It was hoped, perhaps naïvely, that there would be a quick response from the Admiralty, and when no response had come by the end of the first day the determination of many began to waver. Some crews began considering a return to normal harbour duties, while the mood on other ships was to continue to do nothing.

A FACE-SAVING OLIVE BRANCH

The splits and divisions that were beginning to appear in the mutineers' ranks were exacerbated when Cabinet agreed to look into any individual cases of extreme hardship that the pay cuts might cause. This was the announcement that broke the mutineers' resolve, with some rankings seeing it as an olive branch and an opportunity for a face-saving return to work. Early in the evening of 16 September the crew of *Valiant*, the first to openly defy their officers, decided to resume their duties, and the mutiny was over.

The Invergordon mutiny involved more than 12,000 men who did nothing more than refuse orders to put to sea. No officers were harmed, no blood was spilled and it must rank as one of the most polite mutinies in history, though that isn't to say it was without its repercussions. The offices of the Communist Party's official newspaper, the *Daily Worker*, one of the few national newspapers that bothered to cover the incident, were raided and its executive arrested in accordance with the *Incitement to Mutiny Act* of 1797. The government was aware that mutinies had the potential to spark nationwide discontent, even revolution. Foreign currency holders who remembered all too well that the downfall of Kaiser Wilhelm II began with the mutiny at Kiel in 1918 withdrew £33 million worth of gold from London's banks in just three days, precipitating panic on the London Stock Exchange and resulting in England going off the Gold Standard on 21 September, thus preventing the conversion of sterling into gold and any subsequent run on the pound by nervous investors.

PLAYING DOWN THE MUTINY

Just as the military and political establishment in Brazil engaged in decades of suppression to prevent the publication of any lower-deck perspectives on the 1910 Revolt of the Whip, so to the British Admiralty prevented accounts of the Invergordon revolt being published by anyone who was not an officer. In the years that followed, the information the public was privy to was either the product of naval propaganda or leftist opportunism. The Admiralty's papers on the incident weren't released for more than forty years and, voluminous though they were, included not a single perspective from below decks. *The Mutiny at Invergordon* (1937), written by Commander Kenneth Edwards, attempted to reduce the whole affair to nothing more than a botched Bolshevik plot.

The mutiny proved the death-knell for Wilfred Tomkinson's career. Despite his own assessment that forcing the men back to work would result in an unacceptable escalation, the Admiralty felt he was far too lenient and for the next three years Tomkinson was reduced to half-pay. On the outbreak of World War II he was given the rank of flag officer in charge of shipping in the Bristol Channel.

The new First Lord of the Admiralty, Austen Chamberlain, made it clear he wasn't interested in reprisals in a speech in the House of Commons on 17 September 1931, in which he said: 'The past is past. It is in the interest of everyone in the navy or out of it to forget the mutiny. I am not going to look back. I am going to look forward.' He viewed it as neither a revolutionary act nor even particularly mutinous, rather the reaction of 'men who were frightened for their wives and their homes'. In its wake there was not a single reported incident of disrespectful conduct by a ranking man towards an officer, nor were any unpatriotic acts perpetrated upon the flag.

The massive social upheavals caused by the Great Depression had given rise to very real fears among Labour MPs of strikes in the nation's coalmines and urban unrest, and the last thing the government wanted was news of a mutiny to galvanise opposition to its social and economic reforms. It clearly suited the government to play down the incident. There would be no mention of the word 'mutiny', no public inquiry, and no court martials. Trials were held discreetly, out of public sight. Some 200 sailors were subsequently discharged from the service and a few officers were asked to take premature retirement.

As for the hated pay cuts, the Admiralty in the end accepted Tomkinson's recommendations that officers stay on the same rate of pay they were on prior to the budgetary announcement of 10 September and that enlisted men be forced to suffer a reduction in their wages no greater than 10 per cent. The mutineers had won a bloodless victory, and the incident came to be seen in time as one of the finer moments in the history of the Royal Navy.

In 1932 the Atlantic Fleet was renamed the Home Fleet in the hope the change might go some way to helping erase the Invergordon mutiny from the nation's consciousness.

‘NO ONE WILL BE SHOT WITHOUT FIRST EXHAUSTIVELY INVESTIGATING HIS ACTIONS.’

General Carlos Vergara, Chilean Minister of War

1931

LA REBELION DE LOS MARINEROS: THE CHILEAN SAILORS' MUTINY

In 1931 the League of Nations announced that of all the world's developed and emerging economies, none had been more devastated by the stock market crash of October 1929 and the fallout from the Great Depression than that of Chile. In fact Chile's economy was hit not once but twice. The Wall Street crash and the economic tidal wave it triggered coincided with the invention in Germany of a process to synthesise saltpetre, which brought a sudden end to Chile's grand monopoly on the mining of nitrates. Income from the nitrate mines not only underpinned Chile's resource-based stock market but also provided its government with almost 80 per cent of its revenues. In twelve months the nation's

Gross Domestic Product fell a staggering 14 per cent. Net exports and income from mining both declined by almost a third, and the government had gone to its debtor nations cap in hand asking for a moratorium on foreign debt repayments. Chile, once Latin America's most prosperous nation, was bankrupt.

In July 1931 the government of President Carlos Ibáñez del Campo fell, and a month later so did that of his replacement, Juan Esteban Montero Rodríguez. In early September, with no party able to command a clear majority in a fractured parliament, executive control over the country was in the hands of Vice-President Manuel Trucco, and political parties of all persuasions—socialists, conservatives, anarchists, militarists and communists—were falling over themselves trying to fill the political void.

With the economy collapsing and Parliament on the verge of becoming an irrelevance, the last thing Chile needed was a mutiny.

A PASSIVE NAVY

Chile's navy, unlike the more interventionist branches of the country's armed forces, had always enjoyed a reputation of relative passivity when it came to political and military affrays. It played only a minor role in the 1891 Civil War and remained mostly aloof from the coup that overthrew President Arturo Alessandri in September 1924. Despite this separation ending with the election of General Carlos Ibáñez as President in 1927 and his appointment of navy personnel to key government posts, the navy continued to operate within and remain faithful to its own institutional framework and code of conduct. The navy's enviable reputation for professionalism and for remaining calm in a crisis saw the government totally unprepared for the challenges its enlisted men were about to unleash.

In late August the Chilean Fleet, steaming north to escape the coming winter, was about to anchor in the port town of Coquimbo, 400 kilometres (250 miles) north of Valparaiso, to prepare for a series of training exercises. At the head of the fleet was the 32,500-tonne (32,000-ton) flagship *Almirante Latorre*, launched in 1913. It was the most powerful ship in the fleet, boasting ten 36-centimetre (14-inch) guns and a top speed of 23 knots. In addition to its usual complement of 834 officers and crew, *Almirante Latorre* was carrying twenty-one apprentices who had not joined up as teenagers in the usual way but had been brought in as adults to be trained as accounting assistants to the fleet's overworked supply officers. Nobody, it seemed, was concerned or thought it odd that the apprentices, selected solely upon their performances in one open examination, had somehow managed to dodge the usual series of one-on-one interviews and background checks designed to weed out those with a history of social and political activism.

OUTRAGED OFFICERS AND SAILORS

When Finance Minister Pedro Blanquier announced in late August that a series of public sector wage cuts ranging from 12 to 30 per cent would be introduced as part of the government's economic austerity program, there was outrage from officers and enlisted men alike. Their pay was already mediocre enough and offered little by way of compensation for their long absences from home and family. The majority of ordinary seamen had already drawn their pay far in advance and left it with their families so they could meet day-to-day living expenses until the fleet returned home. If the proposed cuts were implemented, the enlisted men and many officers who had also drawn their pay in advance would have no income at all until the end of December.

Sailors had already suffered a halving of their bonuses plus a 10 per cent cut in wages for the good of the nation. There seemed no end to it. Aboard *Almirante Latorre* two trainee accountants and socialist activists Manuel Astica and Agustin Zagal, spoke up. Astica suggested the crew prepare a list of demands, a tactic not without precedent as a means of dissent on Chile's factory floors and nitrate mines, only this time it would be laced with more than a dash of Bolshevik rhetoric. As the list of demands were being discussed, talk of the pay cuts was sweeping through the fleet's wardrooms and mess halls and in no time had reached the ear of Captain Alberto Hozven, the commander of *Almirante Latorre*. Hozven immediately ordered a delegation from every ship in the fleet to convene on the flagship's foredeck. It was time for a little talk.

Hozven, a strict disciplinarian and very unpopular with the lower ranks, lost no time in accusing the representatives from the other vessels, and his own assembled crew, of an almost traitorous lack of patriotism.

Talk of discontent was against the best traditions of the Chilean Navy, not to mention a swathe of navy regulations, was selfish, and must cease immediately. He refused to accept the petition that Astica and others had prepared and abruptly ended his speech with the customary rallying cry, 'Viva Chile!' When the cry failed to be greeted with the traditional three cheers, and the assembled men failed to go about their duties, Hozven must have realised the perilous situation he was in.

STORM THE BRIDGE

That afternoon a meeting of all off-duty petty officers and supply staff was held below decks on *Almirante Latorre.* Astica and Zagal attended the meeting, reminding those present who wanted to set aside the petition that it was their right to demand change and telling them they should refuse to be intimidated. Finally a show of hands on the need for direct action was asked for. Acting on the belief that they had the unspoken support of many of their own officers, whose salaries were about to suffer just as theirs were, it was decided to storm the bridge and take over the battleship on the stroke of midnight, lock their officers in their cabins, and use the mutiny to publicise their grievances to the nation.

At 11 pm on the night of 31 August the duty officers on board *Almirante Latorre* and the armoured cruiser *O'Higgins* were duly locked in their cabins. Petty officers throughout the fleet began organising their enlisted men who, by and large, were happy to oblige. Officers returning from shore leave were immediately led to their cabins and locked in, including Captain Hozven, who taunted his mutinous captors, daring them to shoot him before being forcibly taken to his cabin. By 4.10 am every ship in the fleet had joined the revolt, led by their individual chief petty officers and the six men in seniority below them. The petty officers on *Almirante Latorre* formed an 'Estado Mayor de las Tripulaciones' (EMT or General Staff of the Crews) and elected the ship's chief yeoman, Ernesto Gonzalez, to be their spokesman. Manuel Astica, who before joining the navy had been an active member of the Catholic union movement and a journalist on the Communist Party newspaper *La Razón*, was elected its secretary.

Of the fourteen ships of the Chilean Fleet moored in Coquimbo, only the destroyer *Hyatt* wavered in committing to the revolt. *Hyatt*'s crew was deeply devoted to the ship's commander, Captain Humberto Aylwin, who had heard of the mutiny while still on shore. Aylwin, with the option of staying ashore and keeping away from harm, was confident he enjoyed the loyalty of his crew and decided to go aboard. At this point he could have changed the course of the mutiny. Asked by his crew what course of action they should take, Aylwin responded that their loyalties must lie first with their fellow sailors. It will always be a point of conjecture, but if Aylwin had asked his men to oppose the mutiny they would very likely have done so, and other ships in the tightly knit destroyer fleet may well have joined them. But *Hyatt*'s crew followed the commander's advice and along with the other destroyers fell in with the rebel ships.

THE MUTINEERS' DEMANDS

More than twelve hours later, at 4.55 pm, the mutineers' demands were radioed from *Almirante Latorre* to the government in Santiago, as well as to other ships, inviting their officers and crews to join the revolt. During a recent refit in England *Almirante Latorre* had installed the most advanced radio transmitters of its day and its call to mutiny easily reached the submarine base 800 kilometres (500 miles) to the south at Talcahuano.

The primary points of the communiqué were:

1. Sailors' rates of pay to remain at current levels
2. Former government officials suspected of corruption to be brought to trial
3. The crews agree not to fire their ship's guns on the citizens of Coquimbo
4. The propaganda campaign against the armed forces was to cease
5. The sailors promised to keep the fleet at anchor until the situation was resolved
6. The government must respond to the above demands within forty-eight hours
7. The mutineers stressed that they harboured no political motives or thoughts of anarchy—the action was driven by a desire to improve the living conditions of the Chilean people.

Eight hours after this transmission another more radical set of demands was relayed that called for, among other things, the establishment of a gamut of new civil liberties that would apply to all Chilean citizens, a public works program geared to generate employment, the lowering of interest rates to stimulate investment, and suspension of the government's foreign debt repayments. The language of this second list of demands read with an eloquence that was lacking in the first, causing many in the government to think it could not possibly have been written by the 'lower decks'. It was also more overtly political, with demands centring on land reform and new taxes on the rich giving it a distinctly Marxist revolutionary feel.

THE INEVITABLE CONSEQUENCES

When news of the mutiny got out it quickly generated a number of inevitable consequences. In Santiago mobs marched on Congress. A general strike ordered by the Communist Party failed to achieve the widespread unrest some had hoped for but still managed to bring the capital's buses, trams and taxis to a halt. Reports of looting brought the army into city streets. Vice-President Trucco, fearing the unrest could spread to the mining region of the Atacama in the north, tentatively declared martial law. But it wasn't only the government that was nervous. Chileans remembered all too well the horrors of 1891, by far the bloodiest chapter in the nation's history, in which over 10,000 people lost their lives in the armed struggle between Congress and then president José Manuel Balmaceda. If the mutineers were seen as successful, their protest could spark more widespread revolt in the armed forces, or in the mining sector, to say nothing of what might happen among the tens of thousands of unemployed and disenfranchised. Who knew where it might end? Nobody wanted another civil war.

The government, fearing that an armed response might radicalise the rebels and lead to even greater unrest, decided to attempt a resolution through conciliation, appointing the navy's Admiral Edgardo von Schroeder as chief negotiator. Von Schroeder was well respected and his selection seemed a positive move. But a bizarre order from Vice-President Trucco that von Schroeder would under no circumstances be permitted to board any of the rebel ships was to result immediately in a farcical game of dockside brinkmanship.

When von Schroeders arrived in Coquimbo the rebels' representatives on *Almirante Latorre*, fearing arrest, refused to go ashore to meet him. Von Schroeder begged his superiors in Santiago to reconsider the ban on going aboard, but they refused. Almost an entire day of negotiating time was lost by the time the government agreed to a second request by von Schroeder late on 2 September. By the time von Schroeder boarded *Almirante Latorre*, it was too late to prevent sailors at the submarine base in Talcahuano the following day from sending a small flotilla of the Southern Squadron to Coquimbo to join the mutiny and demonstrate solidarity. On 2 September, the commander at Talcahuano, Admiral Roberto Chappuzeau, had made an unsuccessful appeal to his crews to sign a telegram denouncing the mutiny at Coquimbo.

In the early hours of 3 September a rumour began to circulate through the Southern Squadron that its commanders were considering sending the submarine tender *Araucano*, and a small flotilla of submarines, to Coquimbo to sink what ships they could and force the mutineers to surrender. A small group of rebel sailors boarded *Araucano*. After a brief confrontation with the tender's commander, who stormed off the ship in a rage, they disarmed the remaining officers and took the ship by force. Following this, in one of the more bizarre episodes of the entire mutiny, Admiral Chapuseaux ordered his officers not to assert control of their ships but to abandon them to the mutineers and come ashore. The mutineers in Coquimbo now had another twelve warships allied to their cause and, steaming to their aid, the ageing British-built cruiser *Blanco Encalada*, six submarine tenders and five submarines.

To complicate matters further, the sailors on the Talcahuano fleet issued a series of ultimatums of their own that, if anything, were even more left-wing than those from Coquimbo. Their petition called for the nationalisation of industry, for the wealth of the upper class to be sequestered and used to finance the nation's foreign debt, and the immediate seizing of assets belonging to those politicians who had presided over the bankruptcy of the nation.

Smaller acts of mutiny began occurring across the country. After reading of the mutiny in Concepción's newspapers, mutinous sympathisers overran a cadet school on the outskirts of Valparaiso, and Airforce Group Two assumed control of its base in Quintero, which was an old naval station. Many men stationed there had served with the crews in Coquimbo and had no intention of bombing their former shipmates. Perhaps if von Schroeder's brief had allowed him to board *Almirante Latorre* on his arrival in Coquimbo early on 2 September, the revolts at Quintero, Valparaiso and Talcahuano might not have occurred, and there might not have been a second mutinous fleet of Chilean warships steaming its way north.

A TENTATIVE AGREEMENT

In the wardroom of *Almirante Latorre*, von Schroeder met with the EMT and listened to their grievances. It was agreed he would arrange a review of their clothing allowances and the possibility of the government providing free uniforms, as well as arranging a review of the policy on food rationing and general working conditions, but he was unable to offer any encouragement on the broader social and economic issues such as increased public works programs or the halting of foreign debt repayments. Although a tentative agreement was reached on paper that stated the navy would look at their concerns and there would be no reprisals if all officers were immediately allowed to return to their posts, *Almirante Latorre*'s EMT, aware that the Southern Fleet was steaming north to join them, refused to continue the negotiations until the ships arrived. Von Schroeder, who had spent time in Talcahuano and knew firsthand of the squalid conditions in which the enlisted men and their families were forced to live, was furious that the navy had not moved earlier to lock down the port.

Vice-President Trucco meanwhile had authorised approaches to be made to the United States Government requesting a show of strength from its navy which, it was hoped, might break the mutineers' resolve. It was estimated that at least three heavy cruisers would be required to outgun the Chilean Fleet and form a sufficient deterrent, but the only available ships were moored on the US east coast and were at least nine to ten days away. The US Government denied Trucco's request and told him he was on his own. Von Schroeder, unable to report any progress in negotiating an end to the impasse, was recalled to Santiago, and the mutineers decided it was time to ready the ships for sailing. The time for talking was over.

A SHOW OF STRENGTH

On 5 September, the army was ordered to retake the submarine base at Talcahuano, the rebel strongholds at Valparaiso and Quintero, and a mutinous army base at Las Salinas. At Talcahuano, after a series of requests for the mutineers to lay down their arms went unheeded, infantry and cavalry brigades supported by artillery under the command of General Guillermo Novoa recaptured the base and took more than 2000 prisoners. By the following day a cadet school on Quinana Island had been captured and the rebellions in Valparaiso, Quinteros and Las Salinas had been put down.

The government now faced a dilemma. Needing to demonstrate its resolve to the mutineers at Coquimbo but not having sufficient naval vessels under its command with which to approach them, the decision was made to deploy the Chilean Air Force. Of course any display of firepower, no matter how threatening, had to be measured and carefully targeted. Nobody wanted to be responsible for giving an order that might result in the sinking of the nation's warships.

The recently formed air groups, created from an amalgam of the former navy and army air corps, were under the command of General Ramón Vergara, brother of the Minister of War. Vergara had been boasting to anyone who'd listen that his planes could end the mutiny in minutes if the order was given, and certainly its officers needed little encouragement to flex newly acquired muscle. On 6 September, with diplomatic options exhausted, an order was given to Air Group Two to approach the rebel ships, to shoot over and around them—but under no circumstances was any ship to be targeted specifically. It was hoped the show of strength would be enough to force the hand of the mutineers and result in their surrender. The government took the precaution of ordering aircraft engineers to accompany the pilots on the mission in an attempt to ensure that the planes were free from acts of sabotage from anyone harbouring rebel sympathies.

The aircraft, which included two Junkers heavy bombers and fourteen Falcon and Vickers light bombers, came in over Coquimbo Harbour at a height of about 300 metres (1000 feet) and were immediately met with a withering onslaught of anti-aircraft and small arms fire. Plumes of water erupted around the fleet as the Junkers dropped their payloads of 100 and 300 kilogram (220 and 661 pound) bombs. The ships fired thousands of incendiary bullets at the attacking aircraft and the air force later claimed that not a single plane returned to its airfield that wasn't riddled with bullet holes. None of the rebel ships reported any significant damage, although the submarine *Quidora*, an ageing hulk well beyond retirement, reported it had been made immobile after being hit by shrapnel. One sailor was killed and another injured while the air force suffered the loss of just a single aircraft, forced to crash land in the hills beyond the harbour after being repeatedly hit by gunfire from *Almirante Latorre.*

THE END OF THE MUTINY

By this time public support was squarely in favour of the government, particularly in the wake of the successful restoration of order in and around Valparaiso. This fact was not lost on *Almirante Latorre*'s EMT, who immediately requested the intervention of the Archbishop of Santiago, Monsignor Campillo, in the hope he might be able to negotiate a face-saving exit. But the time for the unconditional granting of rebel demands had passed, and when no response to this request was received, the officers of the Chilean Fleet were released from their cabins and asked by an increasingly anxious EMT what course of action they suggested could be taken.

It was at this time that two destroyers, *Riquelme* and the unsympathetic *Hyatt*, signalled *Almirante Latorre* that they would no longer participate in what was by now an obviously failed attempt at mutiny, and began to make preparations to sail back to their port city of Valparaiso. Then two other ships, the destroyers *Almirante Simpson* and *Orella*, put to sea. To those on *Almirante Latorre* it must have seemed as though the rebel fleet was disintegrating around them.

This led to an ill-conceived threat by Astica and *Almirante Latorre*'s EMT to shell Coquimbo and the nearby port town of La Serena, though what sympathy turning their guns on Chilean citizens would bring them was hard to fathom. The threat of shelling the city was also the final straw for those officers on *Almirante Latorre* who had up to that point been little more than passive onlookers. They stormed the deck, removed key personnel from their posts and restored order. Similar actions took place on other ships. White flags began to be raised across the fleet, and in a display of

Latin American panache the sailors wore their dress uniforms as they steamed back into Coquimbo Harbour. It was 8 September. The mutiny was over.

REPRISAL OF NAVAL AUTHORITIES

Retribution on the part of naval authorities was not long in coming. Court-martial proceedings were initiated within weeks of the surrender and fourteen of the ringleaders were sent to the prison at San Felipe to be executed. When the executions were postponed until after Chile's Independence Day celebrations, the delay gave various amnesty groups and Congress time to organise petitions to commute the sentences. In all, only thirty-three mutineers, including Manuel Astica, were given prison terms. When news came to light that many officers had agreed with the rebels' initial demands and had signed the original list of petitions, public feeling against the mutineers softened. In the end there were no executions, but over 3000 naval personnel were dismissed from the service over the coming months—and despite a major reshuffle of the officer corps only two lieutenant-commanders were dismissed. Others, like the commander of the submarine base at Talcahuano, Admiral Roberto Chappuzeau, slipped into discreet retirement. During the short-lived 100-day Socialist Republic that came to power in a coup on 4 June 1932, seven months after the mutiny, all the participants in the Sailors' Mutiny were pardoned.

The Sailors' Mutiny of 1931 was seen in hindsight by the majority of Chileans to have been not the result of any veiled conspiracies or political movements, but a response to a general malaise and erosion of discipline that paralleled the nation's economic woes throughout the 1920s, compounded by the 'economic blizzard' of the Great Depression and the deep cuts in public sector spending deemed necessary to fight it.

‘WE DO NOT INTEND VIOLENCE. OUR OBJECT IS PROTEST. NO ONE ON BOARD HAS BEEN HARMED.’

Radio message from *De Zeven Provinciën* to the world press

‘HEAVE TO! SHOW A WHITE TARPAULIN ON THE AWNING DECK! SURRENDER AND ABANDON SHIP!’

Cruiser *Java* to *De Zeven Provinciën*

1933

THE MUTINY ON *DE ZEVEN PROVINCIËN*

On the evening of 4 February 1933, Commander Eikenboom and most of his fellow officers of the Dutch cruiser *De Zeven Provinciën* ('*The Seven Promises*'), anchored in the northwestern Sumatran port of Oleh-leh, were spending a leisurely evening in town at an exclusive officers' club. Earlier that night a government spy had tried to warn his captain that a mutiny was likely in the wake of the recent cuts that saw the pay of Dutch sailors reduced by 14 per cent. Eikenboom laughed the suggestion of mutiny off and went ashore to the Afjeh Club determined to enjoy his evening. When he and his officers returned to the dock just before dawn, the 6605-tonne (6500-ton) *De Zeven Provinciën* was nowhere to be seen.

In the early 1930s nothing made mutineers out of ordinary sailors quicker than a pay cut. Just two years earlier the economic downturn resulting from the Great Depression saw cuts to sailors' wages bring mutiny to Britain's Atlantic Fleet moored at Invergordon, and to the Chilean Fleet at Coquimbo. Exports from the Dutch East Indies had been hit by the global downturn in demand, and pressure on the Dutch Government to rein in spending was acute. Civil service pay rates had just been slashed and it was rumoured more cuts were coming. The announcement of the cuts in January 1933 had already led to several cases of insubordination among the crews of the Dutch Fleet at anchor in the port of Surabaya. A mutiny on the cruiser *Java* had also been quickly put down.

THE SMACK OF APARTHEID

Although often referred to as a battleship, *De Zeven Provinciën* was a cruiser-sized warship built for coastal defence. Advances in warship design meant it was obsolete before it had even been launched. Its crew was a mix of Dutch and Javanese and had more than its fair share of militants, with the native Javanese suffering the forms of discrimination common to subjugated nationals: inferior wages and living conditions, few prospects for promotion and forced into their own unions. All Indonesians in the Dutch East Indies Navy worked below decks, and the Dutch Navy wouldn't begin commissioning its first Indonesian officers until just before the outbreak of World War II in 1939. The sailors' treatment smacked of apartheid and was worsened by differences in culture and language that reinforced bitterness and isolation and provided fertile ground for communist infiltrators.

Both the Dutch and the Indonesian sailors' unions had promptly cabled protests to the Dutch Government and organised meetings to discuss the coming cuts. With tensions on the rise, the commander of the Dutch East Indies Navy advised his captains to arm themselves with loaded revolvers and to be on the lookout for any signs of discontent. On 1 February all shore leave for enlisted men was cancelled until further notice.

The Communist Party had a strong presence within the Dutch Navy through the establishment of the Dutch Young Communist League, many graduates of which were sent to serve in the merchant and naval ships of the Dutch East Indies. So when the Dutch Government put down a revolt in the naval garrison at Surabaya on the island of Java and threw more than 400 dissenters into prison, it was a moment in the fight against the colonists that simply couldn't be allowed to pass unanswered. A member of the Comintern (Communist International) movement arrived from Singapore with instructions to the ringleaders of the crew on *De Zeven*

Provinciën to seize the ship, sail it southeast down the Sumatran coast to Java, shell the naval garrison at Surabaya, free the 400 prisoners, and demand an immediate reversal of the announced pay cuts.

OFFICERS IN IRONS

The mutineers struck in the early hours of Sunday, 5 February. Fourteen officers were still aboard *De Zeven Provinciën* when a core group of fourteen Javanese sailors, whose pay cut was even greater than that of their Dutch counterparts, stormed the bridge and held the assembled officers at bayonet before placing them in irons. The remainder of the Javanese crew, which numbered about 185 men, and many but not all of the Dutch crew, joined the insurrection. In the mêlée a junior officer managed to jump overboard unseen, and swim ashore. Some of the Dutch officers on board were completely unaware a mutiny was brewing until the ship loosed its moorings and headed out towards the Indian Ocean. Lieutenant Albert Nicholas Baron de Vos van Steenwijk, was in his quarters when awoken by the sound of the engines and was told via the telephone that mutineers had assumed control of the ship. The mutineers stormed the communications room and broadcast their intentions to the Dutch military.

Furious that his ship had been hijacked, Eikenboom commandeered the small steamer *Aldebaran* and, with a small detachment of infantry in addition to the steamer's complement of forty-five, began to give chase, in full knowledge that *De Zeven Provinciën*'s 28-centimetre (11-inch) guns could easily blow him from the water. Realising it would be essential to track the runaway ship's position in order to coordinate a pursuit, Eikenboom transferred to the faster and more manoeuvrable patrol boat *Eridanus*, while the Dutch military positioned the cruiser *Java* and the two destroyers *Piet Hein* and *Evertsen* at Surabaya to await *De Zeven Provinciën*.

SURRENDER OR WE OPEN FIRE

The renegade ship meanwhile was limping down the Sumatran coast towards the Sunda Strait. Originally designed for a top speed of 16 knots, the vessel was managing only 7 knots due to having been outfitted with massive amounts of heavy side armour that slowed its speed through the water. By now army detachments had been sent to the west Java coast to prevent the mutineers from running the ship aground and escaping. After five days and with the ship almost out of sight of Eikenboom, one of the officers on board managed to access the radio room and transmit precise details of their position. On the morning of 10 February the Dutch Defence Minister Laurentius Decker gave the order to attack. A Dornier flying-boat launched from the cruiser *Java* spotted *De Zeven Provinciën* and dropped leaflets onto the deck saying 'Surrender or we open fire'. The crew were given ample time to comply but there was no radio response, no white flag raised, and the ship neither slowed down nor changed course. It was decided the ship would be bombed, and if that didn't work, submarines would be ordered to torpedo it. The pilot of one of the Dorniers only needed one pass. He took his aircraft to 1200 metres (3900 feet) and released a single 800 kilogram (1760 pound) bomb, which struck the ship just behind the bridge, destroying its funnels and signal station. Twenty-two mutineers were dead and twenty-five more were badly injured. One of those killed was Koliot, a youthful Menadonese crewman from Sulawesi.

Dolf Wattimena, born in the Maluku Islands east of Sulawesi and on his first deployment with the Dutch Navy, was walking near the bridge when the bomb hit but somehow miraculously emerged without so much as a scratch. On picking himself up he heard cries for help from the wreckage surrounding the signal station and saw Koliot lying on his side. As Wattimena approached he could see that Koliot's abdomen had been ripped open. There was nothing he could do.

A BLOODY END

The mutiny had come to a bloody end. Mutineers and officers alike rushed the lifeboats but had no hope of evading capture. The mutineers, including the suspected ringleader, Corporal Maud Boshart, an engineer, were imprisoned on Onrust Island just off the coast from Batavia (now Jakarta). Five Dutch and nineteen Javanese sailors were eventually accused and tried of mutiny and treason and received prison sentences ranging from one to eighteen years.

Why was the mutiny on board *De Zeven Provinciën* treated so ruthlessly when only two years earlier the Invergordon mutiny in Scotland, also ignited in large part by a proposed cut in wages, was ended through negotiation? And when, in fact, those who prosecuted the mutineers could not cite a single example of an act of disrespect by a rating towards an officer? The answer most likely lies in the fact that unrest was widespread throughout the Dutch East Indies and it was felt that when a nation's armed forces were isolated and far from home overwhelming displays of force and intimidation worked better than negotiation.

RESULTS OF THE MUTINY

Few mutinies in history went on to have such profound and far-reaching effects upon government policy as the mutiny on *De Zeven Provinciën*. First of all, the navy conducted a purge of what it called 'undesirable elements', dismissing any enlisted man who had participated in any recent act of insubordination along with many of the administrators of the various employees' unions, which had long been viewed by the naval hierarchy as hotbeds of socialism. Even during the course of the actual mutiny itself, a directive was issued forbidding anyone in the employ of the Dutch Navy to read newspapers that promulgated socialist ideology. The mutiny also resulted in a significant shift to the right in Dutch politics, evidenced in the 1933 general election, which saw the right-wing Roman Catholic State Party win twenty-eight seats in the Dutch Parliament compared to the Social Democratic Workers' Party's twenty-two.

The legislative response soon began. On 22 May the *Civil Servants Prohibition Act* gave the government the authority to dismiss any government employees who were either supporters or members of certain politically undesirable organisations, and a list of associations regarded as being suspect was released on 24 July. In spite of official government inquiries into the mutiny on *De Zeven Provinciën* concluding that the mutiny was directly attributable to the announced pay cuts, not to socialist infiltration of the armed forces, the legislative push in the months after the mutiny suggested that it was every bit as ideological as it was a response to the more usual grievances of poor pay and conditions.

In July 1933 *De Zeven Provinciën* was withdrawn from service and reconfigured as a training ship. In 1936 it was renamed HNLMS *Soerabaja*, and in February 1942 it was sunk by Japanese bombers off East Java.

‘WHEN THE WHOLE CREW OF A SHIP GET TOGETHER IN THE MESS DECKS AND TALK ABOUT WALKING OFF, THERE MUST BE SOMETHING RADICALLY WRONG SOMEWHERE.’

Ordinary Seaman Robert White, deserter, HMCS *Nootka*, 27 October 1947

‘EVERY EFFORT WAS MADE IN THE *ONTARIO* AND 1949 MUTINIES TO HAVE INSUBORDINATE BEHAVIOUR LOOK UNLIKE MUTINY ... BUT THE ATTEMPT WAS FUTILE. THE FOUL STENCH OF MUTINY IS INCAPABLE OF TRANSFORMING ITSELF INTO THE HEALTHY AROMA OF GOOD BEHAVIOUR.’

Louis Audette, member, Canadian Maritime Commission, 1949

1942–49

DISSENSION IN THE ROYAL CANADIAN NAVY

In 1939, before the outbreak of World War II, the Royal Canadian Navy (RCN) consisted of just seven destroyers, four minesweepers, a two-masted schooner and a total of 1585 service personnel. By the time the war was over six years later that number had swelled to 956 ships and more than 93,000 men. Ships were commissioned at a faster rate than it was possible to properly train crews to sail them, and volunteers were taken from the civilian population on an unprecedented scale.

In the post-war period Canada experienced the largest demobilisation of any of the world's navies. A two-year period of transition began in 1945 to move from a wartime service to a peacetime navy of around 10,000 personnel, and was accompanied by an ongoing debate between the government and the navy hierarchy about the role of the navy in the new post-war environment. By 1948 the number of ships in the RCN had dwindled to just over fifty, with 1200 officers and 7600 enlisted men. But the rapid growth and then decommissioning of the service was to bring with it unanticipated problems in the discipline of its enlisted men and the inexperience of its officer corps. Some officers were so inexperienced they even lacked sufficient seagoing and nautical skills, a deficiency that was quickly noticed by their crews and did little to engender loyalty and respect.

MUTINY AND INSUBORDINATION GALORE

The 1940s were years replete with benign examples of mutiny and insubordination within the RCN. In Sydney, Nova Scotia, in November 1942 the crew of the armed yacht HMCS *Reindeer*, when denied an extended period of shore leave, openly questioned the mental capacity of their captain. In January 1944 some of the crew of the destroyer HMCS *Restigouche*, on convoy protection in the North Atlantic, stopped work and refused to resume until they'd received an apology from the ship's doctor who had unfairly accused them of theft. That same month on HMS *Nabob*, a US-built escort carrier in service with Britain's Royal Navy but crewed by Canadians, en route to New York, there was a 'sit-down' protest that almost spilled over into outright mutiny over living conditions.

In January 1945 a group of enlisted men on the corvette HMCS *Rivière-du-Loup* demanded the removal of an executive officer in whom they had no confidence after he was forced to assume command when the captain fell ill. In July 1947 a lock-in of enlisted men was about to be implemented on the destroyer HMCS *Nootka* when a report was received that another destroyer, HMCS *Micmac*, had collided with another ship in heavy fog near Halifax, and all thoughts of a lock-in were forgotten in the rush to get to their stricken comrades. The *Micmac*'s unfortunate collision could well have short-circuited a full-blown mutiny. HMCS *Nootka* was seething with unrest over poor living conditions and had experienced several instances of desertion, the other increasingly popular form of protest.

Examples of frustrated sailors expressing their discontent continued unabated, and it seemed it would be only a matter of time until the unrest spread all the way to the crown jewel of the RCN, the cruiser HMCS *Ontario*.

In August 1947, while at anchor off the coast of Vancouver Island, some of the *Ontario*'s junior ratings wanted to discuss aspects of the daily routine and the appropriate wearing of uniforms with the ship's executive officers. Unfortunately, the RCN tendency not to commit to paper the details of meetings between officers and crew make it impossible to identify why the meeting broke down and what then led to fifty crewmembers adding the removal of the executive officer, Commander J.V. Brock, to their list of grievances and locking themselves below deck in their mess room. The commander, Captain Jimmy Hibberd, was forced to communicate with the men using the ship's loudspeaker system. Rather than ordering the men fall in on deck and risk outright mutiny should the order not be obeyed, he simply spoke to them and after fifteen minutes was able to coax them back to duty. Commander Brock was subsequently, and most unfairly, transferred to another ship.

'SIR, THE MEN WON'T COME OUT'

By the time of the *Ontario* incident an unmistakeable pattern of mass protest in the form of lock-ins and sit-down stoppages had emerged in the RCN, going back to the first recorded instance of mass discontent on the destroyer HMCS *Skeena* in 1936. By 1947 the phrase, 'Sir, the men won't come out' was pretty much one the RCN, alone among the world's navies, could call its own. Acts of insubordination had become so common that Naval Service Headquarters (NSHQ) felt compelled to initiate a study into morale to identify the cause of the discontent. The study was quick to establish as one of the main reasons the complete absence of any officially sanctioned associations or avenues within the RCN designed to promote the welfare or hear the grievances of its sailors, with the result that sit-downs and lock-ins had come to be accepted even by the officer corps as a legitimate and acceptable form of protest. These were essentially harmless practices that provided the fleet with a safety valve for the airing and addressing of grievances that was unique among the world's navies.

A SERIES OF INSUBORDINATE INCIDENCES

In February and March 1949 the RCN entered a fresh period of unrelated incidences of insubordination. On 26 February, during refuelling in the Mexican port of Manzanillo, ninety men on the destroyer HMCS *Athabaskan* barricaded themselves in their mess room and refused to return to duty until their captain addressed their grievances. Early on the morning of 15 March the destroyer HMCS *Crescent*, sent to China to support and assist Western diplomats during the last throes of China's bloody civil war, was at anchor beneath the guns of Kiangwin Fortress on China's Yangtze River at Nanking when eighty-three men locked themselves in their mess rooms and refused to respond to a 9.00 am call to clear the lower decks. On 20 March, just five days after the incident on *Crescent*, the light aircraft carrier HMCS *Magnificent*, on duty in the Caribbean, saw thirty-two aircraft handlers refuse to return to their cleaning stations.

Recent reorganisations in the structuring of officers and enlisted men in the RCN had resulted in a preponderance of officers in relation to lower deck numbers on all three vessels, which was particularly evident when the crews had to perform labour-intensive duties and was certainly a factor in the protests on *Athabaskan* and *Crescent*. After a relatively incident-free 1948, suddenly it seemed it was only a matter of time until the RCN would have to confront its first full-scale mutiny.

When *Athabaskan* had to refuel in Manzanillo, an inexperienced executive officer who had joined the ship's company only two weeks earlier hadn't changed the duty roster to the 'tropical routine' that would have had the difficult job done before the heat of the day took hold. The recent reduction in the number of enlisted men meant there were too few ratings available for what was an unenviable and energy-sapping task, plus there was the prospect of an afternoon's work in the tropical sun due to the unaltered roster. After locking themselves in their mess room the men rose to attention when the ship's commander, Captain Medland, arrived. He addressed them, he said, not as their commanding officer, but as their executive officer intent only on offering advice. It was a cool approach to a situation that was by any reasonable application of the definition, mutinous.

On *Crescent* the crew had been faced with excessive sentry duty while moored on the Yangtze River, just weeks after officer numbers had been increased from 42 to 62 and crew numbers cut from 150 to 125. The night before the lock-in saw overworked sentries hauling crates of beer meant for the British Embassy to the docks, protecting the ship's canteen against looters and replacing the gangplank after it was washed away in the swift current after a night of torrential rain. Breaking point came when the sentries' request to have their shift split into two watches went unheeded. The next morning the overworked sailors had had enough. When the call to fall in was made at 8.00 am on 15 March, only senior hands appeared on deck. Eighty-three crewmen remained locked below and, even as they were being piped to fall in, were busy trying to rally other crewmembers, including the stokers, to join them. Several of the ringleaders had been involved in the *Ontario* incident in August 1947. Although in the RCN what was happening on *Crescent* that morning was just another lock-in, in any other navy it was mutiny.

HMCS *Crescent*'s acting commander, Lieutenant-Commander D.W. Groos, fully aware that he was a long way from home as well as being conscious of the importance of keeping order in the midst of a civil war in a foreign country, arranged for one of the able seamen to come to him and advise him of their grievances. Then Groos went to the mess room and spoke to the men, promising he would work to address their complaints if they came to him one by one. In doing this he was ensuring that the complaints would be heard in a manner consistent with RCN protocols while at the same time avoiding a mess-room confrontation that could well have resulted in the sort of mass insubordination that defines mutiny.

The protest on the light aircraft carrier HMCS *Magnificent* was by far the most benign of the three protests. The first two incidents were unrelated, but those involved in the protest on *Magnificent* had full knowledge of the events on *Athabaskan* and *Crescent* and hoped to achieve similar concessions. Facing a rigorous and demanding schedule of flying programs as part of the exercise in the Caribbean, a group of aircraft handlers briefly refused to return to their stations and aired a series of complaints including leaky showers, bedbugs, overcrowding, and a request for the establishment of a welfare committee which *Magnificent*'s executive officers had previously refused to establish.

On its own this was very much a minor incident and was quickly dealt with, but it had been the latest in an odd series of mischievous acts. Three weeks after the light aircraft carrier was commissioned, a small Carley float, an American-designed lifeboat, had been cut adrift and a quarterdeck rope ladder partially cut through, which could well have led to a serious accident. The wardroom was broken into and more than thirty bottles of wine were stolen. A telescope belonging to one of the ship's executive officers had been thrown overboard. Side ladders had been loosened and allowed to fall into the sea, the radar disabled, sand added to the arrester lines on the flight deck—which could have jeopardised the safe return of aircraft—and an aircraft's reserve oil tanks were found to be empty the day after they had been filled. These incidents took place over many months and during a time of high turnover of personnel, which made the identification of the culprits almost impossible.

The word 'mutiny' was something the Canadian Navy had consistently refused to utter over the years, an attitude exemplified by *Athabaskan*'s captain who, during talks with his recalcitrant crew, had tactfully placed his cap over a list of their grievances to lessen the possibility that their actions might be termed mutinous. Nevertheless, the inescapable conclusion was that these new outbreaks of disobedience represented open challenges to naval authority, clearly deserved to be seen as mutinous, and likely would have been if they had occurred under the rigorous eyes of the British Royal Navy. The Canadian Navy's attitude towards low-level but technically mutinous acts was to let them be addressed without recourse to official inquiries, and to nip any dissent at the coalface.

THE *MAINGUY REPORT*

The late 1940s was a time when many Western governments were increasingly sensitive to the spread of communism in the armed services. With a general election coming up in June, the Canadian Government decided to initiate its own commission of inquiry into the three incidents, and other matters, and in November 1949 its findings, summarised in the *Mainguy Report*, the most thorough and wide-ranging examination into the RCN ever conducted, were presented to the government.

The commission of inquiry, chaired by Rear-Admiral Rollo Mainguy, Flag Officer Atlantic Coast, was a watershed in the history of the RCN. It found no evidence of communist infiltration of the RCN, nor evidence of collusion between the ships' crews, and that the recent protests were in fact poorly articulated, spontaneous and uncoordinated. It acknowledged that not all the men who were locked in their mess rooms were there because they supported the various actions, but once inside felt compelled to stay because of the fear of being seen not to support their shipmates should they leave. The report was also critical of some petty officers and executive officers who, it was felt, must have known of the discontent but due to the relative inexperience that permeated the officer corps failed for whatever reason to inform their captains of their concerns.

The report also cited frequent changes to daily routines without adequate reasons providing a primary cause for discontent, and the absence of welfare committees contributing to crews having no option but to express their grievances in ways that were mostly awkward and poorly articulated. There was also pointed reference made to a largely uncaring officer corps that had inherited many of the aristocratic tendencies of Britain's Royal Navy—which were not representative of a more egalitarian Canadian society. In sum, the incidents that had plagued the RCN over so many years were seen as petty grievances that were easily dealt with, but any one of which could just as easily have escalated into open rebellion. The report, however, failed to properly examine the many strains placed upon the navy's enlisted men and its officers by the unprecedented speed of demobilisation after the war and the complex task of restructuring as it made the transition to a peacetime navy.

Many a mutiny has been sparked by lesser grievances than those that plagued the Canadian Navy in the 1930s and 1940s. In the end it was a mix of good fortune and adequate management that the stain of outright mutiny that has blighted the history books of almost all the world's blue-water fleets did not and has not, so far, left its imprint on the Royal Canadian Navy.

'THE SUPPRESSION OF MUTINY IS THE MOST MERITORIOUS OF ALL MILITARY SERVICES.'

John Jervis, 1st Earl of St Vincent, First Lord of the Admiralty 1801–04

1949

THE *CHONGQING* MUTINY

The warship HMS *Aurora* was an Arethusa-class light cruiser, launched on 20 August 1936 and commissioned into the Royal Navy on 12 November 1937. Attached to the Home Fleet's Second Cruiser Squadron, *Aurora* was destined to see a lot of action. In 1939 it was engaged in the search for the German pocket battleships *Scharnhorst* and *Gneisenau*, and in May 1941 participated in the massive and successful Allied hunt for the German battleship *Bismarck*, which had sunk the battlecruiser HMS *Hood* and cost the lives of all but three of its 1418 crewmembers. In October 1941 *Aurora* was transferred to the Mediterranean where it made up part of the newly formed K-Force with its fellow Arethusa-class cruiser *Penelope* and two destroyers, *Lively* and *Lance*, and engaged in the interception of Italian convoys. *Aurora* also took part in the invasion of Sicily and the Allied landings at Salerno, and gave support at the liberation of Athens from Nazi occupation in 1944.

Aurora had seen more than its fair share of combat during World War II, but at war's end it was just another anonymous light cruiser, always sailing in the shadows of ships with names like HMS *Warspite* and *Ark Royal.* It wasn't known by anyone outside the navy and in all likelihood never would have been. *Aurora* was sold to the Nationalist Chinese Navy of Chiang Kai-shek on 19 May 1948 and renamed *Chongqing.* Preparations were made to sail it to China. Its anonymity was about to come to an end.

SAILING IN CHOPPY WATERS

Since the end of World War II in 1945, Chiang Kai-shek and his Chinese Nationalist Party, which had governed China since 1928, had been fighting a losing battle against the Communist guerillas of Mao Zedong, who were sweeping across China and pushing Chiang's army ever further south. It was a period of military and political decline for the Nationalists, and it was in the midst of this period, on 14 August 1948, that its navy took delivery of the *Chongqing* and made its flagship. But this would not represent any grand rebirth of a mighty Nationalist fleet. Almost as soon as the ship arrived, there were problems with morale.

Just days after the new flagship arrived, almost a third of the engineering and boiler crews deserted. It was hardly surprising. The Nationalists were fast running out of money. The continuing absence of paycheques had been a burning issue with its soldiers and sailors for some time, and wasn't likely to be resolved anytime soon amid the increasing disorganisation and disintegration of the government.

In February 1949, *Chongqing* was given orders to proceed up the Yangtze River, the last great natural barrier to the rest of China, to help prevent the forces of Mao Zedong's People's Liberation Army (PLA) from crossing the river and spilling over into southwest China. Although the Yangtze stretched for many hundreds of kilometres either side of the advancing Communist forces, it possessed relatively few suitable crossing points, and the presence of a heavily armoured warship would certainly make any crossing more problematic.

Reliable information on the precise sequence of events leading up to the *Chongqing* mutiny are difficult to uncover, but according to US Naval Intelligence the ship's new commander, Captain Lu Donggo, had without authorisation ordered it to sea from its moorings in Shanghai Harbour on 25 February, and when a safe distance from port had announced to his astonished crew that he had personally taken over the ship and would be issuing his own orders, and that he expected those orders to be followed. A small number of the crew who felt loyal to the ship's previous popular and respected commander, Captain Deng Zhaoxiang, who was still on board, refused to submit to Lu's actions and threw him overboard. Lu's supporters in turn wrested control of the ship back from the Nationalist sailors and immediately set a course north along the coast in the direction of Communist-controlled Manchuria. Later that day, on learning of the mutiny, the Chinese Communist Party proclaimed the establishment of the Navy of the East China Military Area Command.

Over the next two weeks *Chongqing* sailed northwards. At the port of Chefoo (now Yantai), a small trading centre established by the British in 1862 and now in Communist hands, the ship stopped and the crew allegedly unloaded more than half a million US dollars of Nationalist money before sailing on. Just months earlier, *Chongqing* had overseen the Nationalist government evacuation of the city in the face of encroaching People's Liberation Army units.

CHASING THE *CHONGQING*

The Nationalists, meanwhile, had no intentions of letting their prize flagship escape unhindered and immediately sent their air force in pursuit. Its planes caught up with the vessel along the northern shoreline of Bo Hai Gulf on its way to Dalian in the northeastern province of Liaoning. The Nationalist pilots claimed to have scored several direct hits on the ship and there were even unconfirmed reports that it had been sunk. When *Chongqing* docked at Dalian, however, not only was it not in danger of sinking but appeared to have emerged from the running battle remarkably unscathed. On 12 March the humiliation for the Nationalists increased with a radio broadcast confirming that two warships, names unspecified, that had been sent to enforce *Chongqing*'s return had themselves been sunk by Communist forces with assistance from their Russian allies.

On 18 March, the Nationalists' fortunes began to change. *Chongqing* had been sighted at anchor in the Manchurian port of Huludao. Huludao was the scene of the humiliating retreat of the Nationalist army just four months earlier in the wake of the Liaoshen Campaign, which saw over 470,000 of its troops either killed or taken prisoner and the balance of power swing to the Communists for the first time in the war.

At Huludao the Nationalist air force caught up with the renegade ship. After two air raids and several hits, *Chongqing* began to list to starboard, and although the damage inflicted didn't sink it, Chinese Communist Party (CCP) officials later decided to scuttle it rather than risk it falling back into the hands of the Nationalists. When the ship finally rolled the dramatic scene was captured in a series of aerial pictures taken by Nationalist reconnaissance aircraft that clearly showed the cruiser lying on its side, its superstructure in the water. The CCP, not wanting the Nationalists to claim credit for the sinking, issued a statement claiming that *Chongqing* had been torpedoed by United States bombers and submarines, a claim which, though later retracted, had to wait almost fifty years to be officially laid to rest with a reference in the 1998 edition of the *Chinese Naval Encyclopedia* that its loss was due to air attacks mounted by the Nationalist air force.

The loss of *Chongqing* was a further debilitating blow to the morale of the Nationalist armed forces and its supporters, who had always believed in their so-called 'mandate of heaven', an unshakeable belief that they and they alone had a divine right to rule China. The mutiny and the loss of face associated with its defection caused many Chinese to doubt the mandate's legitimacy, and is universally seen as a key turning point in the war.

One of the problems with analysing the *Chongqing* mutiny is the lack of documentation and any detailed insights into the personalities and agendas of those involved. What was the motivation behind Captain Lu's extraordinary decision to hijack the ship? Was it the promise of half a million dollars of Nationalist money in the hold? Had the Chinese Communist Party conspired with the captain and crew to steal the Nationalists' most potent and symbolic warship, or was it a spontaneous act?

What is not in dispute is that soon after his arrival in Communist-held territory, Deng Zhaoxiang was rewarded with the post of president of the Andong Naval Academy, and in 1960 became deputy commander of the Chinese Navy. This suggests that at some point early on in the mutiny Deng had fallen in with the mutineers, and possibly assisted in getting *Chongqing* safely to Huludao. The fact he didn't join the Communist Party for another fifteen years also tends to suggest that he had nothing to do with the mutiny but only joined in later, which would have caused some to suspect his loyalty.

When the age of steam replaced the age of sail, mutinies lost their ability to inspire and the oceans of the world seemed smaller, and because the details of the *Chongqing* mutiny are difficult to uncover and insights into its protagonists lack the depth of more celebrated mutinies, it's tempting to dismiss it and move on to more adventurous tales of maritime mischief. But the repercussions of the mutiny make it essential knowledge.

THE END OF NATIONALIST HOPES

In the following month, April 1949, the *Chongqing* mutiny resulted in the defection to the Communist side of around thirty Nationalist ships, including patrol boats, landing boats, a destroyer and two of its escort vessels, and several auxiliary craft, as well as more than 1200 sailors, from the Second Fleet of the Kuomingtang Navy under the command of Rear-Admiral Lin Zun. This marked the end of Nationalist hopes of holding their defensive lines along the western banks of the Yangtze, for without a navy to help prevent the PLA from surging across the river, any chance of holding onto southern China was gone. It was only a matter of time before Chiang Kai-shek and his desire for a democratic, free China would retreat with him across the Formosa Strait to the island of Taiwan.

There is also the effect the mutiny had on the CCP. Fearful that a mutiny could emerge from within the CCP's own ranks, it was decided that in order to maintain a greater level of control the Chinese Navy would be split into three separate fleets, much as it had been in the nineteenth century.

For all the enduring romance of the mutiny on the *Bounty* or the horrifying, bloody rebellion on the decks of the *Hermione* they, like almost all mutinies, were extremely isolated events. They had no impact upon foreign policy and apart from the mutineers, officers and their families affected no one else. The *Chongqing* mutiny, by contrast, resulted in one government losing its entire navy to its mortal enemy at a pivotal moment in the midst of a bloody civil war and helped deliver an entire nation to Communism. On this basis alone it remains to this day the most significant and far-reaching mutiny in history.

‘THAT’S THE SILLIEST THING I EVER HEARD.’

Franklin Cave, mother of Clyde McKay, when told her son had become a mutineer

1970

THE SS *COLUMBIA EAGLE* INCIDENT

At the height of the Vietnam War in 1970, more than 300 privately owned merchant vessels were contracted by the United States military to ferry supplies to its troops in Vietnam under the auspices of the Military Sealift Command (MSC). In the four years to 1969 the MSC transported a total of almost 56 million tonnes (55 million tons) of combat equipment and supplies, as well as troops and fuel, into the deepwater ports of South Vietnam. The Vietnam sealift transformed the Pacific Ocean into a maritime highway for the largest expeditionary army in history, and the US merchant fleet had never had it so good. For those who sailed on its ships, the late 1960s and early 1970s were boom times.

The SS *Columbia Eagle* was a civilian freighter constructed and launched in 1945 for the purpose of transporting equipment and supplies to Allied forces in the South Pacific. Originally named *Pierre Victory*, it was purchased by the Columbia Steamship Company of Portland, Oregon at the close of the war and renamed *Columbia Eagle*. On 20 February 1970 it departed Long Beach, California on a supply charter with the Department of Defense, carrying a 4570-tonne (4500-ton) cargo of napalm and detonators bound for American forces in the Thai port city of Sattahip. *Columbia Eagle* transported the cargo of anyone who was prepared to hire it to wherever in the world they wanted it to go. It had no fixed operating schedule, sailed no prescribed routes and had no regular ports of call. It was what was known in the trade as a 'tramp steamer'.

COMMANDEERING THE *COLUMBIA EAGLE*

Two days out from Sattahip, two crewmen entered the cabin of Chief Mate Herrick Morgan and pointed a semi-automatic pistol at his head. He was told to call out to the adjoining cabin and ask Captain Donald Swann to come in. When Swann entered the room he was confronted with a situation no captain in the US Merchant Marine had ever been trained to deal with. Held at gunpoint, Swann was ordered to plot a new course for Cambodia, at that time a neutral country with no extradition treaty with the United States, and to order twenty-four of the vessel's thirty-nine crewmembers to abandon ship. The officers were told there was a bomb on board that would be detonated if the hijackers' demands were not met, and that this was only the first of several mutinies and hijackings planned to highlight opposition to the US-led war. Swann ordered his men to the lifeboats, telling them it was merely a drill, and began to plot a new course for Sihanoukville, Cambodia's only deepwater port. Unbeknown to the mutineers, Swann then ordered his helmsman to steer a slightly circuitous path, in the hope this might allow additional time for any pursuing US vessels to overtake them.

The twenty-four sailors scrambled into two lifeboats and waited an hour for a signal from the bridge to return to the ship, only to see *Columbia Eagle* go full ahead and begin to disappear from view as it accelerated to its maximum speed of 19 knots.

Despite not having a radio the abandoned men did have ample supplies of food and water, the sea was calm, and they were safe in the midst of one of the world's busiest trade routes. Knowing it was only a matter of time until they were spotted, they turned their attention to piecing together what could possibly have prompted the decision to abandon them. Why were they being left behind? Why had the remaining crew not followed them into the lifeboats? Some thought it was a joke, while others began to think the unthinkable. Perhaps there had been a mutiny. But mutinies were a thing of the past. Everyone knew there hadn't been an armed mutiny on a US-flagged vessel in over 150 years. Nobody even used the word 'mutiny' any more unless they were reading from a history book. Surely there must be another explanation?

Later that evening, as the bewildered men were being picked from the waters of the Gulf of Siam by the munitions ship SS *Rappahannock*, its captain was told that while mustering the lifeboats someone thought he'd seen a man on *Columbia Eagle*'s bridge holding a handgun. Throughout the night *Rappahannock* tried without success to make radio contact with *Columbia Eagle*. It wasn't until mid-afternoon of the following day that confirmation came from the hijacked ship that the vessel had in fact been commandeered. The two men, it was emphasised, were desperate. If the Cambodian Government didn't do what they wanted them to do and seize the ship, they were prepared to detonate their bomb and scuttle it. Their sole motive, they claimed, was their opposition to US involvement in Vietnam.

NOTHING MORE THAN A 'HIPPIE-YIPPIE'

The two mutineers, Alvin Glatkowski, twenty, and Clyde McKay Jr, twenty-five, didn't fit the terrorist profile. When told of their stated opposition to the war as the reason for their actions, one of the crewmen rescued by *Rappahannock* claimed neither of them 'could tell Marx from Lenin'. Back home in California, Glatkowski's stepfather referred to him disparagingly as nothing more than a 'hippie-yippie'. Glatkowski's wife Florence, who was expecting their first child, simply refused to believe he was guilty of the anti-US sentiment attributed to him, while the mother of his co-conspirator Clyde McKay said plainly: 'That's the silliest thing I ever heard.'

McKay and Glatkowski had both come from broken families and grown up in environments lacking in love and familial support. They first met at a Seafarers International Convention in Long Beach, California. McKay came from a military family in San Diego, ran away from home when a teenager to join the French Foreign Legion, then signed onto *Columbia Eagle* as a fireman. After marrying Florence, Glatkowski had worked as a gas station attendant and later as a handyman in an apartment complex before enlisting with the Merchant Marine, and on *Columbia Eagle* would be the assistant to the bedroom steward. Glatkowski was described by family as a hardworking individual though prone to being easily led.

Through the latter stages of the Vietnam sealift a shortage of qualified seamen saw many people accepted into the Merchant Marine who might otherwise not have been considered. McKay and Glatkowski had been swept up in the fervour of the anti-war movement, as was confirmed later in interviews with American correspondents in which they both claimed to be sympathetic to the view of the left-wing anti-war movement Students for a Democratic Society (SDS). However, rather than the mutiny being the product of any organised political agenda the consensus, at least among the rescued crewmen, was that the two mutineers had been high on pot for the majority of the voyage and had simply gone nuts. Glatkowski later claimed to have been smoking cigarettes laced with amphetamines in the days leading up to the mutiny.

The argument that McKay and Glatkowski's actions were ill-conceived or spontaneous carries little weight, however. In a hearing after *Columbia Eagle* was reunited with its crew in the Philippines it came to light that the mutineers had brought a .38 calibre revolver on board before departing Long Beach, and had shown it to one of the members of the crew.

PURSUING THE STOLEN SHIP

As *Columbia Eagle* headed towards Cambodian territorial waters, *Rappahannock* radioed the US Naval Communications Center in Manila, which in turn alerted Pacific Fleet Headquarters in Hawaii. Admiral John Hyland ordered the US Coast Guard Cutter *Mellon* and the amphibious transport ship USS *Denver*, the two ships closest to *Columbia Eagle*'s position, to pursue the stolen ship and if necessary take it by force. It wasn't until 1.56 am on 15 March, almost a full twenty-four hours after the incident, that news of the mutiny reached the State Department in Washington DC. Hastily convened talks between President Richard Nixon and the Commander-in-Chief US Pacific Command (CINCPAC) highlighted concerns over the diplomatic complexities of boarding a vessel by force while in the territorial waters of another country, to say nothing of the mutineers' threat to destroy the ship. Hyland's order was reversed.

On *Columbia Eagle* tensions were rising. With Glatkowski and McKay taking turns overseeing the wheelhouse and making certain the ship stayed on course, the officers and crew who remained on board were beginning to discuss how they could best retake the ship. Chief Mate Herrick Morgan was the first to openly challenge the authority of the mutineers when he charged McKay with a crowbar, only to have McKay fire a warning shot above his head. First Assistant Engineer Leopold Tober fashioned a crude but effective blowgun using a length of old pipe and a fire extinguisher for propulsion, but never found an appropriate moment to use it.

On Sunday 15 March, *Columbia Eagle* passed into Cambodian territorial waters. That night McKay and Glatkowski slept in shifts on the aft deck, threatening to shoot their weapons into the detonators stored on deck should anyone be foolish enough to approach them. The following day, two Cambodian warships drew alongside, boarded *Columbia Eagle*, and disarmed McKay and Glatkowski. The two mutineers and Captain Swann were transferred to one of the Cambodian boats and taken to the Naval Chief of Staff Ang Kim Ly, who immediately issued an order for *Columbia Eagle* to be brought closer to shore, gave the mutineers back their weapons and ordered them to return to the ship to oversee its approach.

On Tuesday 17 March, McKay, Glatkowski and Swann were flown to the Cambodian capital, Phnom Penh, and into the centre of a revolution. When they arrived there was rioting in the streets. North Vietnamese businesses and shops were being attacked and burned by angry mobs. Despite immediately being granted political asylum, it was suggested to McKay and Glatkowski that they be confined for their own protection until the violence subsided. In what seems like an unsurpassed act of naïvety, McKay admitted in an interview soon after his arrival in Phnom Penh that he was hoping to provide President Nixon with an incentive to wind down the war by effectively removing *Columbia Eagle*'s cargo of napalm from the battlefield.

In the afternoon of 18 March, still in detention, Captain Swann learned that the pro-North Vietnamese government of Prince Norodom Sihanouk had just been officially brought to an end with an historic vote in the

National Assembly. Prime Minister Lon Nol proclaimed himself the head of state of the new Khmer Republic.

McKay and Glatkowski, who had come to Cambodia in the hope of gaining asylum in a communist nation, now found themselves prisoners of a right-wing regime. The suggestion by the exiled Prince Sihanouk that the hijacking had simply been a plot to deliver weapons to the new government now saw McKay and Glatkowski suspected of being CIA operatives, hardly the sort of anti-US image they were looking to cultivate in their adopted nation. Their hopes of a life in exile had been dashed, and it was only a matter of time until they would be given over into US custody.

INCARCERATION AND SUSPECTED MURDER

On 8 April, Captain Swann and *Columbia Eagle* were allowed to depart Cambodian waters. Rendezvousing with the US Coast Guard Cutter *Chase*, *Columbia Eagle* sailed to the Subic Bay Naval Base on the Philippines island of Luzon where its crew was reunited and its cargo of detonators and napalm loaded onto another ship for the journey back to Thailand. Despite an extensive search of the ship by naval explosive experts, no trace of a bomb was ever found. Later, three members of the crew, among them the man who had been shown the gun at the beginning of the voyage and not reported it, were suspected of passively supporting McKay and Glatkowski and forced to hand in their Merchant Marine cards. Formal charges of aiding and abetting a mutiny were never pursued.

McKay and Glatkowski were held in detention for several months, initially in the pleasant surrounds of Phnom Penh's naval officers' quarters on the banks of the Mekong River, before being transferred on 4 July to a prison ship moored in the river. In the absence of an extradition treaty it's doubtful that either of the two mutineers would ever have faced US justice if Glatkowski had not been adjusting poorly to his semi-incarceration. His wife had given birth to their first child four months earlier and so far he had not received any correspondence from her or any other family member. He was transferred to Tak Hmau Psychiatric Hospital on 6 September after he had reportedly taken to consuming his own excrement and urine. When the US State Department was made aware of his deteriorating mental state, which included two attempts at suicide, it was decided to make the Cambodian authorities aware that the United States would look with compassion on any request Glatkowski made to return home on medical grounds. On 15 December Alvin Glatkowski walked into the US Embassy in a state of near-total nervous collapse, and gave himself up.

Already indicted *in absentia* by a federal grand jury, Glatkowski was sent home in the company of US marshals to face charges of assault, kidnapping and dereliction of duty. In March 1971 he pleaded guilty in a Los Angeles District Court and was sentenced to ten years' imprisonment for mutiny and five years for assault, to be served concurrently.

Meanwhile, minimal supervision on their Mekong River prison ship saw McKay, who like Glatkowski had been indicted *in absentia*, and another American, army deserter Larry Humphrey, able to walk the length and breadth of the ship on their own and even granted permission to go into town for shopping and meals in the company of their guards. On 1 October the two men were taken from the ship and escorted to the Palais du Government official guesthouse, and on the night of 28 October, while dining at a local restaurant, managed to shake off their guards and disappear in a stolen car into the labyrinth of the capital's streets and alleyways. McKay and Humphrey were officially declared missing on 4 November 1970. They were never seen or heard from again.

What happened to McKay and Humphrey became a point of contention for over thirty years. A reported sighting of the two of them masquerading as journalists in Cambodia's Kampong Cham Province was never confirmed. In 1971 rumours arose that they had been murdered by the Khmer Rouge. In 1973 it was claimed they were working agricultural plots overseen by the Vietcong near the city of Kampong Sre. On 1 August 1978, with no evidence to suggest McKay was still alive, all charges against him were suddenly dropped, despite the crime of kidnapping carrying no statute of limitation. If indeed Clyde McKay was out there somewhere in the jungles of Indochina, he was free to come home.

In 2001 a former Vietnam War photographer named Tim Page assisted in the return to the United States of human remains that were identified by the Pentagon as belonging to Clyde McKay. In their book *The Eagle Mutiny* (2001), Richard Linnett and Roberto Loiederman claim the full remains of Clyde McKay were finally returned to his family in 2005.

Columbia Eagle was eventually sold for scrap in Taiwan.

'THE ARMOR OF THE STATE AND PARTY IS SO THICK THAT EVEN DIRECT HITS WON'T MAKE A DENT ... THIS MACHINE HAS TO BE BROKEN FROM THE INSIDE.'

Valery Sablin, Captain 3rd Rank and Political Commissar, Frigate *Storozhevoy*

1975

THE *STOROZHEVOY* MUTINY

Valery Sablin loved his country. He was proud of its proletarian beginnings and was dedicated to the principles of Marxism–Leninism. As a sailor he continued to draw inspiration from the revolutionaries on the battleship *Potemkin* (see pages 112–127) who in 1905 mutinied and challenged the rule of Tsar Nicholas II, demanding equality and an end to being treated like cattle in a poorly equipped, class-ridden navy. He believed with all his heart that Communism, the communism of Marx, Lenin, Trotsky and Engels, would one day deliver the workers' paradise its principles promised it could, and he continued to believe in those principles until the day he died, the day a Russian firing squad, on the personal orders of Soviet President Leonid Brezhnev, ended his life.

Valery Mikhaylovich Sablin was born in Gorky in 1939, into a distinguished naval family with a proud revolutionary pedigree, able to trace their line back to the Decembrists who aided the revolt again Tsar Nicolas I in the revolt of 1825. He was raised with a deep respect for the navy and its traditions. For as long as he could remember all he ever wanted to do was go to sea. In 1955, at the age of sixteen, he was accepted into the Frunze Naval Academy in Saint Petersburg. A youth of uncommon integrity, he became known affectionately as 'the conscience of the class', was elected leader of the Communist Youth Organisation, and went on to become one of the academy's most gifted students. But the communist state the young Sablin saw around him seemed a long way from the workers' utopia spoken of by the October revolutionaries. So the twenty-year-old Sablin decided to write a letter.

A COMMITTED TROTSKYIST

In 1959, at the risk of destroying his budding naval career, Sablin wrote to Premier Nikita Khrushchev complaining of the inequalities and injustices he saw in everyday Russian life. He was fortunate that the only consequence was a postponement of his graduation, and he went on to graduate with honours. A few years later, in a decision that stunned his family and friends, he refused the command of a destroyer at the age of thirty, an extraordinary offer that would have made him one of the youngest commanders in the Soviet Navy, choosing instead to enter the prestigious Lenin Political Academy to come to a fuller understanding and appreciation of the pure Communism of Trotsky and Marx. Their dream of a society where the worker stood shoulder to shoulder with the leadership in a classless, egalitarian world was his dream too, but before he could serve the Soviet state he wanted to better understand the political and philosophical foundations upon which it stood. Or rather, how they had failed to be built upon. No matter where Sablin looked in the new Russia, all he could see was inequality and elitism and at its source a corrupt, privileged politburo, caricatured in the convoys of black limousines ferrying Communist Party apparatchiks through decaying streets to and from the Kremlin. The people were supposed to be in charge! But the purity of Trotsky's theory of 'permanent revolution' barely saw the light of day, trampled under the heels of Stalin's work camps, purges and secret police, which had established an entrenched, generational ruling class every bit as self-serving and ambivalent to the needs of their people as the Tsars they had overthrown.

Sablin realised the last thing the ageing Russian leadership wanted was an ongoing, Trotskyist revolution, but he couldn't help beginning to wonder whether a new revolution wasn't called for. One of the first things he did after enrolling at the Lenin Academy was to seek out the works of Trotsky in the academy's library. But there were none. Sablin was shocked to learn that the works of one of the intellectual giants of the October Revolution had all been censored.

Sablin graduated from the Lenin Academy in 1973 and immediately joined the frigate *Storozhevoy* (*Sentinel*) as its *zampolit* (political commissar), the second in command. The role of the political commissar in the modern Soviet Navy wasn't what it had been prior to World War II. Although still responsible for the political 'instruction' of the crew, no longer was the Communist Party's representative equal in rank to the commanding officer. Unlike the early commissars, who were drawn from the civilian population, commissars now were military men who had more in common with the crews they were there to serve, and no longer seen as mere party hacks or government informers. Despite still being answerable to the KGB, Sablin was very different from other commissars. He dared to be critical of the system and wasn't afraid to say so, and soon became a trusted and valued member of the crew. In his lectures he would often remind the crew of the revolutionary traditions of the navy and the principles that were once considered worth dying for—and soon would be again.

On 7 November 1975, *Storozhevoy* arrived alongside its designated buoy in the Daugava River in Riga, the capital of Latvia, to help the tiny Baltic state, a sovereign nation swallowed up by Russia in 1939, celebrate the fifty-eighth anniversary of the Bolshevik revolution. *Storozhevoy* was a Krivak-class anti-submarine frigate, one of six in service with the Baltic Fleet, with a top speed of 32 knots and a range of 4995 nautical miles. Commissioned in 1973, it had a complement of 230 and carried anti-ship and surface-to-air missiles as well as anti-submarine rockets, four 76 millimetre (3 inch) guns and four torpedo tubes. It was a potent weapon, and Sablin hoped it would provide the security and freedom he needed to plant the seeds of revolution at sea rather than on a factory floor where the ears of the KGB could easily undermine him. The tentacles of the bureaucracy were everywhere, but on board *Storozhevoy* Sablin was the 'tentacles'. There was no one to undermine him—except those he took into his confidence.

The next morning, 8 November, the majority of *Storozhevoy*'s officers and crew left the ship for a long day of festivities in Riga. Captain Anatoli Putorny, however, chose to stay aboard. Unlike most ships' commanders and zampolits, Sablin and Putorny worked well together. They would often talk late into the night and Putorny was considered a family friend by Sablin's wife Nina and his son Misha. Sablin had even tried to convince Putorny to come ashore with him just to get him off the ship, aware that Putorny's mere presence during a mutiny would likely end his career.

AN EXTRAORDINARY SITUATION

That evening at 7.00 pm Seaman Alexander Shein knocked on the captain's cabin door and told him there was a *chrezvychainoe polozhenie* ('extraordinary situation' or 'CP' for short) in a sonar room deep in the lower decks. Apparently some drunken sailors were getting a little out of hand. Shein led the captain to the forward sonar room in the depths of the ship, and promptly locked him in.

Bewildered, Putorny looked around him and spotted an unopened envelope with his name on it. He opened it to discover a letter, signed by Valery Sablin, whose contents shook him to the core. Sablin described what he intended to do and his reasons for doing it. Putorny, realising that his career as a commissioned officer was undoubtedly at an end, nevertheless attempted to do what he could to prevent his ship being stolen. He grabbed instinctively for the telephone, but it had been ripped from the wall. Despite his bloodied hands later testifying to the fact he did all he could to escape, there simply was no way out of the sealed sonar room. There was nothing the captain could now do but sit and wait.

Sablin's plan was to sail *Storozhevoy* into international waters and on through the Gulf of Finland to Leningrad, where he would transmit a list of demands via telegram to navy headquarters. He would then go over the head of the regime and broadcast directly to the Russian people by radio, calling for the establishment of a new political order that would be faithful to the vision of Trotsky and the other October revolutionaries. It was never his aim to abandon his country and the ideals he believed in. Sablin's intention, regardless of how naïve it may now appear, was nothing less than to ignite the fires of a new Russian Revolution.

He realised, of course, that he would not be able to commandeer *Storozhevoy* on his own. A 3860-tonne (3800-ton) ship powered by eight sets of gas turbines would require the cooperation of a dedicated group of men, and Sablin had spent several months studying the crew and determining who could be trusted to join him. His lectures on political theory had been carefully constructed to prepare the men for the possibility of mutiny. One of those he selected was the twenty-year-old rating Alexander Shein. Born in the Altai region of Soviet Central Asia and by his own admission something of a rebel, Shein had already confided to Sablin his disaffection with what he saw as the endless rhetoric of the politburo. 'If there is a war, who are we going to defend with all this meaningless rhetoric?' he asked Sablin late one evening. During the course of the mutiny Shein became Sablin's second in command, in turn influencing others to join them, and began to collect keys to various armouries and compartments.

At 7.20 that evening Sablin made an announcement that the revolutionary film *Battleship Potemkin* would screen on the mess deck for the enlisted men at 7.30, and that there would be a meeting for the officers still on board in the stateroom. Sablin had earlier given Shein a 9 millimetre Makarov pistol, and had told him he was to brandish it if a revolt among the officers looked likely. At 7.29 Sablin took one last, deep breath and proceeded to make the speech of his life.

Over the next fifteen minutes the sixteen officers present became privy to what by all accounts would have brought a smile to the face of Lenin himself. Sablin appealed to them to honour the spirit of the revolution and to put an end to the tyranny that had paralysed their beloved country. He railed against the privileges given to the few and denied to the many, privileges he himself had been given as the son of a prominent naval commander, and was scathing of the graft and corruption characteristic of the Soviet Government since Brezhnev replaced Khrushchev as General Secretary of the Communist Party on 14 October 1964. One of those who chose to side with Sablin, Warrant Officer Viktor Borodai, later described his speech as 'clear, prepared, reasonable, and candid'. Sablin then asked each officer to select a piece from the stateroom's chess set. White meant you were with him, black said you were not. Eight of each colour were taken, and the eight who had chosen black were taken below and locked up, as much to protect their careers if the mutiny were to fail as to have them out of the way. It is an extraordinary testimony to the power of Sablin's words that *any* officer chose to follow him, let alone eight.

Just after 10.00 pm Sablin called formation. Almost all those granted shore leave had returned, and it proved impossible to prevent news of his intentions from spreading. Appealing to their love of country, Sablin announced his plans to more than 150 young eighteen- to twenty-year old crewmen huddled together in their winter overcoats on the quarterdeck. It was an inspiring moment, a potentially historic moment in fact. But still one that required a lie to work. Sablin told the men that ships in the Northern and Pacific fleets were waiting for them to act and then they, too, would join the revolt. *Storozhevoy* was the key to a new beginning for the Russian people. In a scene he had played over and over in his mind, Sablin had the young crew in the palms of his hands, and by the end of his passionate plea for heroism, every crewmember present was with him. From a complement of around 230, he had so far failed to convince only nine officers to start down a path that in the navies of the world, for as long as anyone could remember, invariably led to just one thing. Death.

Meanwhile three officers who had been on shore leave and missed Sablin's stateroom speech decided to arm themselves and retake the ship. Sablin confronted them, all four men brandishing pistols. It's a miracle the mutiny didn't end then and there in a volley of gunfire. An attempt was made to wrestle Sablin to the floor but a group of sailors came to his assistance and dragged him free, though not before one officer had screamed at him that the mutiny was doomed. A fourth had escaped.

As the three officers were confronting Sablin, Senior Lieutenant Firsov had climbed over the rails and swum to the nearby submarine S-263 for help. From there he was taken by launch to Riga where he contacted the duty officer at the nearby Bolderia Naval Base and told him of the mutiny. But getting to the base and convincing them of the extraordinary events all took time. Sablin, not knowing to what extent he had lost the element of surprise and assuming the naval base was now aware of the mutiny, ordered *Storozhevoy* to get under way.

A little after 1.00 am on 9 November, *Storozhevoy* slipped its moorings. Scraping the aft section of an adjacent submarine in the rush to get away, *Storozhevoy* began to steam north up the Daugava River towards the Gulf of Riga. Sablin had reasoned that in all likelihood he no longer had the time to sail to Leningrad, and settled instead on getting through the Irben Channel and reaching international waters where he toyed with the idea of sending a personal plea to the Secretary-General of the United Nations, Kurt Waldheim. In an effort to make the ship invisible he ordered the radar turned off, and hoped that the cover of darkness would do the rest. Sablin couldn't know that the naval commanders in Riga were so paralysed by fear that it would be almost four hours before news of the mutiny reached Moscow.

As *Storozhevoy* was steaming through the Gulf of Riga a radio transmission from a crewmember having second thoughts about the wisdom of following Sablin was intercepted by the Swedish armed forces. In clear Russian, uncoded, it read: 'Mutiny on board *Storozhevoy*: we are heading for open sea.' Over the next few hours the continued monitoring of Russian radio traffic by Swedish surveillance posts would later make it difficult for the Soviets to cover the incident up and prevent news leaking to the West.

SHOW NO MERCY

Defence Minister Marshal Grechko, woken with the news in the middle of the night, immediately ordered that *Storozhevoy* be sunk with all hands. No mercy was to be shown. Grechko's aim was to sink the ship, then announce to the world that there had been an explosion on board, and that the ship had gone down with all hands in waters too deep to mount a recovery operation.

At this point neither Grechko nor Soviet President Leonid Brezhnev knew whether they were dealing with a mutiny or a defection. Although *Storozhevoy* was now heading west towards the Swedish island of Gotland, this was out of necessity. Passage north from Riga to Leningrad at the head of the Gulf of Finland was made difficult by the presence of the two large islands Hiiumaa and Saaremaa, thus the usual route was to head west, then north and northeast into the Gulf. *Storozhevoy* had not yet reached the point where a change of course would signal its true intent.

Brezhnev ordered the chief of staff of the Baltic Fleet, Vice-Admiral Kosov, to immediately mobilise as many ships as he could and set out in pursuit. His orders were slightly more merciful than Grechko's, though equally unambiguous. The air force and ships of the Baltic Fleet would first give the mutineers the option of surrendering the ship. If they chose not to do so, then it would be sunk.

Kosov radioed *Storozhevoy* and demanded to speak to its captain. Sablin advised Kosov that not only was Anatoli Putorny not available, but that his ship was now 'free and independent' of the Soviet Union and no longer accountable to the Soviet Government.

Navy aircraft, including TU-16 Badger bombers and Yak-28 Brewer attack aircraft, were scrambled from airbases on the outskirts of Riga and set off in pursuit, but this led to further acts of insubordination, for their pilots refused orders to fire on their own vessel. The navy planes returned to base but were followed by a wave of brand new Sukhoi-24 air force fighter-bombers whose pilots were more amenable to following orders.

The Sukhoi-24s were armed with 225-kilogram (500-pound) bombs and had orders to disable *Storozhevoy*'s rudder. Although the frigate had ammunition for its machine guns, all heavy weapons had been offloaded just days before in preparation for entering dry dock for a series of overdue repairs. Its surface-to-air missiles, its rounds of 76 millimetre (3 inch) anti-aircraft shells, had been put into storage in Baltiysk. Sablin couldn't have shot back at his attackers even if he'd wanted to. It was a hopeless mismatch. This would be no *Potemkin* incident. In 1905 Russia had no air force to tighten the noose.

To counter the intimidating tactics of the Sukhoi-24s, Sablin ordered a series of evasive manoeuvres, but to no avail. *Storozhevoy* was hit by several 225-kilogram (500-pound) bombs on the main deck, the fo'c'sle, and amidships, and strafed by 30 millimetre (1 inch) cannon fire. The rudder was hit, smoke began to billow from the ruptured stern, and soon the ship was dead in the water. Many of the crew who up to that point had gone along with Sablin and his core of supporters began to waver in their commitment, and Sablin could see that he no longer enjoyed the support of the majority. By 9.00 am, with the ship listing to port, more than a dozen Soviet warships were shadowing *Storozhevoy* through the fogbanks of Irben Channel. The first to pull alongside were Stenka KGB patrol ships from the Latvian port of Liyepaya, but before they could board the rebel ship there was one final act to be played out.

'CEASE FIRE! I HAVE REGAINED CONTROL OF THE SHIP!'

A petty officer and two seamen, seeing that the situation was hopeless, freed the officers from their cabins and with the assistance of the boatswain freed Captain Putorny as well. Putorny was so incensed by Sablin's treachery that he decided to storm the bridge and wrest back control of his ship himself. Taking a pistol and accompanied by two armed groups, he entered the bridge and confronted Sablin but was unable to bring himself to kill a man whom he once respected and considered a friend. Instead he shot him in the leg. Sablin collapsed and Putorny had him taken under guard to his cabin. Then the captain grabbed the radio and screamed: 'Cease fire! I have regained control of the ship!' The time was 10.32 am. *Storozhevoy* was only 50 nautical miles from Swedish waters and five minutes short of turning for Leningrad. The mutiny was over.

Sablin was stretchered onto one of the waiting patrol boats and *Storozhevoy* was towed back to Liyepaya, a naval base on Latvia's west coast. Sablin and his co-conspirators were taken first to the Court of the Baltic Military District in Riga and from there by air direct to GAPTVAC, a military prison outside Moscow, all in the strictest secrecy. Contrary to the usual Soviet approach of publicly naming anyone who disobeys a direct order in the belief that the promise of public humiliation will prove a sufficient enough deterrent to others, in this case the potential for humiliation on a national scale, should it be known Russian sailors had mutinied to draw attention to the failings of their own leadership, was far too great to be aired in public.

The trial of Sablin and fourteen others began in the Military Division of the Supreme Court of the Union of Soviet Socialist Republics (USSR) in May 1976. The trial lasted just three days. Sablin was found guilty of betraying the Motherland under Article 64 of the Soviet Criminal Code, was stripped of his rank and his service medals, and sentenced to death by firing squad. It was a harsh decision. The law only required the imposition of a ten-year prison term, but the influence of the enraged Leonid Brezhnev, the object of so much of Sablin's ire, must also be taken into account. Sablin was buried in an unmarked grave, the location of which has remained a mystery to this day.

Sablin's 'second in command' Alexander Shein was sentenced to fifteen years hard labour in a work camp after defiantly admitting that he had actively supported Sablin from the very start. How many of the crewmembers who sympathised with Sablin were subsequently executed is impossible to say due to the intense levels of secrecy surrounding the trial. Every crewmember was forced to sign a personal letter of apology to President Brezhnev. Those who refused to take part in the mutiny and were held below decks, including Captain Anatoli Putorny and his loyal officers, were demoted and reassigned to distant Soviet Navy outposts. Putorny was deemed derelict by a military court in the education of his crew and in failing to train them as a single armed unit that could have prevented Sablin from getting as far as he did.

There was also the inevitable shake-up in the naval chain of command. Within three weeks of the mutiny the commander of the Baltic Fleet, Admiral Vladimir Mikhaylin, who only months earlier had been awarded the Order of the October Revolution, was removed and reassigned to a desk job in Moscow. The commander of the submarine S-263 and the leadership of the Riga Naval Base were all accused of behaviour that 'bordered on cowardice', and were demoted.

'SABLIN WAS THAT SORT OF NOBLE SPIRIT'

Despite persistent rumours in the West, the Soviet Government continued to deny that a mutiny had occurred. At a news conference in Copenhagen in August 1976, Rear-Admiral of the Baltic Fleet V.V. Sidorov was forced to respond to persistent questions with the following denial: 'Mutiny on a Soviet Naval ship in the Baltic is unthinkable! It must be a hoax played by organs established for this purpose which pursue their thwarting aims in the West.'

In the face of the official denials, however, government speeches began to allude to an acknowledged breakdown in discipline in the armed forces, noting that more attention should be paid to the morale and ideological training of its combatants. At the first Party Congress after the incident Brezhnev spoke of being 'tactful toward people and their needs and aspirations, and to set an example at work ...'. In an article in the Russian military newspaper *Krasnaya Zvesda* in February 1976, Admiral Sergey Gorshkov stressed the need for commanders and party officials to 'pay particular attention to the ideological education of junior officers', and the importance of the 'formation of the ideological and moral potential of the future commander's personality'. New shipboard regulations introduced in 1978 placed more emphasis on the political education of a ship's crew on its commanding officer, as well as an increased level of supervision of the vessel's political commissar.

Pronouncements like these were as close to an admission of the events of 9 November 1975 as the Soviet Government ever got until 1992, when the government of Boris Yeltsin convened a public trial to determine whether Valery Sablin should be rehabilitated. Though a final decision was not reached, in 1994 the Military Collegium of the Russian Federation Supreme Court reopened the original court transcripts and came to the decision that a ten-year term of imprisonment should have been the proper legal response.

Storozhevoy would not be seen again until April 1976 when, staffed by a new crew, it left the Baltic Sea for the last time and sailed via the Mediterranean Sea and the Suez Canal to the Indian Ocean, where it stayed for two months before steaming on to its new home with the Soviet Pacific Fleet, operating out of Petropavlovsk-Kamchatsky on the remote Kamchatka Peninsula. The Soviet Government had decided to send *Storozhevoy* as far away from the Baltic as it was possible for a Soviet Naval ship to go. It was decommissioned in 2004 and sold to India for scrap.

The movie *The Hunt for Red October* contributed to increased public awareness of Sablin's actions within Russia, where today he is seen as a heroic figure. In 2001, at a 25th anniversary reunion of *Storozhevoy*'s crew, Alexander Shein summed up the feeling of those present when he said of his friend: 'Every society needs noble spirits, without them no society can move forward. Sablin was that sort of noble spirit.'

BIBLIOGRAPHY

BOOKS

Alexander, Caroline. *The Bounty: The true story of the mutiny on the Bounty*, Viking Penguin, 2003

Australian War Memorial, *Australian Military Units: HMAS Australia Mutiny*, Australian War Memorial, Canberra, 2010

Baker, Kevin. *Mutiny, Terrorism, Riots and Murder: A history of sedition in Australia and New Zealand*, Rosenberg Publishing, 2006

Bascomb, Neal. *Red Mutiny: Eleven fateful days on the battleship Potemkin*, Houghton Mifflin Company, 2007

Bell, Christopher & Elleman, Bruce. *Naval Mutinies of the Twentieth Century: An international perspective*, Frank Cass Publishers, 2003

Bligh, William. *The Mutiny on Board HMS Bounty*, ABDO Publishing Company, 2002

Bligh, William & Christian, Edward. *The Bounty Mutiny, with an Introduction by Robert Madison*, Penguin, 2001

Bulkeley, John & Byron, John. *The Loss of the Wager: The narratives of John Bulkeley and the Hon. John Byron, with an Introduction by Alan Gurney*, Boydell Press, 2004

Carew, Anthony. *The Lower Deck of the Royal Navy 1900–39: Invergordon in perspective*, Manchester University Press, 1981
Dash, Mike. *Batavia's Graveyard: The true story of the mad heretic who led history's bloodiest mutiny*, Random House, 2002
Dening, Greg. *Mr Bligh's Bad Language: Passion, power and theatre on the Bounty*, Cambridge University Press, 1992
Dienst, Alex. *The Navy of the Republic of Texas 1835–1845*, Read Books, 2008
Dudley Gold, Susan. *Supreme Court Milestones. United States vs. Amistad: Slave Ship Mutiny*, Marshall Cavendish Benchmark, 2007
Edwards, Edward. *Voyage of HMS Pandora: Despatched to Arrest the Mutineers of the 'Bounty'*, Salzwasser-Verlag, 2009.
Edwards, Philip. *The Story of the Voyage: Sea narratives in eighteenth century England*, Cambridge University Press, 1994
Elleman, Bruce & Paine, Sarah. *Naval Blockades and Seapower: Strategies and counter-strategies 1805–2005*, Routledge, 2006
Ereira, Alan. *The Invergordon Mutiny: A narrative history of the last great mutiny in the Royal Navy and how it forced Britain off the Gold Standard in 1931*, Routledge & Kegan, 1981
Goodman, Nan. *Shifting the Blame: Literature, law, and the theory of accidents in nineteenth century America*, Princeton University Press, 1998
Gourgey, Percy. *The Indian Naval Revolt of 1946*, Orient Longman Limited, 1996
Guttridge, Leonard F. *Mutiny: A history of naval insurrection*, Naval Institute Press, 1992
Hathaway, Jane. *Rebellion, Repression, Reinvention: Mutiny in comparative perspective*, Praeger Publishers, 2001
Heffernan, Thomas Farel. *Mutiny on the Globe: The fatal voyage of Samuel Comstock*, W.W. Norton & Company, 2002
Hough, Richard. *The Potemkin Mutiny*, Pantheon Books, 1960
Jackson, Donald Dale. *Mutiny on the Amistad*, Smithsonian, 1997
James, J.M. *The Naval History of Great Britain During the French Revolutionary and Napoleonic Wars, Vol. 2, 1797–1799*, Stackpole Books, 2002
Janvier, Thomas. *Henry Hudson: A brief statement of his aims and his achievements*, Tayler & Francis Group, 2007
Kerr, John. *Germany, 1918–39*, Heinemann Educational Publishers, 2003
Lay, William & Hussey, Cyrus. *A Narrative of the Mutiny on Board the Ship Globe, of Nantucket ...*, New London, 1828

Leys, Simon. *The Wreck of the Batavia and Prosper*, Black Inc, 2005
McFarland, Philip. *Sea Dangers: The affair of the Somers*, Schocken Books, 1985
Melton, Buckner. *A Hanging Offence: The strange case of the USS Somers*, Free Press, 2003
Owens, William A. *Black Mutiny: the revolt on the schooner Amistad*, Black Classic Press, 1997
Otfinoski, Steven. *Henry Hudson: In search of the Northwest Passage*, Marshall Cavendish Benchmark, 2007
Pope, Dudley. *The Black Ship*, Secker & Warburg, 1963
Retallack, James. *Imperial Germany, 1871–1918*, Oxford University Press, 2008
Sherman, Josepha. *Henry Hudson: English explorer of the Northwest Passage*, The Rosen Publishing Group, 2003
Sullivan, Roy. *The Texas Navies: The Civil War in Texas and the Southwest*, Heritage Books, 2008
Valtin, Jan. *Out of the Night*, Alliance Book Corporation, 1941
Weinberg, Robert. *The Revolution of 1905 in Odessa: Blood on the steps*, Indiana University Press, 1993
Woodman, Richard. *Mutiny: Furious, savage and bloody*, Constable & Robinson Ltd, 2005
Young, Gregory& Braden, Nate. *The Last Sentry: The true story that inspired the Hunt for Red October*, Naval Institute Press, 2005

WEBSITES

www.ianchadwick.com/hudson
www.elizabethan-era.org.uk/henry-hudson
www.voc.iinet.net.au/batavia
www.bium.univ-paris5.fr/ishm/.../VESx2003x09x02x022x024.pdf
www.wikipedia.org/wiki/Mutiny_on_the_Bounty
www.royalnavalmuseum.org/info_sheets_bounty.htm
www.library.puc.edu/pitcairn/bounty/mutiny.shtml
http://yomi.mobi/egate/HNLMS_De_Zeven_Provinciën_(1909)/a
www.wikipedia.org/wiki/Spithead_and_Nore_mutinies
www.napoleonguide.com/navy_nore.htm
www.footnote.com/page/1554_the_spithead_nore_mutiny/

http://ageofsail.wordpress.com/category/mutiny/
www.absoluteastronomy.com/topics/Sailors'_mutiny
http://derroteros.perucultural.org.pe/textos/derroteros8/lopez.doc
www.dailymail.co.uk/news/article-1151293/The-bloodiest-mutiny-The-day-cruellest-captain-British-Navy-pushed-long-suffering-crew-far.html
www.jotika-ltd.com/Pages/1024768/Hermione_Front.htm
http://en.wikipedia.org/wiki/HMS_Hermione_(1782)
www.nytimes.com/2002/05/19/books/helter-skelter-on-the-high-seas.html
www.historynet.com/slave-mutiny-on-the-amistad.htm
www.gibbsmagazine.com/Amistad%20part%201.htm
www.latinamericanstudies.org/caribbean/amistad-mutiny.pdf
http://en.wikipedia.org/wiki/USS_Somers_(1842)
www.bbc.co.uk/dna/h2g2/A1162388
http://law.jrank.org/pages/2483/Mackenzie-Court-Martial-1843.html
www.tsl.state.tx.us/exhibits/navy/mutiny.html
http://en.wikipedia.org/wiki/Texan_schooner_San_Antonio
www.answers.com/topic/potemkin-mutiny
www.jmr.nmm.ac.uk/server/show/ConJmrBookReview.116
http://query.nytimes.com/mem/archive-free/pdf?_r=1&res=9D0DE2DE163EE433A25757C1A9639C946996D6CF
http://en.wikipedia.org/wiki/Wilhelmshaven_mutiny
www.newworldencyclopedia.org/entry/Mutiny
www.awm.gov.au/units/event_141.asp
www.navy.gov.au/HMAS_Australia_(I)
www3.interscience.wiley.com/journal/120791973/abstract?CRETRY=1&SRETRY=0
www.seayourhistory.org.uk/content/view/147/234/
www.timesonline.co.uk/tol/comment/columnists/william_rees_mogg/article5408194.ece
www.heritech.com/sea/ceagle.htm
www.time.com/time/magazine/article/0,9171,942206,00.html
www.knowledgerush.com/kr/encyclopedia/SS_Columbia_Eagle_incident/
www.heritech.com/sea/articles/voy2.htm
http://en.wikipedia.org/wiki/Valery_Sablin
www.marxist.com/History-old/realredoctober900.html
http://wapedia.mobi/en/Soviet_frigate_Storozhevoy

ACKNOWLEDGEMENTS

Writing a book that looks back on the most significant and bloody mutinies in history is a bit like having to eat a little chocolate every day for six months. You never tire of it. And having several good people at Murdoch Books behind you as you go doesn't hurt either. I would like firstly to thank my publisher Diana Hill for entrusting this wonderful project to me, and Paul O'Beirne for overseeing and coordinating myriad people behind the scenes.

And last but certainly not least to my editor Anne Savage, who would warn me when about to 'wallop' me with revisions, admitted to her brain being 'fried' at the end of a long day's editing and to sharing my ignorance of German history, and chided me for my habit of making 'whole paragraphs out of one sentence' and using apostrophes inappropriately. My thanks, Anne, for making me a better author.

ABOUT THE AUTHOR

Barry Stone has co-authored the popular books *1001 Inventions that Changed the World* and *1001 Escapes to Make Before You Die* (Quintessence, 2009), and the illustrated reference books *Geologica* and *EARTH* (Millennium House, 2009). He is the author of the Pier 9 history title *I Want to Be Alone* (2010) and co-author of *History's Greatest Headlines* (Pier 9, 2010). He is also the author of *Great Australian Historic Hotels* (Allen & Unwin, 2010) and *Manifesto For Mankind* (Murray Books), a study of how humans are impacting our world, for better and for worse, and suggesting ways we can modify our lifestyles and rethink our needs for the sake of our planet.

In between books he likes to indulge his passion for travel writing and over the years his articles have appeared in some of Australia's leading travel publications, including *Holidays for Couples* and *Australian Traveller*, as well as the international magazines *Destinations* and *DestinAsian*. He has also been a long-time contributor on travel destinations both in Australia and overseas for Sydney's *Sun-Herald* newspaper.

Barry Stone lives on a quiet acre in rural Picton, an hour's drive south of Sydney, with his wife Yvonne and two boys, Jackson and Truman.

Published in 2011 by Pier 9, an imprint of Murdoch Books Pty Limited

Murdoch Books Australia
Pier 8/9
23 Hickson Road
Millers Point NSW 2000
Phone: +61 (0) 2 8220 2000
Fax: +61 (0) 2 8220 2558
www.murdochbooks.com.au

Murdoch Books UK Limited
Erico House, 6th Floor
93–99 Upper Richmond Road
Putney, London SW15 2TG
Phone: +44 (0) 20 8785 5995
Fax: +44 (0) 20 8785 5985
www.murdochbooks.co.uk

Publisher: Diana Hill
Project Editor: Paul O'Beirne
Design concept: Hugh Ford
Design layout: Joanna Byrne
Production: Shannon Haworth
Cover image: Shutterstock / Mark Payne

National Library of Australia Cataloguing-in-Publication Data

Author:	Stone, Barry.
Title:	Mutinies : shocking real-life stories of subversion at sea / Barry Stone.
ISBN:	978-1-74196-634-3 (pbk.)
Series:	True crime and punishment.
Notes:	Includes bibliographical references.
Subjects:	Mutiny—History.
	Seafaring life—History.
	Insubordination.
	Punishment.
Dewey Number:	910.45

A catalogue record for this book is available from the British Library.

Printed by Hang Tai Printing Company Limited, China.